The Mind on Paper

Although the importance of literacy is widely acknowledged in society and remains at the top of the political agenda, writing has been slow to establish a place in the cognitive sciences. Olson argues that to understand the cognitive implications of literacy, it is necessary to see reading and writing as providing access to and consciousness of aspects of language, such as *phonemes*, *words* and *sentences*, that are implicit and unconscious in speech. Reading and writing create a system of metarepresentational concepts that bring those features of language into consciousness as a subject of discourse. This consciousness of language is essential not only to acquiring literacy but also to the formation of systematic thought and rationality. *The Mind on Paper* is a compelling exploration of what literacy does for our speech and hence for our thought, and will be of interest to readers in developmental psychology, cognitive science, linguistics and education.

DAVID R. OLSON is University Professor Emeritus at the Ontario Institute for Studies in Education at the University of Toronto. He is author or editor of 20 books and more than 300 articles on cognition, language and literacy. He is a Fellow of the Royal Society of Canada and the National Academy of Education (US), and he has been awarded honorary degrees by the University of Gothenburg, the University of Saskatchewan and the University of Toronto.

The Mind on Paper

Reading, Consciousness and Rationality

DAVID R. OLSON
OISE/University of Toronto

CAMBRIDGE
UNIVERSITY PRESS

CAMBRIDGE
UNIVERSITY PRESS

Shaftesbury Road, Cambridge CB2 8EA, United Kingdom

One Liberty Plaza, 20th Floor, New York, NY 10006, USA

477 Williamstown Road, Port Melbourne, VIC 3207, Australia

314–321, 3rd Floor, Plot 3, Splendor Forum, Jasola District Centre, New Delhi – 110025, India

103 Penang Road, #05–06/07, Visioncrest Commercial, Singapore 238467

Cambridge University Press is part of Cambridge University Press & Assessment, a department of the University of Cambridge.

We share the University's mission to contribute to society through the pursuit of education, learning and research at the highest international levels of excellence.

www.cambridge.org
Information on this title: www.cambridge.org/9781107162891

DOI: 10.1017/9781316678466

First published 2016

A catalogue record for this publication is available from the British Library

Library of Congress Cataloging-in-Publication data
Names: Olson, David R., 1935– author.
Title: The mind on paper : reading, consciousness and rationality /
David R. Olson, OISE/University of Toronto. Description: Cambridge,
United Kingdom: Cambridge University Press, [2016] |
Includes bibliographical references and index.
Identifiers: LCCN 2016026752 | ISBN 9781107162891 (hardback)
Subjects: LCSH: Reading, Psychology of.
Classification: LCC BF456.R2 O57 2016 | DDC 418/.4019–dc23
LC record available at https://lccn.loc.gov/2016026752

ISBN 978-1-107-16289-1 Hardback

In memory of Jerome Bruner, mentor and friend, 1915–2016

Contents

Figures

Preface

It is, by now, widely acknowledged that reading and writing and literacy in general have played a critical role in the formation and operation of a modern bureaucratic society, the world I described in an earlier work, *The World on Paper*. At the same time, it remains much in dispute whether reading and writing in such social circumstances play a decisive role in the formation of the modern mind. Opinions range from the claim that the mind-brain is the universal, indeed biological, property of human cognition, to the view that the mind is a social construction shaped to reflect an existing social order. Between is the view, often traced to Vygotsky, that the biological resources of the mind are amplified or extended through the technologies of the culture.

One such technology is that of writing, whose uses extend into almost every institutional and intellectual undertaking in a modern society. Just how and why it does so remain open questions. Although concepts such as the "literate mind" and "literate mentality" have found a permanent place in classical, historical and cultural studies, and although the language arts largely define the curriculum of the school, writing has been slow to find a place in cognitive sciences and in the philosophy of mind. This book is an attempt to find such a place, to find "the mind on paper."[1]

While it is uncontroversial that writing is a useful tool for planning action and for solving problems, the central claim of this book is that the cognitive significance of writing lies elsewhere: namely, in the fact that writing brings a new consciousness to speech. It is that consciousness of language that I explore and that provides a bridge

[1] Thanks to Janet Astington for offering this expression as a title for the book.

from children's earliest efforts in learning to read to the specialized rational thinking of educated adults.

I was first drawn to this topic when, under the direction of Jerry Bruner, I was attempting to show how children's acquisition of a spoken language made their thinking about spatial relations conscious and deliberate, and I came across Jack Goody and Ian Watt's classic paper "The Consequences of Literacy." The article was the first clue to the possibility that the invention of a written form for representing speech could have allowed speakers, perhaps for the first time, to realize that their speech was actually composed of a small set of distinctive elements. Their view of literacy and mind provided a key to my understanding of what McLuhan had been up to with his discussion of the media. McLuhan, of course, is well known for his sometimes extravagant claims about the effects of the media, including writing and printing, on both culture and consciousness. Vygotsky's *Thought and Language*, published in English at just this time, 1962, offered the possibility of examining the implications of writing and reading from an empirical developmental perspective. These advances provided the larger perspective that turned reading theory into literacy theory, thus raising new questions about the nature and uses of writing, and in the present case, the relations between reading and mind.

There is a deep irony in the fact that although educators since the rise of humanism in the 18th century have insisted on the importance of education for the development of mind and have mounted extensive and energetic literary programs to achieve that goal, the cognitive sciences have, by and large, ignored the relation between speaking and writing and the relation between writing, reasoning and rationality. Consequently, this book attempts to address two quite different audiences: one concerned with the development of literate cognition, primarily those concerned with education and human development; the other concerned with the role of writing in the formation of mind, primarily those concerned with the cognitive sciences. One recognizes the importance of education in the development of the modern mind; the other examines the mental processes involved in achieving this goal. These two audiences are, I believe, increasingly becoming one. One cannot improve education without a fuller understanding of mind, just as one cannot fully understand the mind without a fuller account of the role of reading and writing and literacy in general on human rationality.

In this book I warm to the task by sketching in some facts about writing and the currently available theories of writing and mind, particularly those of Dewey's Pragmatism, Vygotsky's sociocultural psychology and contemporary theories in the cognitive sciences. I then turn to the specific domains in which we may expect to locate the cognitive implications of learning an alphabetic script, namely for representing phonemes, words, sentences and written prose. Finally, I examine two contexts in which this specialized literate knowledge is central, namely in learning to read and in the development of rational thought. The final chapter pulls together the relations between reading, consciousness and rationality.

Although the topic of writing and mind is very broad, the question I address is somewhat narrow, focusing on one kind of writing, alphabetic, in one kind of society, a modern Western one, for one kind of competence of broad applicability, reading and writing prose. This allows me to examine in a more precise way the relation between reading and consciousness of language and how that consciousness plays out in modern reflective thinking. But at the same time I'll disappoint readers hoping for an exploration of the broader question of the relation between literacy and literature.

I am grateful for the thoughtful advice and critical comments on the multiple drafts of this work by friends and colleagues including Marilyn Jager Adams, Janet Astington, Alf Bang, Eric Bredo, Christina Erneling, Joseph Heath, Keith Oatley, Frank Smith and Brian Stock. And thanks to Frances, a true Dorothea to this Casaubon, for everything.

PART I Introduction

Reading, Writing and the Mind

1 Awakening

Reading and Consciousness

I imagined that God had created light so that people could read, and through reading, see other worlds. (French mathematician Evariste Galois (1811–1832), as portrayed by, T. Petsinis, 1997, p. 40)

To a skilled reader a text is a window to the world. The act of reading brings into consciousness a world otherwise unknown. For such readers this is so much a matter of course that it is difficult if not impossible to imagine a life and a mind unacquainted with writing, to imagine a world, as it is fashionable to say, *avant la lettre*. Though we may have lost track of our own awakening to literacy, we may have observed children as they learn to read and have witnessed, as a sort of miracle, the birth of this new consciousness.

AWAKENING TO THE WRITTEN WORLD

Consider the example provided by Marilynne Robinson in her recent book, *Lila* (2014), the story of a nameless outcast child who, some years later, was to become the wife of the aging Calvinist minister John Ames, whom readers met earlier in her Pulitzer Prize-winning novel, *Gilead* (2004). "There was a long time when Lila didn't know that words had letters and that there were other names for seasons than planting and haying" (2014, p. 10). Lila, unlike her friends, does learn to read and with it to distinguish the words from the things they represent. When she reads aloud a sign that says "General Store," her friends, lacking such distinctions, mock her ability: "Well, anybody can see that's a general store, so what them words going to say? County jail? It don't look like nothing else but a store, does it?" (p. 42). One theme of the novel is the interplay between what Lila knew through pain and deprivation and the world as represented in language. When Ames tells her that religion has to do with existence, Lila thinks: "All right. She knew a little bit about existence. That was pretty well the only thing she knew about and she had learned the word for it from him. It was like the United States of America – they had to call it something" (p. 74). A word is a gift that somehow opens up a world.

Best known, of course, is the account by Helen Keller of the awakening provoked by the simple recognition that signs, in this case signed spellings, could represent things – that here was a web of words that could be laid over and in a sense disclose a shared world to the mind, a discovery she experienced as no less than miraculous.

Many writers have tried to capture the way that becoming a reader opened up a world previously not suspected to exist. William Cobbett, who in the 18th century grew into adulthood before learning how to read, later becoming a noted statesman, described this awakening. He said that buying and reading Jonathan Swift's *Tale of a Tub* "procured what I have always considered a sort of birth of intellect" (Carlyle, 1947, p. 17);[1] he became aware of the fact that in reading he entertained not only the author's thoughts but, more importantly, his own thoughts. It is as if encountering another's thoughts in a written form invites a new consciousness of one's own. At other times it is as if the writer is speaking one's own thoughts.

So too the novelist John Williams in *Stoner* (1965) recounts the life of a Missouri farm boy whose mind is gradually awakened if not brought into existence through the study of English literature. Even in the second year of university, although he read and reread his literature assignments, "the words he read were words on pages, and he could not see the use of what he did." That all changed when he

[1] Michael Clanchy pointed this out to me.

began to feel that the literature spoke to him and took him out of the present:

> The past gathered out of the darkness where it stayed, and the dead raised themselves to live before him; and the past and the dead flowed into the present among the alive, so that he had for an intense instant a vision of denseness into which he was compacted and from which he could not escape, and had no wish to escape. Tristan, Iseult the fair, walked before him; Paolo and Francesca whirled in the glowing dark; Helen and bright Paris, their faces bitter with consequence, rose from the gloom. And he was with them in a way that he could never be with his fellows who ... walked unheeding in a Midwestern air. Indeed, years later when he looked back to the time before his awakening, "he was astonished by the memory of that strange figure [himself], brown and passive as the earth from which it had emerged." (1965, pp. 11–16)

The world into which one enters when becoming a reader is not always a commonly shared one. Carlo Ginzburg (1980) recounts the life and death of the 16th-century Italian miller Menocchio, newly literate presumably via the recently established school for poor children in the area, who found himself able to read the Bible. His eyes were opened. On the basis of his somewhat idiosyncratic reading he began to doubt the teachings of the Church just at the time that the Inquisition reached its peak. Among other heresies Menocchio claimed that God had not created the world: "in my opinion, all was chaos, that is, earth, air, water, and fire were mixed together; and out of that bulk a mass formed – just as cheese is made out of milk – and worms appeared in it, and these were the angels" (pp. 5–6). When he refused to recant, he was burned at the stake. Reading, while providing a route to a unknown but existing other world, also invites the reader to imagine another of his or her own making to rival that offered by a writer.

An equivalent "consciousness-raising" has been reported for reading and learning to read prose texts. Stewart's (1922) early study of the effects of teaching adult illiterates to read is extended by the recent findings by Allen (2013) that by careful reading and discussing the words of the US Declaration of Independence her adult learners "found themselves suddenly as political beings, with a consciousness that had previously eluded them. They gained a vocabulary and rhetorical techniques for arguing about it" (p. 35).

Becoming a reader opens up, as well, the world of literature. Many North American children have encountered Emily Dickinson's song-like poem:

> There is no frigate like a book
> To take us lands away,
> Nor any coursers like a page
> Of prancing poetry.
> This traverse may the poorest take
> Without oppress of toll;
> How frugal is the chariot
> That bears a human soul!

More literary readers may prefer John Keats' "On First Looking into Chapman's Homer":

> Much have I travell'd in the realms of gold,
> And many goodly states and kingdoms seen;
> Round many western islands have I been
> Which bards in fealty to Apollo hold.
> Oft of one wide expanse had I been told
> That deep-browed Homer ruled as his demesne;
> Yet did I never breathe its pure serene
> Till I heard Chapman speak out loud and bold:
> Then felt I like some watcher of the skies
> When a new planet swims into his ken;
> Or like stout Cortez when with eagle eyes

He star'd at the Pacific – and all his men
Look'd at each other with a wild surmise –
Silent, upon a peak in Darien.

It is somewhat of an irony that the world opened to Keats in reading Chapman's translation of the Homeric epics was a world created through oral not written composition. It has been argued (Powell, 1991) that the Greek alphabet took the form that it did in the attempt to capture the subtleties of the sound of Homer's oral poetry. So even while celebrating the importance of literacy it is imperative to remember that very complex thinking may be carried out in the absence of writing. What writing adds may remain unrecognized because those additions are manifest only in the options they make available in the spoken language.

AWAKENING TO LANGUAGE

Each of these cases of intellectual awakening is distinctive in that they demonstrate not only a new awareness of some property of the world but of a consciousness of the language used to express that content. This awareness of the language, the ability to think about language, lies at the base of the famous "critiques" set out by Kant, of aesthetics, morality and knowledge. All critique is thinking about thinking and so all involve a specialized language to do that thinking in. It is the nature, origin and development of that critical metalanguage that we may attempt to trace to the history of writing and literacy.

Much has been written on the ways that literature stocks the world of the imagination (Oatley, 2013). But writing not only opens one to the world of literature it also is a gateway to the world of the mind. It does this, I shall argue, through a new consciousness of language. For it is this consciousness that gives rise to the forms of systematic knowledge and the ways of critical thinking that shape and have come to dominate the modern intellectual world. Thus while the account of reading and consciousness that I set out may not compare with "the wild surmise" experienced in opening Chapman's Homer, I hope to show something equally important, namely, that there is a world of mind, hidden in the recesses of the unconscious that is brought into awareness in reading and writing and that can be examined and perhaps explained within a scientifically testable theory of the mind. At the same time it should indicate the responsibilities of education for developing this knowledge.

To understand writing and its relation to consciousness we shall need to avail ourselves of recent accounts of how learning a language makes possible a consciousness of the world and then how learning to read and write produces a new consciousness of language. This consciousness of language in turn can help to explain more reflective forms of thinking that have come to define rationality. The concepts that writing and literacy add to consciousness necessarily find a place back in oral spoken language in such a way that the natural language remains a primary medium of thought.

UNCONVINCED

Although educators and the general public place great value on literacy, their enthusiasm rests on a shaky intellectual foundation. The founder of modern linguistics, Saussure (1916/1983, pp. 23–24), insisted that writing was not language in that "the spoken form alone constitutes the object" and he viewed the attention to the written as "the tyranny" of the alphabet. Levi-Strauss spoke for many when he wrote:

> Writing is a strange thing. It would seem as if its appearance could not have failed to wreak profound changes in the living conditions of our race, and that these transformations must have been above all intellectual in character. Yet nothing of what we know of writing, or of its role in evolution, can be said to justify this conception. (Levi-Strauss, 1961, p. 291)

Levi-Strauss's dismissive attitude is shared by some contemporary writers. Although researchers influenced by Vygotsky were among the first to recognize writing as an intellectual tool, more recent work in that tradition has tended to subordinate writing to oral discourse and to the social practices of the society into which writing is introduced. Important early work, such as that of Scribner and Cole (1981), looked for the cognitive implications of writing and reading by examining learning to write in an essentially non-literate culture and concluded that what little effect it had (it did produce a consciousness of syllables, the writing system studied being a syllabary) was completely overshadowed by the social practice, letter writing, it served. However, the deeper implications of writing may be revealed only when writing reaches its fullest flower, when examined from what Standish called "the vantage point of the present" (Standish, 2013, p. vii). Only when pushed to its limits in philology and science, dictionary making and logic, and when perpetuated in a culture of literacy, does the nature and significance of writing become clear. The inventors of writing had no idea that writing could represent speech; some modern writers seem reluctant to admit that it could serve as an instrument for deductive reasoning. Yet those were among the features of writing that modern societies continue to elaborate, exploit and advance through a literate education. At the same time it is important to remember that there are many kinds of writing, employed in many different cultures for many different uses and with diverse effects.

Critics point out that anything that may be said in writing may be expressed in oral speech, that unwritten law precedes written law, that dialogue is more productive than monologue, that social argument is more important to thinking than prose writing, that computer skills are more important than reading (Spiro et al., 2015). Socio-cultural and educational theorists such as Wells (1999) argue that attention to written texts distracts from the importance of practical hands-on experience and oral discourse. Some see writing as little more than a record of what is worked out in talk. To address such concerns it is necessary to return to the more basic questions of the relation between speech and writing, between writing and consciousness and between writing and rationality.

Modern readers immersed in a reading culture and equipped with a literate consciousness may find it difficult to recover an "innocent eye," an eye untainted by the experience of reading and writing. Reconstructing a world without words, letters, sentences and documents cannot be reached by introspection alone but is a task for research and theory.

READING, CONSCIOUSNESS AND RATIONALITY

To proceed with the task of tracing the links between reading, consciousness and rationality it may be useful to outline how these concepts are to be used.

Reading. Reading and writing are used not only to refer to the decoding and encoding of signs, but as general terms that include the ability to read and write both simple texts and complex ones characteristic of the literary, governmental, scientific and educational institutions of a modern bureaucratic society; in a word, the model of literacy that defines the language arts from primary school through the university – from word identification to essayist prose. Thus, reading and literacy are to be seen as somewhat analogous to knowing a natural language. Once one is a speaker of a language, one can converse on virtually any topic with anyone who is also a speaker of that language. So too with writing as a representation of a natural language; to be literate is to be able to participate in a broad range of literate discourses, discourses based on writing.

Consciousness. Consciousness is both a condition for knowledge and a consequence of knowledge. Gerald Edelman (2004, p. xi) pointed out that "consciousness is the guarantor of all we hold human and precious. Its permanent loss is considered equivalent to death, even if the body persists in its vital signs." But "consciousness" is ambiguous in that it sometimes refers to a kind of awareness or vigilance common to all animals and essential to all learning, and at others to something specific, to be conscious of something as something. Robert Brandom (1994) expressed this distinction in terms of *sentience*, the consciousness we share with primates and other animals, and *sapience*, the consciousness, uniquely human, that one has of a thing in thinking or saying something about it, that is, casting something into linguistic form. Most verbalizable thoughts are about objects and events in the world that one can refer to and comment on. But others, more important to my argument, are thoughts *about* the language itself. As we shall see, that is where reading and rationality come into the picture.

Consciousness of language plays a critical role in an account of language and literacy. Children seem not to know that their speech is composed of elements of sound called phonemes. Such linguistic processes are unconscious, or, as I shall say, transparent. Even most adults do not realize that "is" is the third-person, present, singular form of the verb "to be" and yet they routinely manage subject–verb agreement. Learning to read makes some of this opaque or unconscious knowledge conscious and explicit. Neither the nature of this implicit knowledge nor the means by which it is made explicit is well understood. To some, phonemes are as real as cats and need only to be brought to consciousness in learning to read an alphabetic script. To others phonemes are as ephemeral as fairies, the only reality the visual marks and the meanings assigned to them. Our task ahead is to characterize implicit knowledge of language and to provide a model or mechanism by means of which such implicit knowledge is made explicit as an object of thought.

Rationality. It is widely agreed that all humans display a form of rationality defined by the ability to give reasons for what they say and do. This form of rationality, perhaps better thought of as reasonableness, is intrinsic to the acquisition of a first language. Sapient consciousness, consciousness of the world enabled by language, allows one to construct what Wilfred Sellars (1997) called "the space of reasons" and hence to give reasons for one's utterances and actions.

But in addition to reasons for justifying actions and beliefs, there are, I suggest, reasons about reasons, metareasons that may be used to evaluate reasons in terms of relevance, evidence, validity, clarity, ambiguity and the like. This is the language of formal rationality that, I shall further argue, derives to some degree from writing and a written tradition. Reasonable and rational are usually seen as synonyms and for most purposes they are. But to understand how reading and literacy contribute to a distinctive way of thinking, it is necessary to distinguish those actions that are reasonable, that is, those justifiable by reasons, from those that involve the scrutiny of reasons that we may more narrowly describe as, strictly speaking, rational.

READING AND LEARNING TO READ

Long before reading and literacy became a topic for science and philosophy it was a topic for those concerned with the practical arts of teaching children to read and write. These teaching practices have remained much the same since classical times (aside from the size of the class and the strictness of the masters). Grendler (1989, p. 409) provided a vivid description of 18th-century schools: "Teachers and textbooks taught by breaking a skill into the smallest components, drilling them intensively, and then assembling the bits to make the whole." Although this sounds eerily familiar, there was a period in the 1920s when the teaching of reading took a decisive turn against drill and practice methods (Ontario Teachers Manual, 1920). Concerned that some children merely called out the letters and words without thinking about their meanings, reformers developed the "word method" in which children learned to recognize words with "clear, vivid meanings," primarily words that had become familiar through memorized nursery rhymes and words that carried emotional weight. Larger units of meaning such as songs and stories received equal attention. Later on, the Dr. Seuss books essentially implemented these practices. Only when a rich body of words was known by "sight" did instruction begin, if it began at all, on breaking known words into the phonemes represented by the alphabet. The entire program was devised to emphasize meaning, story and the desire to read. The approach came to a shuddering halt when it was discovered, in the 1950s, that "Johnny can't read."

Contemporary reading theory as exemplified in the widely adopted Common Core Curriculum in the United States and supported by a large body of empirical research is in a sense a reprise of the 18th-century view. The Common Core Curriculum emphasizes the Basic Skills such as letter knowledge and letter–sound relations that have been shown to correlate with reading comprehension. Critics of the Common Core insist on the importance of meaning, believability, interest and understanding and they relegate the "basic skills" to the implicit and largely unconscious workings of the brain.

The theory of writing advanced herein may allow us to approach the controversy in a new way. As we shall see, writing not only preserves speech, it represents it in a new medium. Learning to read requires that one learn a set of metarepresentational concepts, beginning with the concept of *word*, that brings both a new consciousness of language and a grasp of what the reading task entails. This is the subject of Chapter 11.

WHY IT MATTERS

Although it is universally agreed that education and literacy are essential to both human development and to a civil society, the social and educational practices designed to bring this about are diverse, often incoherent and often unsuccessful. Consequently, proposals for reform come from many sides – sometimes from testers promising to raise standards, brain scientists promising to rewire the brain, psychologists promising better diagnosis, publishers promising new materials – but few acknowledged the central fact that the development of children's learning and thinking requires the often prodigious efforts of educators. Shortcuts to the development of literate competence through test-prep agencies or brain exercises promise an effortless route to a skill that educators know can only be achieved by the effort and sometimes drudgery of patient study. Nostrums are a boon to politicians willing to shred educational budgets while pinning high hopes on computer technology and the brain sciences rather than on pedagogy. Although mental development is in part a matter of brain growth, education is a normative discipline concerned not only with what happens in nature but also with what *should* happen and what one must take responsibility for. Rational thought, self-control and the understanding of rules and laws are urgent outcomes of literacy and schooling that may be addressed with a more adequate theory of reading and consciousness.

THE WAY AHEAD

A theory linking reading, consciousness and rationality has at its base the claim that reading is less a matter of learning visual symbols than a matter of discovering the implicit properties of speech. Support for the theory comes both from the history of writing and from empirical studies of children learning to read. The conceptual shifts involved in the invention of writing and those made by children when they are learning to read are much the same. In both cases it involves the discovery of underlying properties of language that the visual signs can represent. In this way learning to read is homologous to the invention of writing. The concepts invented in the course of devising a writing system, like those children acquire in learning to read, disclose a previously unsuspected world, the world of language. It is that awakening that defines a new literate consciousness. This general perspective was introduced in my earlier book, *The World on Paper*. While that book examined writing and literacy in terms of social and cultural diversity, this volume addresses the cognitive processes involved in turning language from a medium of communication into a means of thinking about thinking, for explicating and formalizing knowledge and for the critical reflection we think of as rationality. The argument is advanced as follows:

Part II sets out the theoretical background for the work. Chapter 2 provides a brief summary of the history of writing to show that the invention of a writing system was at the same time the discovery of the implicit structures of speech. Chapters 3, 4, and 5 provide reviews of how the Pragmatists, the Vygotskians and the Cognitive Scientists address the relation between writing and mind. In Part III, Chapters 6, 7, 8, 9 and 10 examine the cognitive structures uniquely associated with writing, namely, phonemes, words, sentences, extended prose and "test questions." Part IV examines the uses and implications of those cognitive structures. Chapter 11 examines theories and claims about reading, learning to read and the assessment of reading competence. Chapter 12 examines the relation between ordinary reasoning and formal rationality. Part V, Chapter 13 attempts to pull together the links between reading, consciousness and rationality and to justify the claim that a literate education is central to the development of a modern mind.

The basic claim, to be advanced in the course of 12 chapters, is that reading and writing provide both the structure and occasion for talking about language, that talking about language requires a metalanguage and that a metalanguage is the key to the development of a particular form of rationality.

PART II Theories of the Relation between Writing and Mind

2 Inventing Writing

The History of Writing and the Ontogeny of Writing

The civilization created by the Greeks and Romans was the first ... to become literate in the full meaning of the term, and to transmit its literacy to us. (Eric Havelock, 1982, p. 40)

To the non-reader the script in Figure 2.1 may as well be an example of infant doodling. The English script is just as puzzling to children learning to read as that of Linear B is to us. Linear B, a script from Crete and Mycenae that dates back to 1400 BC, was deciphered only some 60 years ago, the discovery announced in 1952. Deciphering it was difficult not only because one did not know where to begin but also because it was unclear just what sort of cognitive or linguistic unit each of the marks was meant to convey. Did the marks represent inventories of objects? Did they represent an aspect of language in an unknown tongue? Did they represent the sound patterns of a language? Cryptographers at least had knowledge of how their own writing system worked. Children lack even that.

Cryptographer Michael Ventris solved the puzzle of Linear B when he recognized the signs as representing the syllables of spoken Greek. Like many before him he had been misled by the fact that the script was found not in Greece but in Crete.

Ventris had an advantage over children when they are first exposed to writing. Ventris assumed, correctly it turned out, that the visual signs were representations of a language rather than a non-linguistic system of communication using visual signs. The distinction may be seen if we compare a writing system such as that studied by Ventris, or, for that matter, a modern alphabet, with a non-linguistic writing system.

FIGURE 2.1 NAMA Tablette 7671 Linear B: A Mycenean form of writing, *c.* 1400 BC, found in Knossos, Crete, that registers the amount of wool to be dyed.

SIGNS FOR PRESERVING AND COMMUNICATING INFORMATION

Consider the pre-contact pictorial writing system developed by the Blackfoot, a Canadian Aboriginal people in Southern Alberta, Canada. Their writings were inscribed on buffalo-hide teepees to serve as a "Winter count," a kind of chronicle for representing major yearly events in the history of the people. The figures shown in Figure 2.2 were copied into a notebook with their interpretation in English added by an Anglican priest around 1940, which is now stored in the Glenbow Museum in Calgary. Here are three typical entries:

Thus "The year that many horses got drowned" was depicted by painting a circle representing the lake with several stick-figure horses enclosed within it. The filled black box beside the drawing indicates that the drawing is to be taken as indicating a particular year as in a chronicle. Viewers "reading" that chronicle could then associate family events, such as the birth of a child, with the year visually chronicled as "The year many horses got drowned."

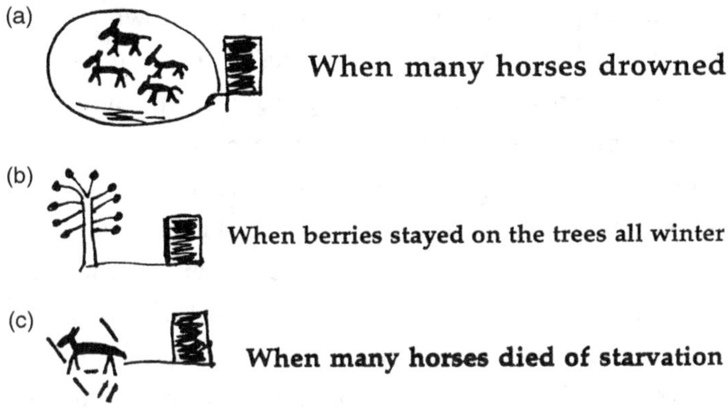

FIGURE 2.2 Blackfoot Winter Count.

This is a kind of visual communicative system. It is not a language in that the signs are not drawn from a limited inventory. Yet the fact that visual signs for communicating information could be devised without appeal to the particular properties of a verbal language has inspired some inventors to attempt to create a universal visual language that could be read in any ordinary language just as mathematical notations are. A number of attempts, going back to Leibniz's 17th-century proposals for a "Characteristica universalis," have attempted to design such a visible international language. One of the most ambitious was that made by Otto Neurath in the 1940s (Koterski, 2015), which used icons to denote objects and graphs to indicate relations. While such sign systems are widely used, they serve a limited function; no such system has yet been invented that matches the conceptual range afforded by a "full" writing system, one that represents a natural language. Visual languages serve a limited range of functions such as regulating pedestrian traffic or as diagrams, graphs and charts used for representing information. Mathematics perhaps comes closest to the ideal of an autonomous visual language, although computer languages may turn out to be of equal revolutionary significance. Yet neither of these formal languages have the semantic range of even the most primitive form of ordinary language.

Iconic or pictorial signs are important in showing that meaning can be communicated without appealing to linguistic form. But such visual signs convey meaning by designating events, not the *language* about those events. All of the world's writing systems (Daniels, 2009) represent meaning by means of signs for representing the language that expresses that meaning. The hypothesis I advanced in my earlier work (Olson, 1994), and that I elaborate herein, is that language is largely transparent to its non-literate users. Prior to the invention of writing there was no adequate metalanguage for talking about the properties of language that could serve as candidates for visual signs to represent. Hence there were no signs for phonemes, syllables, words and so on. A metalanguage for denoting entities suitable for representing by visual signs was a product, indeed a by-product of a long and complex history of writing. The history of writing can be summarized as a number of steps, with each invention building on the preceding one and each step revealing an unforeseen level of linguistic structure. This general hypothesis is applied to the specific cases of the discovery of phonemes, words and sentences in subsequent chapters. Here I will show only that the history of the invention of the alphabet provides evidence for the general claim that the invention of writing provided the occasion for developing consciousness of the implicit properties of speech.

THE INVENTION OF SIGNS FOR LANGUAGE

Aristotle (350 BC) in *On Interpretation* claimed that language is composed of signs for things and that writing is a set of signs for signs: "Spoken words are the symbols of mental experience and written words are the symbols of spoken words." This definition is sufficient to exclude alternative forms of visual communication. Indeed, it is now widely agreed that any full writing system is capable of rendering in visual form anything that is spoken.

Students of the history of writing further agree that the earlier historians such as Gelb (1963) and Diringer (1968) erred in thinking that the inventors of writing systems were attempting to represent spoken utterances, implying that earlier writing systems were largely failed attempts to achieve that goal. Early forms of writing are now seen as directed to creating a functioning system of visual communication and not an attempt to represent language. Cooper (2008, p. 83), for example, concluded that "no writing system was invented, or used early on, to mimic spoken language." Representing language was a slow and largely unintended achievement: "For the Egyptian and Mesopotamian scripts … a relatively full notation of language, including its grammar … was reached perhaps half a millennium after their first appearance" (Baines, 2008, p. 150).

Why, one wonders, did they not just set out to create a system of visual marks to represent the structure of the spoken language? The earliest writing served a narrow set of purposes, primarily keeping records of business transactions. But business transactions were verbal agreements. Why not represent the actual verbal expressions? One reason, as I mentioned above, is that an appropriate set of concepts about the properties of language that could be visually represented was not available to the inventors. In inventing and borrowing writing systems, they were discovering the properties of the language they spoke.

This should not strike readers as wildly speculative. The inventions of grammar and logic, explicit concepts for talking about the structure of language, were major achievements of the classical Greeks. The inventions of grammar and logic are important discoveries about language, sufficiently novel and important to have drawn enthusiastic audiences to scholars such as Socrates and, in the Middle Ages, to Abelard, and at Oxford to students of the *trivium* of grammar, logic and rhetoric. Only in the past century did Ferdinand de Saussure set out a modern theory of the structure of language and in our time Noam Chomsky advance a conception of grammar more adequate to an account of the production and comprehension of language. Linguists continue to make fascinating discoveries about the implicit properties of grammar (Pinker, 1994). So we should not be surprised that pre-reading children and adults with no exposure to written language have limited insight into the mechanics of their own speech. Linguistic processes are in large part implicit, essentially unconscious and hence did not volunteer their properties to the inventors of writing. The history of the alphabet is the history of discovery of some of these unconscious properties and processes.

THE INVENTION OF THE ALPHABET

Figure 2.3 is a sound spectrogram for the utterance "Hispanic costumes are quite colorful." Not only are there no breaks in the utterance corresponding to particular words, even the final syllable of "Hispanic" completely overlaps with the first syllable of "costumes." Yet listeners have no difficulty in distinguishing the two words while remaining oblivious to their overlap. But how then could this stream of sounds of speech be represented by visual signs? What should the signs represent? As we shall see, attempts to use visual marks for

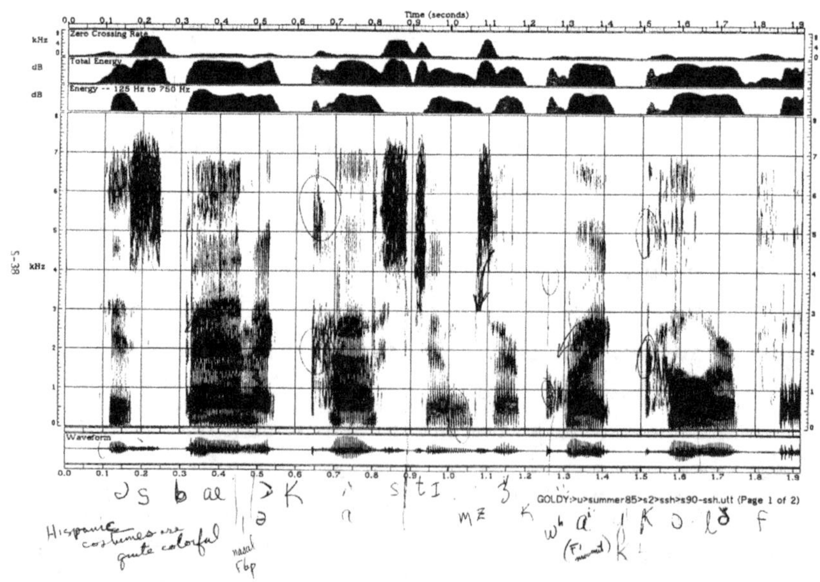

FIGURE 2.3 Sound spectrogram of "Hispanic costumes are quite colorful."

communicative purposes led to a variety of attempts to create distinctive signs adequate to the preservation and communication of an unambiguous meaning. Important discoveries about language came with the invention of signs that represent the implicit properties of speech, including words and syllables, and then, primarily but not exclusively in alphabetic scripts, phonemes.

Word signs. The procedure adopted by the Blackfoot is ancient indeed. "Art was age-old when writing began," wrote Denise Schmandt-Besserat (2007). Carved stones and antlers carrying images of bison and deer and painted images on cave walls go back some 15,000 to 20,000 years. In the 8th and 7th millennium BC, Near Eastern farmers decorated their houses with paintings and pottery and made reliefs in stone and plaster. Writing as we know it, that is as a representation of spoken expressions, came later, beginning in Ancient Sumeria around 3000 BC.

Visual marks and signs began to serve as symbols with fixed, conventionalized meanings around 7500 BC when tokens were first used to represent objects and goods as part of commercial transactions. A cone, a sphere or a disk could represent different quantities of grain, a cylinder a particular animal, a geometrical shape a unit of labor and so on. These combined with seals representing particular owners could then represent a transaction, providing a sort of record associating a particular person with a certain number of animals or a certain quantity of a commodity. A clay token for a vat of oil resembled an actual vat; two vats of oil would be represented by two similar tokens. A major step toward writing as we know it was taken when signs came to represent transactions in a language-like way with separate signs for number and object numbered, as shown in Figure 2.4.

FIGURE 2.4 Two ways of representing objects and quantities: Three ducks and "Three ducks."

The transition from token to verbal sign is an oft-told but dramatic story.

Schmandt-Besserat (1992) argued that the decisive step occurred when instead of using six sheep-like tokens collected into a container to represent a transaction involving six sheep, the ancient Sumerians came to represent the six sheep by two word signs, one for the entity and one for the number 6, inscribed into a clay surface. The result was cuneiform, in which signs for objects could be combined with signs for number, as in Figure 2.5.

This figure of a cuneiform tablet from Ur in Mesopotamia, dated to 2960 BC, lists the contents of a warehouse. That in the third column, topmost row – a cross-hatched triangle representing a vat of beer (the vat laid on its side) – is combined with a series of indentations representing the number of vats. Thus the signs are to be read by combining the signs to express a proposition just as speech does, and could be read as 12 vats of beer. Thus the visual signs changed from representing things to representing the words for things, thus producing the first *logographs* or word signs. As word signs they could be combined syntactically with other word signs to convey a meaning. Not only is this an economical notational system, it directs attention to the language used as opposed to the event represented. This is what is meant by consciousness of language.

So began the concept of *word,* first for names and nouns and then for the possibility of lists of words, lexical lists and eventually the more modern idea that any utterance is composed of combinations of words. Word knowledge, that is, knowledge *about* words as opposed to knowledge of the things words pointed to, was first articulated by means of such visual sign systems (Watson & Horowitz, 2011, p. 160).

Syllable signs. We may be more certain that the signs were taken as representing aspects of spoken language when a *logographic* sign representing an object was borrowed to represent a sound or a syllable of a word for a different object, the so-called rebus principle.

FIGURE 2.5 Syntactic writing. Cuneiform tablet from Ur, 2960 BC, itemizing contents of a storehouse.

Word signs for "bee" and "leaf" could be combined to represent a different word, "belief," thus each sign changed from a word sign to a syllable sign. This involves a new kind of metalinguistic ability, namely, the ability to separate the sound from the meaning, and then using the sound as a constituent of a sign for a different word.

A clear example of borrowing signs for objects to serve as signs for sounds may be seen in Egyptian hieroglyphic writing, where each sign now represents a syllable. A series of such signs enclosed in a cartouche represented the names of the monarch, Cleopatra and Ptolemy; this provided a clue to its decipherment. Jean-François Champollion's decipherment of ancient Egyptian in 1822 came with the recognition that the series of signs for representing the name Cleopatra, shown in Figure 2.6, contained a sign (the lion) in the second position that also occurred in the fourth position in the sign for

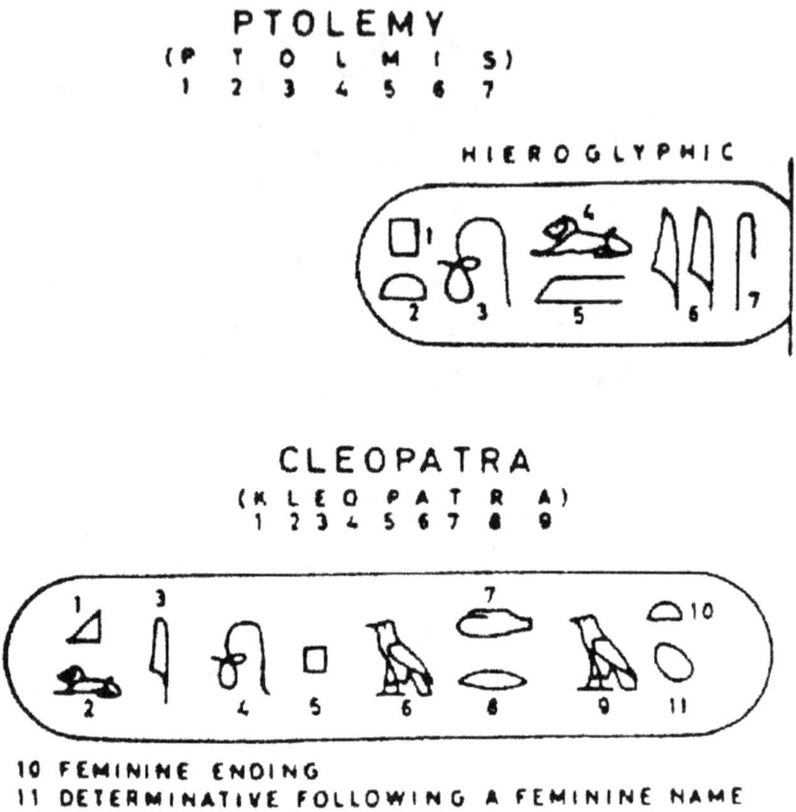

FIGURE 2.6 Egyptian hieroglyphic signs for the royal names: Cleopatra and Ptolemy.

Ptolemy, from which he could infer that it represented the sound /l/. Deciphering the royal names thus distinguished some of the sounds that occurred in the ordinary words, thereby opening up to modern readers the extensive inscriptions of an otherwise lost tradition. Landgrafova (2013) calls such signs consonant signs, but as there were no signs for vowels, they can equally well be called syllable signs. She shows that some hieroglyphic signs represent single consonants, some two consonants and some three. Other signs represent whole words and still others represent "classifiers" that indicate the conceptual class that the word falls into, for example, the sign for "bear" would carry the unpronounced classifier "animal," and the cartouche drawn around the name Cleopatra carries the unpronounced classifier "royal name."

The same phonological principle, that of the rebus, was used when the signs representing words in one language were borrowed to represent the similar sounds that occurred in quite a different language, Akkadian. Thus signs originally used to represent words in Sumerian came to be used as signs for syllables in Akkadian. In each case, the invention of signs involved the discovery of implicit properties of speech, from words to syllables to phonemes.

Prior to the invention of the alphabet no one could have predicted or intuited that their speech was composed of some 40 phonemes that could be represented by some 26 distinctive letters that in combination represent the entire lexicon of English. English is composed of some 600,000 words, of which an ordinary speaker knows about 20,000 and the average high school graduate knows about 45,000 (Nagy & Anderson, 1984).

How syllables came to be analyzed into consonants and vowels is perhaps the most dramatic part of the story. Although signs for syllabic sounds were invented in all of the writing systems of the world, the alphabet with distinctive signs for vowels was invented only once and that by the classical Greeks sometime around 750 BC. Although sometimes celebrated as a work of genius, it is now more commonly recognized as the consequence of borrowing a writing system that was adequate for the representation of one language to represent a different language for which it was less suited. The result was that word signs became syllable signs and syllable signs became signs for phonemes.

This was the case when an existing Semitic script, presumably Phoenician, was borrowed for writing the Greek language. As we noted, the earlier form of Greek writing called Linear B had disappeared. The Semitic script represented a class of syllables that shared an initial sound or "onset" by means of a single sign. Thus syllables /be/bi/bo/bu/ were all represented by a single sign "b" representing the sound /b/. However, there were no signs for vowels. Gelb called such a writing system an unvocalized syllabary, although it could equally appropriately be called a consonantal alphabet. When borrowed to write the Greek language, many of the syllabic signs adequately represent sounds in Greek; these were adopted to represent the consonants. But unlike a Semitic language, Greek and other Indo-European languages, including English, use vowel sounds as single words and vowel differences are used to make lexical distinctions, so some new signs were needed. Signs from Phoenician that had no equivalent sounds in Greek were borrowed to represent the Greek vowel sounds. And once vowels were represented explicitly as independent sounds, those vowel sounds could be heard as embedded in syllables. So the syllable was divided into two signs, one for the vowel and one for the consonant. Thus what had been represented by the letter *b* could now be represented distinctively by letter pairs as *ba, be, bi, bo* and *bu*. Thus was the alphabet born.

The Greek invention was prompted, it has been argued (Powell, 1991), to represent the complex linguistic forms of the Greek language found in the great orally composed Homeric poems, *The Iliad* and *The Odyssey*. The Semitic script was perfectly adequate for representing commercial and other business transactions, so the novel task of representing the ancient treasured works of Homer may well have served as the occasion for its invention.

Thus, the invention of the alphabet was not an explicit attempt to represent phonemes; it was rather that the inventors discovered such properties in their attempt to make a writing system adequate to representing unambiguously the meanings of spoken Greek. Only with an alphabet does the written code acquire resources more or less equal to those of spoken language. Even then, the letters of the alphabet are at best an approximation to the phonemes of the language and it was only in the 20th century that Jakobson and others produced a modern theory of phonology.

Although there are many writing systems in the world, at least two of which were invented independently, that in ancient Sumeria and that in ancient Mesoamerica, all full writing systems represent some of the underlying properties of a spoken language. In the case of the alphabet that history consisted of the invention of visual marks to represent increasingly abstract properties of speech, each invention bringing with it a new consciousness of an aspect of language. Thus the history of writing reveals a history of the discovery of the implicit and largely unconscious properties of our most universal human accomplishment, namely, our ability to speak. Through a long history of invention and revision the inventors ultimately hit upon word-like and phoneme-like constituents. Discovery of those constituents was a remarkable achievement analogous to that begun 3,000 years later, and yet to be completed, of identifying the underlying constituents of matter.

The obstacle to the invention of the alphabet was not only, or even primarily, that of creating an inventory of distinguishable visual signs for communicating meanings. It was primarily a problem of finding suitable things in spoken language for the signs to represent if one was to have a manageable inventory of signs and if they were to be capable of representing everything that could be said.

The history of writing is not confined to the invention of scripts but must also take into account the institutional practices for preserving, using and teaching that script. The importance of the institutional context for teaching and learning to the rise of Greek literacy has been demonstrated by Leiper (2013).

HOW CHILDREN REINVENT WRITING

If the invention of writing was in large part a matter of bringing increasingly abstract properties of language into consciousness, it is reasonable to expect that some aspects of this discovery process will recur as children learn to read and write. Yet it remains controversial if not implausible to claim that adults who are competent speakers as well as pre-reading children, avid word learners all, are not aware of words, phonemes and other underlying properties of their language. Let us consider some informal observations that suggest that language processes are largely unconscious even when the reference or meaning, the product of those processes, is conscious.

Young children's language flows out of them, often unprompted, in what seems like an automatic and unconscious way. Ruth Weir's (1962) *Language in the Crib* and Katherine Nelson's (1989) *Narratives in the Crib* documented this productivity in the verbal and narrative soliloquies of 2-year-old children.[1] Such observations suggest that young children are never lost for words. Far from being rendered speechless by their limited vocabulary and grammar, their thinking seems to take shape in the very act of speaking. While they are clearly conscious of what they are talking about in that they require answers for questions and actions in response to requests, they seem to be unaware of the linguistic processes involved in doing so. Of course, we as adults have no idea either of how we generate an utterance or type a sentence into our computer. The language just magically appears while we monitor the meanings expressed. A useful analogy is the action of whistling a tune; we have no idea of how we do it but we recognize the tune produced.

On the other hand, children, especially those in literate households, play word games, try out different sounds, imitate the language they hear including meaningless nursery rhymes. And they acquire some metalinguistic concepts such as *say*, *ask*, *promise*, as well as *story*, *song* and to *yell* and *whisper.* But, critically, they tend not to acquire concepts of *word* or *phoneme* until they are taught or otherwise pick them up in the context of parents reading books to children (Aram, Fine & Ziv, 2013).

Consciousness of the internal structure of language comes more from attempts at representation than from the activity of speaking.

[1] I recently overheard a neighborhood 3-year-old generate an endless streak of comprehensible speech as she walked along with her mother. I stopped the mother and asked what the child was saying. She replied, "Oh nothing. Just was daddy home? Where was he? When would he be home? and so on and on." The child is clearly aware of what she was talking about but the language flowed effortlessly and unconsciously. It took a theoretical linguist, Chomsky, not a child psychologist to first insist on this point.

One expression of children's earliest interest in symbolic activities is in their attempts at drawing. From an early age children distinguish drawing from writing yet remain unsure about the difference. Informal observations confirm those documented by researchers. If in pausing after reading the sentence "My porridge is too hot!" in the story of Goldilocks, a pre-reading child is asked "Where does it say 'My porridge is too hot'?" the child is likely to point to the accompanying picture of the hot porridge. Children a few months older, but still pre-readers, when asked the same question are likely to point vaguely to the printed page of the text itself. Still later they begin to search for the actual expression. But by then they have become readers.

In the course of more systematic investigations on the relation between reading and awareness of words (Homer & Olson, 1999), pre-reading children were asked to write a number of expressions. One such child protested that she did not know how to write. She was prompted to "pretend to write 'cat'." As the copy of the actual transcript collected on that occasion and shown in Figure 2.7 shows, the child made a long squiggly line. She was not tempted to draw a cat; writing was obviously different.

But what did the squiggly line represent to the child? That was sorted out by asking follow-up questions: "Can you write 'Two cats'?" She made two squiggles, pointing to each squiggle in turn: "One cat, Two cats." Asked to write "Three cats," she made three squiggles. Asked to write "No cats" she paused, then waved the pencil slightly above the paper and said: "There are no cats so I didn't write anything." The point to note is that she had yet to make a fundamental discovery. Writing is about the language, what was "said," rather than about the world, what was "meant" or referred to. Even after children know letters they may write "dog-dog" to represent two dogs rather than represent the word "two" in writing, as the transcript of such an interview made by Bruce Homer (Figure 2.8) indicates.

Other developmental psychologists have observed a similar pattern when pre-reading children are asked to write something. The

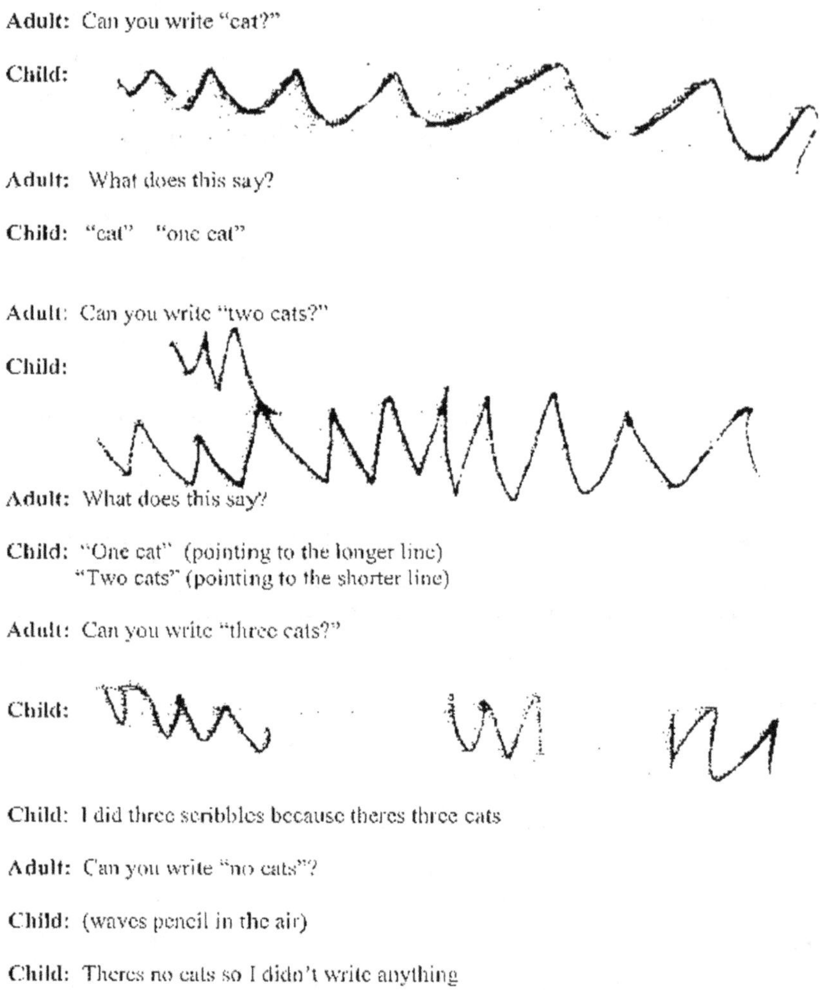

FIGURE 2.7 Can you write "Three cats"? Copy of the original data sheet; printed text inserted later.

practice of picturing the world gives way to representing the properties of language. Ferreiro (1985, p. 251) (see also Ferreiro & Teberosky, 1982; Vernon, 2002) found a series of stages in children's learning to use written signs. Their earliest attempts used a single known letter such as a /k/ to represent a thing, duplicating the sign to represent two things. Later they began to select from their limited inventory

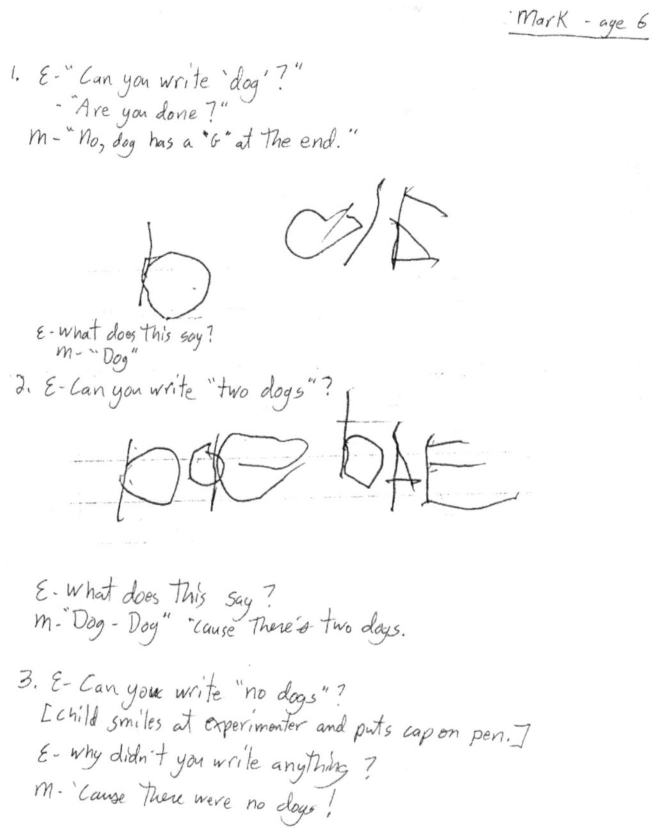

FIGURE 2.8 Can you write "Dog"? Copy of original data sheet for one subject.

of signs to produce letter strings, using each letter to represent a part of the thing represented rather than part of a word. Thus one child attempting to write "barco" (boat) claimed that one letter or even two was not enough, it said only "ba"; another letter, chosen arbitrarily, must be added to make "bar-co." "With one letter missing it is still an 'incomplete boat' the child insists."

Children's developing understanding of how visual signs may be used to represent a meaning is shown in a study by Pelletier (2002), who found that if preschool children were asked to represent

FIGURE 2.9 Write "Three hockey sticks."

"three hockey sticks" they often drew the three hockey sticks then appended the numeral 3 to the drawing. Only later did they recognize that the message could be adequately represented by the numeral 3 and a single hockey stick, one sign for each word. These children were well on their way to using written signs to represent linguistic forms.

When they do begin to use their inventory of written letters to represent the sounds they can detect in their own speech, their constructions are marvels of invention, as shown in Figure 2.10. "Hockey" is rendered "hoocee" and "sticks" as "sdeecx." One can fairly hear the sounds being squeezed out of the words by the beginning writer.

Eskritt, in her study of children's move from depiction to notation (Eskritt & Olson, 2012), asked young children to represent such objects as a red triangle, a blue circle or a green rectangle by pictorial means. The youngest simply drew a triangle and colored it red. Somewhat older children produced a patch of red followed by, redundantly, a red triangle! Only the most sophisticated children produced a red patch followed by a colorless triangle, thereby duplicating in their drawing the very syntactical properties of a spoken expression. Their visual signs had become word signs and the sequence of

FIGURE 2.10 "Dad has 3 hockey sticks."

signs represented the sequence of spoken words. Furthermore, the less able children accepted both depictions of red and of triangle as acceptable representations of the red triangle, while the more able children rejected such partial representations as ambiguous and also recognized the possible ambiguity of verbal messages. As we shall see later, children at this stage are also willing to accept as true such statements as "Some elephants have trunks" even if older children reject them. This suggests that children's understanding of notations reflect their developing awareness of the structures of language.

Although the youngest children enjoy drawing and showing their drawings to others, their talk is primarily about the content of the drawing, not the shapes and lines that they explore to express that content. Consequently, when they encounter or invent written signs they tend to regard them as thing-signs, not word-signs. They have yet to learn to think about an utterance as composed of a string of isolatable words. This hypothesis brings together two independent claims. One from Vygotsky who claimed, as we shall see in more detail in Chapter 4, that language is transparent to young children, the other from Goody (1977), who argued that writing was responsible for the invention of the concept of *word* as a linguistic object.

I have reviewed some of the evidence from the history of writing and from learning to write to show that what literate adults take as obvious is a hard-won conceptual achievement. It was not apparent to the inventors of signs for writing, nor is it to children learning them, that visual marks should map on to spoken utterances, specifically to the underlying constituents – sounds, words and sentences – of spoken language. Thus begins a lifelong practice of thinking about language and its properties. The metalinguistic concepts instrumental in thinking about language, as we shall see, are just those required for thinking about thinking, indeed for rationality. Our next task is to see how three lines of contemporary theory, Pragmatism, Vygotskian theory and cognitive science, address the role of writing in mind with a view to building a more comprehensive and adequate theory.

3 Dewey and the New Pragmatists

Reading, Writing and Mind

If letters devised for the purpose, presumably, of facilitating commercial transactions had not developed into literature, they would still be technical equipments, and we ourselves might live amid hardly a higher culture than that of our savage ancestors. (Dewey, 1934/2003, p. 327)

A PLACE FOR WRITING IN PHILOSOPHICAL AND EDUCATIONAL THEORY

Although language has become central to all philosophical and psychological accounts of human cognition, writing has been slow to find a place in such theories. Writing is commonly seen as a simple, transparent cipher for speech, lacking in significance in its own right. Even when writing has been seen as a "tool of the intellect," like other tools it is seen as facilitating certain tasks rather than as altering the functions or structures of the mind. Consequently there is little in the sciences of mind that could explain the complexities of creating and learning a writing system that were examined in the last chapter.

Nor could theories of cognition that overlook or minimize the significance of writing account for the conspicuous prominence of writing and written documents in modern life, indeed in the very creation of what we think of as modernity. Whereas the teaching of writing and literacy has now reached some 85% of the world's population, the study of writing as a theoretical problem has languished. The place for writing and literacy in the formation of knowledge, in the ways we think and reason, in our consciousness and sense of self, in a word, in the theory of mind, is largely ahead of us.

The sources of this neglect in the sciences are not difficult to find. Although the human capacity for speech has become central to the study of mind, writing has remained secondary, often seen merely as a convenient recording device. Consequently writing has been slow to earn a place in the psychology and philosophy of mind. As mentioned, Saussure (1916/1983, pp. 23–24) insisted that the spoken form of language was the appropriate object of study. He then set out a purely formal description of language as an abstract system independent from use. Thus "structuralism" has become the dominant model for modern linguistic, psycholinguistic and literary theory. And as the structures of writing are essentially those of speaking, one theory, structuralists assume, should be adequate for both. Linguists (Joos, 1967) chose to distinguish "registers" of speaking rather than distinguishing speaking from writing. The consequence was that linguists, with notable exceptions, have been slow to find a place for written language. Socio-cultural theories, to be considered more fully in the next chapter, while taking literacy seriously, either subordinate writing to existing social practices (Scribner & Cole, 1981), treat it as one among many "mediational means" (Wertsch, Tulviste & Hagstrom, 1993), or insist that all literacies are local (Street, 1984). Hence, the study of language development, logical development and rationality often proceed without due attention to the significance of writing and the role played by the written tradition in the formation of the modern mind. The irony, then, is that while reading and writing are at the top of the political and educational agendas worldwide, little in the prevailing theories of language and mind appears to justify this commitment.

Not all writers have dismissed writing and a few have considered writing as a transformative technology. Unlike Saussure, C. S. Peirce (1872, cited by Misak, 2013, p. 42), the father of Pragmatism, argued that thinking in logic and mathematics depends upon certain visual properties of writing. Thinking, he wrote, "consists in constructing an icon or diagram the relation of whose parts shall present a complete analogy with those of the parts of the object of reasoning."

He never extended this argument to the spatial properties of written linguistic texts themselves, but he invited such thought and his colleague John Dewey seized on this idea to justify his claim that writing was an important "tool of the intellect."

These two founding fathers of semiotics, Saussure and Peirce, had very different conceptions of language. Saussure set out the systematic form or structure of a natural language as a shared means of communication, whereas Peirce examined the possible uses of that system for thinking and reasoning for oneself. Peirce's primary concern was with the ways that a natural language was used in thinking, adding that only writing offered a new spatialized medium for operating on those signs. Peirce was not the first to recognize the importance of the spatial properties of the medium of writing. Kramer (2012, p. 12) has shown how philosophers ranging from Socrates, to Descartes and to Leibniz offered "a vision of radically turning our mental attention in cognitive processes to the acts of writing down, reading, and manipulating inscriptions perceivable by the senses, without having to be distracted by questions of interpretation." But these remained minority reports until recently.

Peirce's lead was taken up by Dewey (1980, p. 64), who, as mentioned, saw writing as a prominent tool for thinking. Yet Dewey provided no analysis of just how the tool functioned nor why it was distinctive. In spite of these nods to the importance of writing, writing remained unaddressed in the philosophy and psychology of mind and knowledge until quite recently. As the epigram to the chapter indicated, psychologists and educators have tended to see reading and writing as skills that could be taught through practice rather than as a symbolic system with a unique but unspecified relation to speaking.

The turning tide, if it is so, was marked by Richard Rorty (1981), a modern Pragmatist who contrasted 19th-century "idealism" with 20th-century "textualism." Instead of examining ideas, modern philosophers have devoted attention to language and texts. Lyotard (1984, p. 3) announced the project: "Our working hypothesis is that the status of knowledge is altered as societies enter what is known as the postindustrial age and cultures enter what is known as the postmodern age." He distinguished the modern and the postmodern on the basis of a new concern with language and discourse. Whereas the modern concern was to give a complete description of the world – to see nature as it truly is – the postmodern changes its focus to the language in which the world is described. Science comes to be seen as a kind of literate discourse, "a branch of literature" as Popper (1972) put it. Lyotard continues:

> It is fair to say that for the last forty years the "leading" sciences and technologies have had to do with language: phonology and theories of linguistics, problems of communication and cybernetics, modern theories of algebra and informatics, computers and their languages, problems of translation and the search for areas of compatibility among computer languages, problems of information storage and data banks, telematics and the perfection of intelligent terminals, paradoxology. (1984, pp. 4–5)

But aside from announcing that something is afoot, Lyotard can do little more than insist that "knowledge cannot survive unchanged within this context of general transformation" (1984, p. 4).

The "linguistic turn" in philosophy may be seen as one expression of this more general textualism. Psychology too, with its concepts of analytical rationality and the extended mind, reflects this turn. But to understand the new linguistic pragmatism we must review the first pragmatists.

DEWEY'S PRAGMATISM IN EDUCATIONAL THEORY

Dewey's Pragmatism has particular appeal to educators because he began his career as a teacher and knew first-hand the complexities of classroom teaching. Furthermore he recognized how self-defeating routines of drill and practice and memorizing authoritative texts were to learners, a practice he sometimes denounced as "book learning."

Dewey came to recognize that the reform of education was blocked not only by a reactionary public but also by an obsolete philosophy of knowledge and a mechanistic behavioristic psychology. Knowledge then, and for many even now, was thought of as that body of objective truths far removed from the everyday experience of ordinary people, truths that had to be instilled in children through a discipline of training and testing. Dewey's Pragmatism set out an alternative.

Dewey found his allies among a group of colleagues who called themselves, somewhat ironically, for they disavowed metaphysics, the Metaphysical Club, whose activities are now well known because of the celebrated book of that name (Menand, 2001; but see also Misak, 2013). Dewey, along with friends and colleagues Charles Peirce, William James and Oliver Wendell Holmes, advanced their alternative approach to knowledge under the label of Pragmatism to emphasize the importance of action, of doing and undergoing, and of formulating truths appropriate to action and judgment. Dewey's utilitarian theory of knowledge was offered as an alternative to what he called "the spectator theory of knowledge." To the Pragmatists, knowledge was practical and action-oriented, a consequence of doing and trying to do, of experimenting and discovery. Peirce's model was derived from his knowledge of modern laboratory science and is fully congruent with the way that scientific knowledge is now thought to progress. Thinking was seen as dependent upon the tools available or invented, first language, but also mathematics, the laboratory and, in an unspecified way, writing.

Although Pragmatic principles continue to guide and inform practical educators, Pragmatism lost its place in educational theory and policy making in the 1920s in part because of its perceived permissivism and lack of standards (Arendt, 1954) and in part due to the availability of a more objective alternative, namely, Behaviorism in the form of Thorndikean "testing and measurement" empiricism (Lagemann, 2000). Behaviorism swept away the "mysteries" of agency, meaning, intentionality, judgment and responsibility as unobservables and replaced such mysteries with measurable outcomes of practical skills. Reading and writing, once seen as basic skills, came rather to be seen as the output of still more basic skills or subskills – analyzing speech sounds and sounding-out letters among them – that may be systematically taught and objectively assessed. Empirical findings turned reading research into a hard science with a degree of objectivity that Dewey's child-centered theories were unable to match. What was lost, Dewey's followers insist, was a concern for the learner's subjective experiences, their beliefs, feelings, understandings and goals. Attention to what the child is doing and thinking may be essential if teaching is to succeed. Furthermore, attention to learners' intentional actions is essential if we are to understand how learning to read and write contributes to consciousness of language and mind.

It matters practically because, as Dewey and the Pragmatists noted, the teaching of reading was not only often unsuccessful, it had become an overprescribed, over-regimented drudgery in the attempt to raise test scores. It was seen as sacrificing children's ingenuity, their willingness to think, to try, even to fail, and to take on any responsibility for their own successes and failures. Behaviorism had displaced the agency and responsibility for learning from the child and on to the teacher, thereby depriving the child of some of the satisfactions of personal achievement while attributing learning failure to teacher failure. Behaviorism, critics claimed, turned learners into passive recipients of hand-me-down knowledge rather than explorers of the world both directly and through notational systems. It overlooked children's own experience and intuition and reduced learning and thinking to mere compliance with an adult-imposed standard, in the worst case "drilling children into stupefied acquiescence," as Alan Ryan once expressed it.

Current criticisms of the now predominant "standards and accountability" movement are a reprise of those leveled by Dewey in the early 20th century. While, as mentioned, teachers are now more Deweyan in outlook, researchers and policy makers remain in thrall to measurable outputs of children's skills rather than to children's experience, knowledge and understanding; in a word, their consciousness. So although policy makers continue to "turn the screw" in the attempt to mandate higher scores, much of the world looks in admiration at the Finnish schools that manage to obtain high scores without the regimens of testing (Sahlberg, 2011). I discuss this issue more fully in Chapter 11.

The revival of Pragmatism and of Deweyan aspirations in educational thought may be seen in Jerome Bruner's introduction to *The Process of Education* (1960). That book, a report of a workshop composed of leading scientists and educators, addressed the "renewal of concern for the quality and intellectual aims of education" (Bruner, 1960, p. 1). Researchers, Bruner added: "had turned their attention with great effect to the study of aptitude and achievement and to social and motivational aspects of education, *but did not concern themselves directly with the intellectual structure of class activities*" (1960, p. 4). Those intellectual aims were to be addressed by rethinking how the content of various scientific disciplines could be approached as problems to think about rather than as facts to be learned. In fact, the curricula of all the major disciplines were then reorganized to make them more problem-oriented topics for research and argument. And while reading and writing are now seen as a part of "the language arts," analogous problem-solving approaches to learning to read have largely failed to overturn the traditional focus on narrowly defined testable outcomes. As long as reading is thought of as a skill to be mastered rather than as a distinctive form of knowledge, such a reformation is unlikely to take place.

In fact, a re-reading of Dewey's classic *Art as Experience* (1934), especially chapter 3 in which he offered the concept of "experience" as a possible solution to the classical dichotomy between subject, what is in the mind, and object, what is in the world, and chapter 13 in which he distinguished instrumental perception from critical judgment, the distinction I address in terms of "metarepresentation" will find little in need of revision. It could, nonetheless, benefit from being brought into more modern discourse. Janack (2012) has argued that current initiatives such as situated cognition, Gibsonian ecological perception and theories of agency fit nicely within Dewey's Pragmatism.

THE NEW PRAGMATISTS

Pragmatism as a branch of philosophy has recently had something of a revival in the hands of linguistic philosophers such as Richard Rorty, Donald Davidson, Robert Brandom and David Bakhurst, all of whom trace their own work through Dewey back to the idealism of Immanuel Kant in the 18th century. For Kant judgment was the critical act in the formation of knowledge. Judgment is something one does, that one is conscious of and that one is responsible for. It is an action and not something that just happens to one, but rather something for which one is responsible.

For modern pragmatists, then, judgment is an aspect of every act; one judges whether an action was a success or a failure, every utterance as correct or incorrect, true or false, understood or misunderstood. For Rorty, knowledge is not an objectively correct mental picture of the world but rather a guide to practical social action (although see Misak, below). For Brandom, what is distinctive about judgments and intentional actions is that they are *normative*, that is, they are correct or incorrect, right or wrong, successful or unsuccessful. They are intentional actions that we are conscious of and *that we are responsible for*. Pragmatism places the actor as the agent of his or her knowledge; rewards and punishments, rather than affecting behavior directly, as the Behaviorists claimed, are seen as having an effect only in terms of their relations to the intentional action of agents. Furthermore, learning simple habits becomes thinking only when what is learned is cast into concepts expressible in a public language. To speak a public language is to honor agreements about usage with other speakers of the language. Those agreements are what constitute the *norms* for correct and incorrect usage. For the Pragmatists the habits, dispositions and brain processes recruited in speaking and reading must be seen as in the service of social practices carried out intentionally by conscious and responsible persons. In this way writing and literacy may be incorporated into a modern pragmatic theory of knowledge, mind and education.

What did Dewey actually say about language and literacy? Dewey wrote a great deal about language, referring to language as the "tool of tools" (Dewey, 1986a, p. 134). He wrote: "Language ... is the medium in which culture exists and through which it is transmitted" (Dewey, 1986b, p. 28). And again: "Any theory must face the problem of the extraordinary differences that mark off the activities and achievements of human beings from those of other biological forms ... The development of language is the key to this transformation" (Dewey, 1986b, p. 50). Yet as Brandom (2011, p. 28) points out, Dewey lacked a theory of language adequate to spelling out either how language "demarked" the shift between humans and other animals or what "leverage" the acquisition of language gave humans in coping with the world. Brandom concluded that Dewey would never be numbered among the philosophers of language. Dewey discussed language primarily as a social process for coordinating cognition between persons useful for reducing egocentrism and allowing persons to cooperate in building their knowledge of the world. He never saw language as key to distinctively human thought. The laboratory was, to the Pragmatists, a more appealing model.

And although Dewey took literacy as important, his more immediate goal was to subordinate "book learning" – what he took to be the incarnation of the "spectator theory of knowledge" – to first-hand experience, a view sometimes caricaturized as learning chemistry through gardening, and the like. He objected to the classical view that knowledge was embedded in books and that a thinking person was one who knew what was in them. Rather, for Dewey every child was an experimenter building up a picture of the world; books were to be seen as an additional resource in advancing and sharing one's own understanding with the wider world. On the other hand, when Dewey emphasized the importance of language he referred to language "in its widest sense – that is, including all means of communication," including writing. There is an apparent contradiction between valuing writing and yet disparaging book learning, a contradiction that may be resolved by distinguishing between texts as objects to be learned and resources to think with, Dewey's real goal.

So although Dewey never disparaged writing he saw it as merely one means among many, not as a distinctive intellectual resource. Indeed, he promoted literacy around the world. Early in the 20th century he advised Kemal Ataturk on his initiative to reform the Turkish writing system from one based on Arabic to one based on a Roman alphabet in the attempt to achieve universal literacy and to move Turkey from the Ottoman Empire into the modern Western world.

Misak (2013) has pointed out an important limitation of Dewey's pragmatism, a limitation perhaps more in the uptake of Dewey than in Dewey himself. This was his willingness to make "truth" secondary to practical usefulness, sometimes glossed as "truth is what works." In fact, it was William James who made that claim; Dewey identified truth with the revisable knowledge that the most advanced sciences currently take to be true. Yet as Misak shows, he is vulnerable to the charge of "relativism," making "truth" relative to practical social activity rather than to a defensible objective standard that could be pursued and is worth pursuing. Dewey's conflation of truth with usefulness undermined the credibility of his more general theory.

The source of the difficulty lies in the fact that Dewey wrote long before the so-called "linguistic turn" in philosophy and psychology, the turn associated with Wittgenstein's *Philosophical Investigations* (1958) and Hacking's *Why Does Language Matter to Philosophy?* (1975). Dewey assumed continuity between practical action, habit formation, problem solving and reflective thought. Although he distinguished "primary or first-hand and secondary or reflective experience" (Murphy, 1990, p. 68) and insisted that all reflective thought must be grounded in primary experience, he took the transition to be natural and developmental, continuous with what had gone before.

Children, he claimed, were as engaged in deep thought about falling objects as was Newton; both looking for what happens and what works in the attempt to build a general model of the world. But that leaves unclear just what was distinctive about Newtonian science and about theoretical language-based thinking more generally.

The New Pragmatist philosophers such as Brandom and Bakhurst state the relations more boldly, arguing that the functions of language in mind are unique in creating what philosopher Wilfred Sellars (1997) called "the space of reasons," a kind of verbal discourse in the mind that identifies thinking with the giving of reasons. Conceptual capacities are to be seen as linguistic capacities; "Assertion [is not] the expression of an interior act of judgment; judgment, rather, is the interiorization of the external act of assertion" (Dummett, 1993). These philosophers make the case that the linguistic forms on which reflective thought depends are culturally invented and taught rather than an inevitable higher stage of development. Bakhurst (2011) emphasizes the importance of education to human development. He argues that through the acquisition of language and other social activities including education, human beings acquire conceptual structures and forms of reasoning that enable scientific thinking.

The New Pragmatists adopt from Peirce the notion that speaking is a pragmatic act. Peirce argued that an assertion is something that speakers take responsibility for (Misak, 2013, p. 36). This social relation was explicit in Peirce's theory of symbols for which he introduced the notion of an "interpretant," specifically, that a symbol represented something *to* someone. That is, saying something is not merely about something about the world but a commitment to others; that others can "take your word for it." For the New Pragmatists a concept is a social agreement, a rule on how a thing shall be called. It is this social agreement, the agreement with another person, that makes language novel and exciting to infants when they learn a word; in most cases the reference was already known. As with speaking, so with thinking. Thinking is the internal manipulation of the inventory of concepts in a public language that are available to the thinker. How one generates a sentence, like how one generates a thought, are of course not available to consciousness, while the meanings expressed in that language, even when used privately, are. Whatever else it may be, writing is an enlargement of this verbal inventory and with it a new range of thoughts and a new consciousness.

To the New Pragmatists thinking is little more than talking to oneself. In Vendler's (1970) description, thinking is like pretend typing, running your fingers over the keys but without actually pushing them down. To extend the metaphor, the thoughts are limited by the set of keys available and those keys are the conventions negotiated in learning a public language. And although thoughts are private, they are not idiosyncratic as they are shaped and judged by the norms implicit in the speaking practices of the larger community.

What distinguishes the old from the New Pragmatists, then, is that the latter turned their attention away from the problem of how one knows about the world to the problem of how language is used in formulating that knowledge. However, although the New Pragmatists turned their attention to language and consciousness of language, they continue, I suggest, to overlook the ways that writing gives rise to the very conceptual resources they take as central to this consciousness of language. Yet, this "linguistic" or "textualist" turn is just what we require if we are to explain the relation between writing and the mind.

To this point I hope to have established that language is less the expression of thought than the medium of thought. Language is a social product shaped by agreements within a speech community. The mental states we entertain are the interior side of speaking. Conversely, the thoughts and beliefs one can entertain are limited by the resources, the concepts available, for forming those thoughts. Sellars (1997) makes this point in citing Kant as saying "Intuitions without concepts are blind." Put more starkly, feelings are not thoughts but may become such through verbal concepts.

But even with their emphasis on language the New Pragmatists fail us in that they fail to give proper regard to the role and effects of writing on language and mind. On the other hand, their emphasis on the central importance of linguistic concepts provides a suitable basis for the further claim, to be elaborated in the next chapter, that writing is the proprietary discourse or medium for creating concepts about language, thereby bringing language itself into consciousness. Writing, I shall argue, adds not only new concepts but a new dimension to that stock of concepts for thinking about language and mind and hence a new medium of thought.

4 Vygotsky and the Vygotskians

The word is a direct expression of the historical nature of human consciousness. (L. Vygotsky, 1986, p. 256)

Technology is explicitness. (S. Giedion, 1948)

While Dewey's pragmatism, along with his theory that language and literacy were tools of mind, slipped into obscurity, Vygotsky's proposals along these lines have become increasingly influential. Thus, many contemporary theorists trace their interest in language and literacy to Vygotsky (see, for example, Lantolf & Poehner, 2014). Vygotsky, like Dewey, has immediate appeal to educators because he took culture seriously and because he recognized education as essential to human development in a modern society. For Vygotsky, human mental development was less an expression of a maturing biological brain than of the mastery of cultural and social practices, primarily those based on language. He wrote: "The internalization of socially rooted and historically developed activities is the distinguishing feature of human psychology, the basis of the qualitative leap from animal to human psychology" (1978, p. 57). Yet, as Vygotsky acknowledged, only "the barest outline of this process is known." Indeed, how the mind "internalizes" social knowledge remains as puzzling as the more traditional problem of how the brain relates to the mind.

VYGOTSKY ON LANGUAGE

The social practice of greatest concern to Vygotsky was language, to which he harnessed his reflections on writing. He promised to overturn the classical notion that speech is the expression of thought, the view we associate with Descartes and John Locke, with the view that "thought is not only expressed in words, it comes into existence through words" (1986, p. 218). Vygotsky noted that aphasic patients, those who have lost the power of speech, also lose their ability to think and to plan (1986, p. 134), suggesting that speaking and thinking are much the same thing. Vygotsky's theory of language was up-to-date in other ways as well. Like the New Pragmatists, he claimed that words could only be understood in the context of sentences and those in turn in the context of situation (Kozulin, 1986, p. xxxvii). But he also insisted that words could be taken from context to become objects of knowledge and contribute to a distinctive form of abstract rationality. Thus, unlike the Pragmatists, he introduced a distinctive place for writing.

Although it seems clear enough that culture is transmitted from one generation to the next, Vygotsky's account of how social practices become psychological ones remains central and, in my view, unresolved. How does a communal practice become the possession of an individual mind? For some theorists it doesn't; the social is irreducible, a mechanism in its own right with individuals as role players in these social practices. Private thought is said to be social such that any word or utterance is "half someone else's" (Wertsch, 1991, p. 59), and the notion of an independent mind is sometimes dismissed as a version of an outdated "individualism" (Wells, 1999, p. 73). Others, while agreeing that thinking is embedded in social practice, insist that persons are autonomous, minded creatures and responsible agents who become so only through the acquisition of a shared public language (Bakhurst, 2011; Derry, 2013). Vygotsky links the social and the personal by suggesting that the learner first practices an activity such as speaking with another person, an interpersonal function, that later becomes an intrapersonal function, used by the self for private thinking. So, for example, promises made to one can become promises made by one (Olson, 2007). But as we shall see, there is no agreed account of what the language learner brings to the task of learning a language or of how language itself can become an object of thought. These questions will be addressed in terms of metarepresentation in the next chapter.

Vygotsky's metaphor that language as a tool for thinking is perhaps his most conspicuous legacy. Although Dewey called language the "tool of tools" he subordinated language to practical action in the formation of thought. Vygotsky, on the other hand, insisted that language was definitive of thought itself and that the mind should be seen as an assembly of internalized cultural tools, language primary among them.

While the concept of a tool is unproblematically applied to technologies such as writing systems and magnifying glasses, used by persons for particular purposes, its appropriateness for describing the role of language in thought is problematic. Brandom pointed out that tools are designed with an end in view and can be judged in terms of their effectiveness in meeting that end. Language, on the other hand, defines thinking, not simply aids it. What language brings into existence and that could not exist without language is the formulation of justified valid beliefs, a unique form of cognition. To collapse language into the general category of tools or "mediational means" may hide Vygotsky's more important claims about the link between mind, language and knowledge. Language is less a tool than the very medium of thinking.

Jan Derry (2013) in her book *Vygotsky Philosophy and Education* attempts to rescue Vygotsky from his interpreters who, she claims, combine their postmodern critique of objective rationality with a political commitment to multiculturalism. To most Vygotskians, this is not a criticism. Vygotsky's cultural-historical perspective is of particular importance in revealing the underlying rationality of marginalized groups whose claims had traditionally been rejected as irrational and those of children whose actions are often seen as pre-rational. Derry's worry is more specific, claiming that Vygotsky's interpreters err in calling "the possibility of knowledge itself into question" by substituting the pluralist concept of "voices" of the mind (Wertsch, 1991) as an alternative to the traditional concept of objective truth. For Derry, objectively valid knowledge is not merely one among many cultural forms but the foundation for both education and democracy. The very goals of education and development are jeopardized by treating discourse as if it were equivalent to teaching, by treating street math as in some way equivalent to real mathematics, and more generally by failing to distinguish informal social practices from literate, rule-based bureaucratic ones. Schools are charged with negotiating between the two, not siding with the former.

Furthermore, although Vygotsky emphasized that language use was pragmatic and context-dependent, he accorded an important place to treating language as an object, in effect lifting language from its context. An undue emphasis on contextualization leads modern Vygotskians such as Wertsch to dismiss "decontextualized" semantic structures "that belong to nobody and are addressed to nobody" (1991, p. 59). However, the features that belong to nobody actually belong to everybody who is a speaker of that language, although they may remain largely implicit. As we shall see, when words and sentences are decontextualized, or as I shall say *metarepresented* and brought into consciousness, they turn out to be critical ingredients of critical thinking and abstract rationality.

Derry defends Vygotsky's theory of language and his account of knowledge while distancing herself, as we have seen, from some of Vygotsky's interpreters. She points out that whereas beliefs may be personal and subjective (although formulated in a public language), knowledge is not subjective but rather consists of those claims and beliefs that have been subjected to scrutiny by the best critical and scientific methods available. Such knowledge may be taken as "objective," all the while acknowledging that all knowledge is revisable. A firm conception of valid knowledge is what underlies the authority of the teacher and the cultural institutions that the teacher represents (see also Olson, 2003). Derry's further concern is that human agency and responsibility are undermined when agency is attributed to tools, signs, discourses, programs and culture itself, as some Vygotskians and some computer scientists do (pp. 41–43). Yet, though critical, Derry, like Bakhurst, remains thoroughly Vygotskian.

Derry and Bakhurst, whom I would include among the New Pragmatists, have done much to bring the writings of Vygotsky and his Russian colleagues Ilyankov and Luria into the fold of the modern pragmatic philosophy of mind. Vygotsky's theory of meaning was advanced independently of the "linguistic turn" that the New Pragmatists attribute to Frege, Wittgenstein, Davidson and Brandom. Yet they all agree that thought is made possible by language and that language is a social institution such that the uses of language are social practices. Wittgenstein's (1958) claim that "there is no private language" would no doubt be endorsed by Vygotsky.

As we saw in the last chapter, what makes language a social product is that words are not merely signs for things or ideas, as Locke, for example, had argued, but rather, or also, social agreements, relying on what Peirce referred to as interpretants (self or others). Consequently beliefs, concepts and word meanings are *normative*, something that may be correct or incorrect, right or wrong, that are shared with others, that one is conscious of, that have meaning and that one is responsible for.

The Pragmatist view of mind linking concepts and consciousness is fully compatible with Vygotsky's insistence that the language of thought is a natural language acquired in early childhood (Olson & Campbell, 1993). Vygotsky's colleague Luria (1961) published a series of studies designed to show how the acquisition of language could serve as a second signaling system for "regulating behavior." His demonstrations were meant to show that whereas the eye–brain automatically imposed "figure-ground" perceptual organization, after learning language a verbal command could alter what was taken as the figure and hence alter the response. Subsequently the child could use his or her own language to plan a response. Such findings now seem quite unremarkable. What else could one expect if the child understood the expression? Furthermore, there are many ways to redirect attention, including conditioning. So what is special about language remains puzzling.

VYGOTSKY ON WRITING

Although Vygotsky was primarily concerned with the role of spoken language in the formation of mind, he was no less prescient in regard to writing. Vygotsky (1986, p. 179) argued that writing was not only useful as a practical resource but also brought "awareness, abstraction and control" to speech and thought. Whereas oral language, speech, is transparent to its users, learning to read and write makes language, in both senses, visible, to the eye and to the mind's eye. With writing, language becomes not only an instrument for communication but also a possible object of thought. Writing is instrumental in bringing language itself into consciousness. Wertsch (1991, p. 39) and Roberts (2011, pp. 47, 48) generalize this idea by suggesting that writing brings language awareness through what they call the "decontextualization of mediational means."

Bringing language into consciousness, Vygotsky claimed, was the task of the school, where language becomes the object of discourse not only the medium of discourse: "not as a means of communication but as a form of knowledge" (1962, p. 27). When words (and sentences) become the object of discourse they create a new type of concept that he called a "true" or "scientific concept." "Scientific concepts, with their hierarchical system of interrelationships are seen as the medium through which awareness and mastery first develop. Reflective consciousness comes to the child through the portals of scientific concepts" (1962, p. 92). Vygotsky was less explicit about the link between a culture of writing and scientific concepts. It is not clear that Vygotsky thought that the concept of word was a scientific concept, although that would seem to be implied. Schooling, Vygotsky added, "plays a decisive role in making the child conscious of his own mental processes" (1986, p. 171). This consciousness is essential for deliberate control and planning: "Written speech requires what might be called deliberate semantics – deliberate structuring of the web of meaning" (1986, p. 182). For Vygotsky, schooling is "explication"; "systematicity and consciousness do not come from the outside displacing the child's system of spontaneous concepts, but ... on the contrary, they presuppose the existence of rich and relatively mature representations" (1986, p. 172).

As I suggested earlier, to make something explicit is to say something about it, to name a property or to give a reason. Explication is both an effect of writing and the task of schooling, but the two are not systematically distinguished by Vygotsky. Although he argued that "Writing brings ... awareness to speech" (1986, p. 183), he more often attributed advanced, reflective thinking to schooling. Yet schooled concepts are just those that are brought into awareness, invented by and preserved in literate culture and that are then taught and monitored in school contexts. Schooling is the set of programs and practices that institutionalize the norms and standards of written culture. In reading authoritative texts learners are acquiring not only knowledge but also the rules and norms for what constitutes a clear distinction, defensible theory, valid argument or a sound reason in a written-document culture. And that set of norms and standards is then to be carried over and used to judge one's own views whether written or spoken. Vygotsky's "scientific concepts," I suggest, are literate concepts, concepts that have gone through and found a place in the extended critical written discourse as well as a useful place in the operations of mind. Schooling is the institutional practice that establishes and maintains the norms and standards of literate discourse (Olson, 2003).

Vygotsky's claim about the transparency of speech is more controversial, partly because the scope of the claim is not clear. Language has both a form and a meaning; only the former, the semantics and grammar, is assumed to be transparent. One is aware of the meaning intended, including the objects or events referred to. But not all aspects of form are transparent. All speakers distinguish language from music, for example, or English from French. Second, children are avid word learners; a single pairing of a phonological form with an object is often sufficient for bringing a word into productive use, a fact that would seem to imply a certain consciousness of the linguistic form as well as its meaning. Children enjoy word play including play with nonsense. Moreover, there is considerable evidence that young pre-literate children notice and comment on numerous features of their own and others' speech. Children have been observed to comment on mistakes in pronunciation, grammar and choice of words in actual speech (Tunmer, Pratt & Herriman, 1984). Two- and three-year-old children have been reported to make linguistic "repairs" to their own and others' phonological, lexical and syntactic errors (Grieve, 1990). Yet at other times they seem completely oblivious to the grammatical form, attending only to the message conveyed (Gleitman, Gleitman & Shipley, 1972; Huttenlocher, 1964). While pre-literate children notice patterns such as rhyme and alliteration as well as deviation from expectation, as we shall see some aspects of form remain implicit while attention falls on the world as represented by the language. Told "Doggy" when pointing to a dog, the child's attention, the object of discourse, is the dog. Hence the child is more likely to ask "Will he bite me?" than "Does Doggy mean 'little dog'?" or "Do Daddy and Dog start with the same sound?" Moreover, they insist that what was said is what they had taken it to mean (Robinson, Goelman & Olson, 1983), again indicating that the language is transparent to its meaning. Minimally, what is claimed by saying that language is transparent to its users is that attention normally lies elsewhere.

But the transparency of language means something more than the locus of attention. Making language opaque, an object of thought, implies something more than the registering of anomalies. Special efforts and resources are necessary to bring aspects of linguistic form into consciousness, something to think about, namely, learning new concepts. Concepts do more than point to knowns; they are devices for bringing those detected features into "the space of reasons," that is, as something that may be attended to, talked and thought about.

What pre-reading children have yet to learn, and what schooling fosters, Vygotsky claimed, is attention to the language. To bring language into consciousness is to turn it into something to think about, to analyze into grammatical constituents, beginning with words: "Writing brings awareness to speech" (1986, p. 183). Attention to the language, it may be argued (but see Chapter 11), is required when children learn to read, for then they must analyze their speech into categories that match the conventions of the script. This is a massive project of translation. Distinguishable features of speech must be found for each corresponding feature of the written form: What are the features of sound organized in time that are to be depicted by marks organized in a two-dimensional space? We saw earlier how this task was solved by the inventors of writing systems. Basically, they tried everything imaginable, settling on signs for messages, for words, for syllables and, for the Greeks, for phonemes. Learners face the same problems. Primary among them is the task of analyzing the complex patterns of continuous sound into the limited inventory of the 26 discrete alphabetic signs. Even this problem Vygotsky seems to have anticipated, pointing out that "the child is unconscious of the sounds he pronounces" and has great difficulty in "dividing a word into its constituent sounds" (1986, p. 195). In learning an alphabet, each phoneme, once discovered, is to be signified by a sign. The visual signs, when grasped in relation to the sounds they represent, I suggest, provide the concepts children need for thinking about their speech.

WRITING AS A COGNITIVE TOOL

As we have seen, Vygotsky insisted on the importance of writing in the development of consciousness of language and, I have suggested, in the development of scientific concepts. Some later Vygotskians discount the significance of writing for thinking. Cole and Cole (2006, p. 320), for example, write: "Vygotsky clearly was wrong about the consequences of writing for thought processes," seeing writing as a cultural tool secondary to the variety of social practices it contributes to. Consequently many Vygotskians focus on particular forms of writing such as lists, recipes, essays, charts and diagrams that serve as cultural tools or "mediational means" that are instrumental in and constitutive of social practices. Indeed, the uses of writing are of major concern in both research and educational practice.

Vygotsky's theory of cognitive tools or "mediational means" (Wertsch, Tulviste & Hagstrom, 1993, p. 344), writing among them, has received increased attention not only from Vygotskians but also from cognitive scientists devoted to showing how biological brain processes are embedded in cultural resources or tools that extend the processes of thinking and reasoning (Theiner, 2011). These situational and cultural resources, sometimes represented by the acronym DEEDS (dynamic, embodied, extended, distributed and situated), are appealed to in describing thinking and problem solving in an attempt to show that humanly designed artifacts make us smarter than our biological brains would seem to allow. Some artifacts give access to new forms of information (magnets and microscopes, for example), some to store and retrieve information (written notes, for example), others help us process information (computers, for example), or to share tasks (in organizations, for example). Much of the world's work is accomplished in just these ways (Coulmas, 2013).

Cognitive tools are so much a part of thinking and planning that some theorists claim these technologies to be part of the "extended mind" (Clark & Chalmers, 1998; Theiner, 2011). Some have suggested that some of our thinking goes on outside the mind. The agency once at the core of personal identity and responsibility is said to be distributed between persons and their tools and that mediational means "have agency in their own right" (Wertsch, 1991, p. 72). The boundary between computer science and science fiction, in some accounts, dissolves. Ray Kurzweil, director of engineering at Google, predicted that "we will blend with our machines; we will upload our consciousness into them" (Frank, 2015, p. 27). Humanists are suspicious of such claims partly because it leaves the issue of responsibility for action unresolved.

Writing as an extension of mind is one version of the theory of the mediated mind. Clark (2008, p. xxv) discussed the claim made by Nobel Prize-winning physicist Richard Feynman that his discovery of quantum mechanics was not thought out in his mind but was worked out on paper. "It's not a record, not really. It's working. You have to work on paper and this is the paper. Okay?" (Gleick, 1993, p. 409).

Apparently this is not unknown in the mathematical sciences. Wojciech Sady (2013) described how Max Planck arrived at the concept of *quanta*. In applying the statistical concept of entropy to the distribution of energy of black body radiation, Planck noticed that "the classical and statistical formulas are identical if and only if the energy of resonators was a multiple of *hv*. Radiation came in chunks, quanta."

Clark (2008, pp. 162–182) generalized his claim saying that "language is a species of external artifact [that has a role] in re-shaping the kinds of computational space that our biological brains must negotiate in order to solve certain types of problems ... If our brains were a computer, then language would be the 'ultimate upgrade'." Keith Oatley and I (Olson & Oatley, 2014) showed how rethinking may occur in the revision of first drafts of written documents, a process we described as "working on paper."

Theiner (2011, p. 233) presented an elaborate defense of the extended mind:

> Against the lopsided emphasis on the brain, the extended mind thesis stresses the importance of dynamic brain–body–environment couplings, the opportunistic exploitation of bodily morphology, the canny performance of epistemically potent bodily actions, the generation and use of external representations, and the multiple layers of cognitive scaffolding provided by tools, aids, and social-cultural practices.

The extended mind thesis complements earlier claims about "tools of the intellect." When thought of as a tool, writing is valued for its memorial or computational advantages, as a means or device that allows one to do more efficiently and effectively what could more laboriously be done by non-technical cognitive means. But is that all there is to writing?

LIMITATIONS OF THE "TOOL" METAPHOR

Less explored are the intellectual consequences of taking writing as an explicit representation of speech. Whereas tools are local and fitted to a practice, a language is a general resource applicable anywhere. In the same way, thinking of writing as a "tool" may hide a more basic fact about writing, namely, that writing is a "technology of explicitness" (Giedion, 1948), a technology that brings existing but unnoticed structures to light. Consequently, writing has all the resources of speech plus a degree of consciousness not available to speech uninformed by writing. Giedion argued that any technology makes explicit what was implicit and automatic in the process it replaces. Industrialization involved making a machine do something previously done only by a skilled craftsman. Creating the technology required implementing the expert's knowledge but just as often it allowed the expert to discover some steps in the procedure that had been simply taken for granted. So too for creating a written representation of a spoken utterance; it is not clear at the outset what aspects of the spatial medium should be used for what aspects of the temporal sound pattern of speech. The attempt to represent language in a new spatial medium, I argued, may lead one to invent new concepts that make one conscious of the properties implicit in the spoken medium. These are the concepts critical to the pursuit of objective knowledge, the central concern of Derry's critique. And, as we shall see, this consciousness of language provides the concepts essential to a critical rationality.

WRITING AS CONSCIOUSNESS OF LANGUAGE

The metaphor that casts writing as a tool for thinking, however useful, occludes the very property of writing, the explicitness and hence the consciousness it brings to speech. It is this explicitness that may be appealed to in explaining the intellectual implications of writing. Writing invites an awareness of the form and meaning of the language itself that was elaborated over time. The history of writing showed that creating a writing system that exposed the implicit properties of speech was less the design of a tool for a fixed purpose than an adventitious achievement. Baines (2008, p. 150) pointed out that writing systems could be part of an evolved visual culture without representing speech: "Even though writing systems … have been developed from their various points of departure to focus more and more on language, that is not necessarily what writing was intended to notate at the point of origin." But it was an endpoint in the history of writing, including alphabetic writing, an explicit representation of the implicit properties of speech. The explicit representations of phonemes, words and sentences bring consciousness to properties of language, providing new things to think about as well as new ways to think about existing things. Making language into a conceptual object is not merely one use among others of a tool but rather the elaboration of a "written language" useful for many purposes including something as general as our thinking.

To understand the intellectual implications of reading and writing, then, we must set aside the notion that writing is one tool among others that is to be examined only for its possible uses and replace it with the concept of writing as a distinctive medium of representation. In fact, this idea was the critical insight of the "media theorists" of the 1960s. They claimed that writing was not merely a useful tool but rather the portal to a new consciousness of language and mind. Making knowledge about language explicit requires a metalanguage, the topic of the next chapter.

5 The Cognitive Science of Metarepresentation

When we introspect we never find anything mental; we are only aware of what those mental states tell us about the world. (Wiseberg, 2014, p. 113)

The claim that the mind is in some sense social puts Vygotsky and the New Pragmatists at odds with much of Cognitive Science. Because Cognitive Science is the attempt to provide a model or account of the thinking and acting of individual subjects it has rarely made any, let alone proper, accommodation for the social (Proust, 2013, p. 304). As a consequence many Vygotskians are tempted to abandon the cognitive ship (Greeno, 1997) and others to advance a parallel social science of mind (Cole, 1996). But the Cognitive Sciences increasingly have incorporated language, consciousness and social learning, topics formerly monopolized by pragmatic and social-cognitive theories. Moreover, the cognitive sciences provide a rigor seen as lacking in more social and social-constructivist theory (Bakhurst, 2011), so the attempt to bridge the gap is an appealing task.

The Cognitive Sciences are the disciplines ranging from brain sciences to the social sciences that share the goal of formulating a comprehensive scientific model of human behavior, thought and rationality. They adopt the view that the currency of the mind is the set of computational states much like beliefs and desires but without explicit linguistic form and largely independent of consciousness. In the hands of such writers as Dennett (1991), Eagleman (2011) and Proust (2013), beliefs are seen as composed of syntactically related concepts much like a sentence, which are then organized into if–then procedures to satisfy desires, the entire process mechanically implemented in the brain. Simply, if you want a drink (a desire), you go to the well (an if–then procedure) because you believe there is water in the well (a belief). Many of these procedures are seen as shared with other simpler species, and indeed, aspirationally with those of a modern computer. Language is seen primarily as an input–output device, with acting and thinking as the product of largely unconscious processes in the brain. I say "largely" unconscious because the role of consciousness is treated as "after the fact" confabulation by some (Dennett, 1991; Wilson, 2014), but as critical to higher-order controlled processing by others (Kahneman, 2011; Proust, 2013; Shallice, 1988).

The extended mind theory that I associated with Vygotsky has a perfect counterpart in perhaps the dominant version of the cognitive science of mind, the Two Process theory of thinking and reasoning. Whereas the former examined the cognitive tools involved in thinking without, I suggested, sufficient analysis of the role of consciousness of language, the latter examined conscious, deliberate reflective thought, but does so with little regard for the roles played by technology, in particular writing and literacy, in its evolution and by schooling in its development.

A bridge between these two sets of concerns may be found in the concept of metarepresentation. Proust (2013) contrasted the norms governing ordinary activities – those having to do with success or failure – with the norms governing mental activities such as thinking and planning – those having to do with "normative dimensions such as accuracy or coherence." The norms for evaluating thinking are *about* thinking and hence are metarepresentational.

Although metarepresentations may be about any form of representation, including various art forms as in Kant's third critique, the metarepresentations themselves are necessarily linguistic and are composed of saying something about a representation, its meaning, truth or validity, for example. The concept is meant to cover a variety of categorical distinctions that have been advanced over the centuries to account for just this distinction. Most important is that between *use* and *mention* that marks the distinction between "A robin is a bird" and "'Robin' is a five letter word." Bernstein (2010) points out that prior to the linguistic turn this distinction was not made. Although lacking the distinction, Aristotle covered some of the same ground by distinguishing ordinary from philosophical use of terms, and modern philosophers (Goldstein, 2015, p. 48) acknowledge that the language we actually speak is "richer and wilder than the fastidious language of the logicians." In addition to use–mention, other distinctions that overlap that of metarepresentation include: assert or state vs. quote, on-line vs. off-line, contextualized vs. decontextualized, pragmatic vs. formal, utterance vs. text, sentence meaning vs. speaker's meaning, to which I would add the Two System or Dual Process theory of cognition (Stanovich, 2009).[1]

The use–mention distinction may be taken as the most fundamental. It is sometimes marked in writing by the use of quotation marks, brackets or italics, but the distinction remains largely implicit in speech. Yet, there are subtle intonational differences between the following two sentences: "Can you draw three little pigs?" and "Can you write 'three little pigs'?" One can almost hear the quotation marks in the latter, and by age 5 or 6 most children notice the distinction. Saenger (1982) has noted the lack of punctuation marks in early written texts for distinguishing quoted from paraphrased language.

As noted, some cognitive theorists have recently been drawn to these metarepresentational processes. Two Process theorists (Heath, 2011; Kahneman, 2011; Stanovich, 2009) propose that the cognitive processes may be sorted into two broad categories. System One mental processes are low-level, unconscious, fast, algorithmic, efficient and, some claim, shared with other animals. System Two processes are reflective, analytic, slow, deliberate, conscious, logical and "rational." Indeed, Stanovich and West (2000) designed a series of tasks to measure the skills taken as representative of System Two. These System Two reflective processes are essentially those that the

[1] Julian Jaynes' (1976) theory of the bicameral mind, an early version of the two-mind theory, distinguished the modern mind in terms of its capacity for metaphor.

Vygotskians take as dependent upon such cultural tools as speech and writing and that Uccelli and her colleagues (Uccelli et al., 2014) hope to capture with a test of academic language skills.

System Two processes are important to our concerns as they are more correctly seen, I suggest, as metarepresentational. Although Kahneman (2011, p. 418) acknowledges the existence of System Two processes – how else would he know the "correct" answers to the tasks presented to his subjects? – he challenges the view that System Two gives a realistic account of human thinking and he provides abundant evidence to show that even educated adults have a limited understanding of logic and probability and are subject to a variety of "biases" attributable to System One. The work extends that of March (1978), Simon (1996) and others who showed that limited computational resources may result in decisions that are less than fully rational. And it extends the claims of Henle (1962), who found that even educated adults appear to follow the rules of logic (System Two) only insofar as they generate conclusions with which they happen to agree (System One). Although language has an implicit logical form, it is easily overridden by concrete functional and situational considerations. The relation between ordinary reasoning and logic, other than asserting their difference, remains unclear.

But if logic is not an operating principle of the mind, what is it? And what place does it have in reasoning? Jaynes (1976, p. 41) pointed the way in his suggestion that "Logic is the science of the justification of conclusions we have reached by natural reasoning ... Logic is how we ought to think. Logic is to thinking as conduct is to morality." In a later chapter (Chapter 8), I advance the claim that the rules of logic hold only in a stipulated, well-defined artificial world, the world where language is to be treated as *mentioned* rather than *used*. Logic, then, provides a normative standard against which ordinary decisions may be judged as valid or invalid, true or false. Logic holds a place in reasoning analogous to the place that definition holds in meaning; both depend on making explicit and conventional what is ordinarily implicit in speech. In a word, logic is metarepresentational; it is less a theory of thinking than a metalanguage for thinking about thinking.

Given the goals of Kahneman's research program, namely to demonstrate the biasing effects of System One on System Two judgments, it is appropriate that his proposals for improvement of the reasoning processes focus on limiting the effects of System One rather than on elaborating the knowledge required for System Two. To enhance attentive, knowledgeable valid reasoning, Kahneman proposes that students acquire "a precise vocabulary" for their application of concepts (2011, p. 418). However, the vocabulary he proposes is one for detecting biases and learning various "nudges" that help resist them. Consequently, Kahneman's proposals include "knowing the vulnerabilities, environmental factors, symptoms" and the anchoring and framing effects that distort logical and statistical reasoning.

System Two theorists seem untroubled by their assumption that there is a valid and logically correct answer to the questions they pose. Consequently, they pay insufficient attention to the metalinguistic concepts that are required to think about words and sentences, as well as the principles of evidence and inference that make up System Two. The best defense against bias, it may be argued, is systematic knowledge about the rules of inference and the contexts in which they can be usefully applied. These are the concepts that arguably are articulated in metalinguistic talk about words, sentences and prose texts that I examine in Chapters 8 and 9.

Although the Two Process theory is useful in differentiating vernacular, that is, everyday cognition from more formal educated reflective thinking, it seriously underestimates the rationality of ordinary, unreflective talk and thought. Grice (1989) has proposed that there are two logics, one for formal discourse and one for ordinary conversation including narratives. Davidson (2001, p. 148), too, argues that before dismissing an act as irrational one must assume that the action makes sense to the actor and then attempt to sort out the reasons for action. Only after that is it appropriate to evaluate the validity of those reasons. This is a well-known pedagogical principle. What many lack and what an education can provide is a metalanguage for talking and thinking about the truth of their beliefs and the validity of their inferences.

Finally, the account of System Two processes is blind to the role of technologies such as writing and other "mediational means" in reflective thinking. As Sousa (2004, p. 11) noted in another context, "What is lacking [in most thinkers] is the metarepresentation that is required for beliefs to be examined, criticized and made the object of self-conscious inference."

Metarepresentational processes are embedded not only in the minds of educated thinkers but also in institutional structures such as science, government, the school and the academy that have responsibility for maintaining the standards of rationality. It is primarily in learning to do science that one learns the rules for sampling, controlling variables, distinguishing hypotheses from observational data and so on. And it is in preparing papers for publication that one learns to anticipate counter-arguments and challenges to valid inference. Some of these rules may be carried into everyday events but equally often we turn to experts in those domains to do the thinking for us. It was the recognition of the importance of public institutions that allowed Montaigne (1580/1993) to claim that public law was more important than private virtue. What is true of morality is equally true of rationality; good thinking is not only possessing good mental habits but knowing how institutions such as law and science make judgments.

If thinking is tied up with language, at least some of the differences set out in the Two Systems account of mind may be recast in terms of the differences between language in use and the metalanguage for talking and thinking about that language. For it is here that we may seek to establish the link between literacy and rationality.

REFLECTION ON LANGUAGE AS METAREPRESENTATION

If thought is based on language, reflective thought is thought about language.

We may recall the claim of the New Pragmatists that it was the very act of putting something into language that created the thought. Equipped with a language one's thoughts are already belief-like and tied into a system of beliefs subject to implicit normative standards or rules of language use. Feelings, expectancies and other states and processes are then organized in terms of these conscious beliefs. Even habitual actions are based on a complex network of beliefs acquired over time such that even 6- and 7-year-olds recognize themselves as agents, accept responsibility for what they do and often can explain their actions in terms of their beliefs and desires.

In sum, consciousness (as sapience) is the product of learning a language; language gives explicit verbal form to implicit social non-verbal practices of pre-linguistic children. The knowledge implicit in a social practice such as, for example, passing a toy back and forth to a child is made explicit by learning the expression "Give me the ball." Only then is the ball lifted from the more general social practice to become the object of a conscious thought. To be sapiently conscious of something is to be in a position to be able to say something about it: "It's a ball" and "I'm giving it to you" and so on.

Here we arrive at the critical part of the argument. Talking, too, is equally a social practice that, as Vygotsky pointed out, gives only limited conscious access to its form; speech is largely transparent to its object; one is conscious of the content of what is being talked about, but not of the language used to talk about it. On hearing a story, young children are conscious of the events in the story, though they are largely unaware of the fact that it is composed of words, indeed, that it is just a story. This was Vygotsky's claim about transparency of speech. But speech may be rendered opaque and subject to consciousness largely through concepts invented for talking *about* the language. Language becomes something to talk about primarily in literate contexts, book reading, learning to read and write and talking about what is read. Thus we complete our explanatory circle linking literacy (reading), talk about talk (reflectivity) and rationality (critical thinking).

To this point I have argued that a mind equipped with public language is what distinguishes sentient beings from sapient (thinking) beings (Brandom, 1994). And thinking in a language creates what Sellars (1997) has called the "space of reasons." This space is defined by the set of concepts one has available for perceiving, thinking, planning and justifying actions. Furthermore, concepts are organized by means of a grammar or syntax that permits one to generate an unlimited set of thoughts. The grammatical devices that perform this operation remain unconscious and implicit in speaking. Special concepts are required to bring those unconscious processes into consciousness, something to think about. How is this achieved?

LANGUAGE TRANSPARENCY AND METAREPRESENTATIONAL DEVELOPMENT

Learning a language, as is well known, involves connecting a linguistic form with a meaning. Although linguistic form is a "problem space" in which learners have to sort out phonological, semantic and syntactic devices relevant to the meaning that is expressed (Karmiloff-Smith, 1992), these linguistic processes themselves are largely unconscious. Indeed it has taken generations of linguists to even penetrate those structures. Consciousness is tied primarily to what the language is about, the meaning communicated and the worlds disclosed. Jackendoff (2002) compares the procedures and rules involved in language processing to those involved in stereoscopic vision, complex and largely unconscious, to be discovered not by introspection but by science. Some of the more important concepts such as that of *word* were discovered in the course of inventing a writing system.

Although Vygotsky never claimed that one can learn a language without an awareness of language, it would seem to follow from his claim about the transparency of language. Further, it is in line with Jackendoff and other linguists who claim that grammatical knowledge is unconscious. And it is congruent with the argument of this book that aspects of linguistic form such as phonology, lexicon and syntax are brought into consciousness only through the acquisition of an appropriate metalanguage (some of which was invented in devising a writing system). Still the claim that language learning is largely unconscious seems radical and remains controversial.

Two prominent reading theorists, Smith (1971) and Krashen (1989), have argued that in learning a language as well as in learning to read, linguistic structures remain implicit and out of consciousness. Indeed, Krashen (1989) has argued that linguistic competence is acquired subconsciously and automatically when one understands the linguistic input. If we distinguish linguistic form from what the language is about and claim that the former is largely unconscious, or, as I shall say, implicit, the claim seems justifiable and I shall assume it to be a valid expression of the transparency of language argument. As we shall see (Chapter 12), much depends upon just what aspects of language are and remain transparent.

Although the linguistic resources including the grammar involved in creating thoughts remain unconscious and implicit, the thoughts generated with the language are objects of consciousness, the things we think about. Of course, these were the very things shared with pre-verbal children and nonverbal animals. So what is involved in moving from the pre-verbal world to the world of verbally structured thought? The obvious answer: Learning a language.

FROM NORMS IMPLICIT IN PRACTICE TO RULES EXPLICIT IN LANGUAGE

We may take our lead from the general formula advanced by Brandom (1994, p. 20) to frame the language-learning question, namely that of making explicit: "norms explicit as rules presuppose norms implicit in practice." Brandom's agenda is somewhat different than the developmental psychologist's in that as a philosopher of language he is primarily interested in what is implicit in the act of making a statement. However, what is implicit in making a statement is precisely what the learner must bring to the task of learning a language. So Brandom's claim that language makes explicit the rules and norms that are implicit in social practices can lead us to look for the social practices that must be in place if a child is to learn a language. He continues: "One cannot address the question of what implicit norms are, independently of the question of what it is to acknowledge them in practice" (1994, p. 25). We find such practical norms in the social routines and games that pre-verbal children engage in with adults (Bruner, 1983; Tomasello, 2014).

Consider what implicit knowledge is drawn on when the child first understands an assertion such as "Kitty's hungry" or even "Kitty is a cat." Clearly the pre-verbal child knows what a cat is, perhaps even that it is hungry, but, lacking a language, cannot entertain, so I have argued, the thought "Kitty is hungry." Yet, the complexity and sophistication of pre-verbal children's knowledge is impressive and continues to be explored (Moore, 2006, pp. 37–39).

How pre-verbal knowledge relates to learning a language is controversial (Astington & Baird, 2005). The two approaches on offer differ, as we might suspect, in how seriously they take the social dimension. Perhaps the most widely held view is that expressed by Perner (1991), who deserves the credit for much of the original research on metarepresentational thought and metalinguistic language. Perner proposed that behavioral rules constitute the implicit knowledge that is then made explicit when one learns a language. Behavioral rules may link situations to actions without the intervention of any representational or mental activity; behavioral rules become thoughts only when one learns a language. Proust (2013, p. 39) seconds this proposal, suggesting that these behavioral rules may be largely unconscious, attention falling on securing desirable outcomes as in Skinnerian learning. Learning a language, on this view, is essential for communication, not for cognition.

However, unlike behavioral rules, linguistic rules are designed less to regulate behavior than to capture social agreements. Learning a language builds on social practices that make explicit in the form of rules what had been implicit in social activities. A "norm" is a standard or convention or rule against which an act may be experienced as correct or not. It allows a distinction between what one does and what one "ought" to do. It is a standard one has agreed to and that is monitored by others. Consequently, only socially shared routines, not privately held behavioral rules, allow the formation of a norm. Norms have the further property in that because they are socially shared one is not free to change them to suit one's purposes; one is responsible *to others* for honoring the rule. Humpty Dumpty was wrong:

> "When *I* use a word," Humpty Dumpty said, in rather a scornful tone, "it means just what I choose it to mean – neither more nor less." (Lewis Carroll, *Through the Looking Glass*)

Norms and social rules are anathema to most cognitivists because they appear to reach outside an individual mind. Consequently most cognitivists reduce social learning to ordinary learning, learning that just happens to involve other people.[2] The New Pragmatists, on the other hand, insist that norms are not just learned by training and reinforcement but rather by imitation, initiation and participation in patterned cooperative social activities that allow the formation of rules and norms recognized by participants and, importantly, are known to be held by others as well as by oneself.

A norm or rule, then, is something more than a behavioral regularity. Indeed, there appears to be an unbridgeable gap between a behavioral rule and a social norm. McDowell (1994, p. 342) asked how one could distinguish learning "blind" behavioral responses to situations from acting according to a rule. "The answer is: by belonging to

[2] In moral philosophy this distinguishes the consequentialists from the deontologists.

a custom, practice, or an institution," just as Wittgenstein had argued in *Philosophical Investigations* (1958). The norms for customs, like the rules for language, remain implicit; language is, in part, just an elaborate custom. But it is a custom that allows the formation of utterances that may be shared with others and may be judged as true and false.

Bruner (1983) and Tomasello (2014) are primarily responsible for this second view, the view that cooperative social practices shared by child and adult provide the conceptual basis for language learning. The sociality of humans relative to apes, Tomasello suggests, is part of the explanation of why apes are unable to learn a language and he points to the "common standards of correctness" that are involved in imitation and in any cooperative social practice or routine such as games of "pat-a-cake." Learning these social routines come to include linguistic ones. Premack and Premack (1996), too, noted the simultaneous appearance in children of norms in such diverse activities as the ability to imitate others, to pretend play and to practice an act until it can be done successfully.

Learning a language is learning the implicit conventions for participation in a social practice. The rules of the language are the implicit norms that are honored in producing and understanding language. What is made explicit and brought into awareness through language is the meaning or content expressed in the social practice. What remains implicit are the grammatical structures that are responsible for the generativity or productivity of language. Thus in learning a language one is learning both a linguistic form that remains implicit and unconscious, and a meaning or content of which one is conscious. It is the duality of form and content and not just its normative quality that makes language uniquely associated with mind.

Both implicit norms and explicit rules are social in that they are monitored by others; others hold the actors responsible and accountable for following the rules first in cooperative action and later in speech. When we speak of concepts, beliefs and representations we are talking about the norms, the social agreements that make language and thought possible.

Developmental changes in behavior may be understood in terms of making behavioral practices explicit as rules. Zelazo and Jacques (1996) report a card-sorting experiment in which 3-year-old children are trained to sort cards into boxes on the basis of their color, thereby establishing a behavioral routine, a kind of social practice. But when the experimenter announced a rule change, these children continued to put the cards in the same place. Four-year-old children, on the other hand, alter their sorting to comply with the new rule. This suggests that they have begun to think about the rule as a rule, that is, they begin to metarepresent their practice as rule-based and revise their practice in the light of the new rule. With the new rule their sorting changes. Explicit rules are rules in the language and it is the language, not the world, that now offers the options. This is just what Luria (1961) had attempted to show in his early experiments on the role of language in realigning figure and ground. Not the explicit stimulus but the linguistic rule shaped the action. Later, with writing and literacy, children will acquire metarepresentational concepts to apply to language itself.

At this point we have arrived at a conception of beliefs as explicitly held verbally structured thoughts and, further, an account of how what was implicit in earlier social practices may be made explicit through language. This allows us to advance to the heart of the metarepresentational problem, namely, beliefs about beliefs and language about language. I say heart because it is through the elaboration of metarepresentational concepts that reading and literacy more generally contribute to consciousness.

METAREPRESENTATION AND THE THEORY OF MIND

Vygotsky (1962, p. 92) included in his description of scientific concepts a discussion of a "self-referring system of signs." "Self-referring" signs are metarepresentational signs, words or concepts that take other linguistic signs as their content. The cognitive significance of such concepts became clear primarily in the 1980s with the discovery of what has come to be known as "children's theory of mind" (ToM) (Astington, Harris & Olson, 1988; Wimmer & Perner, 1983). When children reach the age of 4 or 5 years they begin to recognize that another person may look in an empty box for a candy because that person "thinks" it is there. They allow that another could hold a belief they themselves would deny, thereby passing the false-belief task. The metarepresentational concept *belief* or *think* turns an implicit mental state into an explicit object about which one may say something, such as, that it is false. Surprisingly, children who fail to recognize false beliefs in others also fail to recognize them in themselves (Gopnik & Astington, 1988). They lack, not a theory of others' minds, but a theory of mind in general. Success in distinguishing beliefs from reality is closely related to a number of mentalistic distinctions such as that between appearance and reality (Flavell, Flavell & Green, 1983).[3]

Long before they acquire a theory of mind, children have been making and understanding assertions such as "The cat is hungry" or "I want a candy." But as Searle (1983) has pointed out, speech acts such as assertions and requests have "sincerity conditions" that are implicit in saying things. To say that "The cat is hungry" has the sincerity condition that the speaker *thinks* that the cat is hungry, that asking implies *wanting*, promising implies *intending* and the like. In spite of their fluency in saying, requesting, promising and the like, children seem to remain unaware of the sincerity conditions, the beliefs, desires and intentions, that lie behind or are implicit in them.

The implicit sincerity conditions are made explicit in the acquisition of a ToM. Once made explicit, that is, represented by a verbal

[3] Much of the interest in children's theory of mind is on the intuitions about the social actions of others that develop prior to an explicit theory of mind, leading some to propose that two quite different systems, similar to those of the Two Systems theory, are involved (Apperly, 2011). I would prefer to say that the theory of mind makes explicit what is implicit saying things.

concept such as *think*, *mean*, *intend* and *want*, these mental states may be attributed to others to explain, for example, false beliefs, unsatisfied desires, insincere intentions and the like. Beliefs have become the objects of thought. The concepts essential for thinking about beliefs and thoughts generally are, as mentioned, metarepresentational concepts, concepts for talking about what is said, meant and thought and characterizing those thoughts in various ways (see Astington & Olson, 1990).

Thus, ToM is a paradigm case of an explicit verbal representation of what had been left implicit in assertions, requests, promises, declarations and other speech acts. Metarepresentational concepts for representing these intentional mental states bring what was implicit in saying into consciousness, that is, into objects of thought. The most important of these is the metarepresentational verb "thinks" with its complex grammar that allows one saying to be embedded in another (de Villiers, 2005). In saying that "John thinks that the candy is there," it becomes possible not only to think about John's thought but also to think about the thought "the candy is there" independently of John, as entertained rather than asserted (Rozeboom, 1972). Thus language makes thinking as opposed to doing possible. Thinking about thoughts without believing them is what makes reflective thought possible.

Metarepresentational concepts allow one to talk about thought, to turn thoughts into objects of discourse, to make them objects of consciousness. In fact there is an enormous vocabulary for talking about what was said and what was meant in saying it. In many cases there is a direct relation between the verbs of saying and the verbs of thinking such that "John said *p*" is equivalent to "John thinks *p*"; the same holds for *asks for* = *wants*, *promised* = *intended*, *explained* = *understood*. These relations can be multiplied almost endlessly for subtleties of saying: *say*, *tell*, *insist*, *proclaim*, *declaim* on one hand and *thought*, *felt*, *inferred*, *construed*, *understood* and the like on the other. One may be surprised to find on looking into a common thesaurus that the bulk of words in the language are not about objects in nature but about language and communication. But this metalanguage does not come free.

LITERATE METALANGUAGE

Some considerable part of this metalanguage is tied to the practice of reading, writing and interpreting texts in a literate culture. Some evidence for this general claim comes from the borrowing into the English language of a rich set of concepts for talking about thought as English became a medium for legal, scientific and bureaucratic discourse. Classical Latin had for centuries served as the language of law and literate scholarship. English began to be used for those purposes only in the 17th century. A typical case is that of William Harvey, an Englishman who had studied in Padua, who wrote his treatise on the circulation of the blood in English as well as in scholarly Latin. When English concepts were lacking, he simply brought Latin words into English. Some of the terms brought into English in that period include: assert (1604), argue that (1548), admit (1532), concede (1632), contradict (1570), explain (1513), mention (1530), predict (1546), remark (1633), remind (1635), state (1641) (Olson & Astington, 1990). Corson (1985) pointed out that such terms are part of the vocabulary of written language, and ignorance of them constitutes a "lexical bar" to less advantaged students, limiting their access to the essentials of complex knowledge. To some this suggested the importance of learning Latin; for others it suggested the importance of reading and studying academic texts (Adams, 2011).

Many of these technical literate concepts had earlier versions in Old English (Traugott, 1987) and the Latin terms brought only subtle changes. Consider the Old English term "foretell" that yielded pride of place in the Early Modern period to the verb "predict." Predict is clearly drawn from Latin, roughly pre–before, dict–saying. But the semantic shift is significant. Foretell carried a mystical element, the insight of a prophet. In *The Iliad*, the poet Homer claimed that only the gods could foretell, that is, see into the future. "Predict," on the other hand, is restricted to scientific causality. Young children and gamblers are weak on this point. A similar distinction may be made between dragons and dinosaurs, the former mythological and the latter scientific. Even modern dictionaries shifted imperceptibly from listing all meanings of terms, including their metaphorical meanings, to their exclusively factual ones. By the 17th century: "there can no longer be any signs except in the analysis of representation according to identities and differences ... [species] exists in itself only in so far as it is bounded by what is distinguishable from it" (Foucault, 1970, pp. 144–145). In general, definitions were altered to allow strict inference.

Two other concepts underwent significant change. With the invention of statistics "probable" came to be distinguished from "plausible" and "likely." But naive subjects may fail to note the difference, as Kahneman's studies showed. The meaning of the words "experience" and "evidence" have undergone a similar transformation. Clanchy (1993) pointed out that medieval courts relied on evidence in the form of testimony provided by an authority. Only with early modern science did evidence come to rely on an eyewitness testimony. Correspondingly, an observation shifted from an offhand comment to something witnessed under ideal conditions (Wiersbicka, 2010, p. 297). Consequently until the 17th century there was no concept of evidence that allowed one to pose the problem of induction, namely, how to use evidence of the senses to justify a rule. With the new concept, "evidence can be critically examined rather than immediately assented to." The relevant concept "did not exist beforehand" (Hacking, 1975, p. 31). While some concepts were developed for legal purposes and others for early modern science, still others came with the invention of a critical discourse about literature (Stock, 2015). Such literate concepts make their way into ordinary thinking primarily through education.

As mentioned at the outset, although the classical Greeks distinguished ordinary from philosophical uses of terms, they lacked the use–mention distinction. Philosophical terms are abstract and decontextualized but it is important to note that abstract terms are not necessarily metalinguistic. What metalinguistic concepts do is refer to properties of the language itself, not the things the language refers to, turning those properties of language into objects of thought and talk. The result is a new world, the world of language, analogous to the world of mathematics, something one may think about somewhat independently from what the language is about.

Vygotsky identified self-reflective concepts as part of "schooled concepts," whereas I prefer to trace their literary roots. However, the boundary between schooled and unschooled, like that between those in speech and those in writing, is permeable. Some basic terms such as "ask," "say" and "tell" may be used metarepresentationally and are acquired in the course of learning to talk and thus are part of ordinary spoken language (Mead, 1934). Others are tied to specific registers or genres in societies both with and without writing (Feldman, 1991; Heeschen, 1978). Even archaic terminology referred to language in general terms such as song, speech, story. However, other concepts were unique to writing; those that made reference to grammar and linguistic form and came only with Greek literacy: "neither *epos* nor *logos* originally signified the separated word," Havelock (1982, p. 289) pointed out. Hence the concept of *word* as a grammatical and semantic entity is plausibly a metalinguistic concept that originated with literacy.

What one can say about those metarepresented entities matters as well. To say of a word that it rhymes with another word is quite a different matter than saying that it has the same meaning as another word. Clearly the concept of word is only the first step in the metarepresentational domain but an important step in exposing the links between reading and consciousness.

By claiming that learning a public language is learning a language for thinking, it is important to remember the link between concepts and consciousness. Becoming a language user does not endow the learner with unlimited reflective competencies. Reflective abilities depend upon the specific concepts for talking about talk and thought as true or false, mine or yours, clear or confused, as well as the more technical concepts such as *implied, concluded, valid, conjectured* and the like. Judgments of this sort contribute to the formation of clear and distinct ideas, the ideas that Vygotsky called "scientific concepts" and that cognitive scientists would include as part of System Two. But as I have argued, they arise through literacy, through learning a language about language, a metarepresentational theory of language and mind.

In the next chapter I shall show how the history of writing was not only the invention of visual means of communication but rather, or in addition, a series of discoveries about the internal structure of language including the discovery of words and phonemes. And although I begin with phonemes, it is important to remember that phonemes are phonemes by virtue of what they contribute to the identity of words, that words have meaning in sentences and that sentences have meaning in discourse. It is these higher-order structures that are normally present to consciousness and the lower-order ones brought to consciousness through analytic, metarepresentational concepts.

PART III Reading and the Invention of Language about Language

6 Phonemes and the Alphabet

Consciousness functions in the decision as to what to say, how we are to say it, and when we say it, but then the orderly and accomplished succession of phonemes or of written letters is somehow done for us. (Jaynes, 1976, p. 27)

If anything is "given" in speaking surely it is the sound patterns or at least the phonemes of the language, for it is these sounds that distinguish meanings. The notion of the "given" is misleading in that the Pragmatists showed that a stimulus becomes an object of thought only by its association with some concept or meaning. Language learners have the task of sorting out the patterns of sound associated with those meanings; they have to associate linguistic forms with meanings. The argument to be developed in this chapter is that whereas the meaning, including the objects referred to, are readily brought to mind and commented on, the sound pattern, the phonology, remains implicit, to be uncovered only by special means, among them learning the alphabet. The sounds, as we say, are transparent – there, responded to, but not objects of thought.

Clearly, not all aspects of sound are out of consciousness, for some aspects of the sounds of language capture not only the attention of infants but also of punsters and poets. Poets have long worked with the sounds as well as the meanings of language. Alexander Pope's injunction "The sound must seem an echo to the sense" encouraged writers to pay attention to the form as well as to the meaning if one is to produce literary art. Although the meaning of an expression is both conscious and closely tied to the events in the world, the sound patterns are arbitrary and, as we suggested earlier, largely unconscious. The invention of writing, I argued in Chapter 2, involved the discovery of some of the elementary constituents of language, eventually the phonemes that could be represented by the letters of the alphabet. This was not always seen as a benefit. As Saussure pointed out, familiarity with the alphabet had blinded earlier linguists to the fact that alphabets are only a crude model of the elements of speech sounds, the phonemes, the discovery of which awaited the invention of recording machines. Recording machines created fixed texts suitable for examination and re-examination of patterns of sound so as to isolate their structure, much as writing had earlier done for spoken utterances.

A phoneme is an elementary unit of sound that makes a distinctive contribution to meaning. Phonological structure itself is enormously complex. Jackendoff (2002) described four subcomponents of sound with segmental structure, the string of discrete phonemes at their core. Phonemes are decomposable into a restricted set of distinctive features and at the same time are embedded in syllabic and prosodic structures. For most of us, our knowledge of the phonology of the language is restricted to what we have learned to hear in learning to read and spell. Thus, most of us hear a /t/ in the word "pitch" even if, we are told, there is no /t/ present in speech and that "pitch" and "rich" are identical except for the initial *phoneme* or *onset*. The spelling patterns create a kind of "orthographic illusion," the tendency to hear only the sounds represented by the spelling.

The alphabet provides only a rough model of the phonological structure of words as the letters of the alphabet are inconsistently mapped to phonemes. For example, the regular plural suffix is represented by the letter *s* but has three different pronunciations: /s/ as in cats, /z/ as in dogs and /uhz/ as in horses, the choice of which depends on the final sound of the word that the suffix is attached to (Jackendoff, 2002, p. 7). Thus *s* in this case represents not a sound but a unit of meaning, namely, plural. Hence, as Nunez and Bryant (2009, p. xiii) have shown, in learning to read, children treat the letter *s* in this position as an indication of meaning, plurality, rather than as an indication of sound. They show that spellings cannot be predicted from the way that the words sound but become predictable when the morpheme they occur in is taken into account. Leong (1982), too, showed how letters of the alphabet represent morphemes, that is, units of meaning, as well as units of sound. An enormous research literature has shown that reading involves the detection of structure at several levels, that of the phonemes indicated by individual letters, syllables represented by letter combinations, morphological constituents or "roots," as well as whole words (Snowling & Hulme, 2005).

The growth of understanding of what letters represent is also apparent in children's learning to write. Ferreiro (1985), Tolchinsky (2003) and others have shown that when children invent spellings they sometimes used the letter *b* pronounced as /bee/ to represent the first syllable of a complex word, so "beet" becomes "b-t." In learning to write, children explore many possible uses of letters: as signs for morphemes, for syllables, for phonemes or even as a visual sign for a whole word, all in the effort to convey a meaning. The alphabet provides an inventory of signs associated with sounds from which learners assemble the meaning of words and sentences. Some aspects of the phonology can never be represented and brought into awareness because, as Jackendoff notes, the distinctive features of a phoneme, those aspects of speech production that distinguish one phoneme from another, cannot be heard because they are not even distinctive sounds.

The loose fit of letters to sounds was shown by Householder (1971), who pointed out that the rules for mapping in one direction, from sound to letter, were far more complex than that for mapping letters to sounds. Valtin (2014) has cited research showing that children invented as many as 119 different spellings for the single word "elephant." "Mapping" is perhaps an unsuitable metaphor for describing the relations between letters and sounds in that there is not a one-to-one relation either between a physical sound and a phoneme nor between a phoneme and a letter.

A more suitable metaphor for describing the relation between letters and the phonemes they are designed to represent may be found in the invention of the well-tempered clavier, the clavichord. The problem for keyboard instruments was that if the strings were tuned for each of the tones and semitones of the key of C they were then unsuitable for playing in any other key. A composition in G sharp minor, for example, would sound, experts say, wildly out of tune if played on an instrument tuned to the key of C. The problem could be solved by having one instrument tuned for each key, as some classical guitarists in fact do. For a clavichord as for a modern piano(forte), that solution is obviously out of the question. The alternative, adopted at the time of Bach, was to "temper," that is round off, the notes to minimize the discord, dividing the octave into 12 roughly equal intervals, using the same string for C sharp and D flat with the result that music in any key sounds slightly off but only to those with a professionally trained ear or a tuning fork. Some 40 or 50 distinctive sounds in an octave are thereby represented by only 12 keys of the keyboard. While the Do-Re-Me may be sung in any key without compromise, the octave on the piano represents sounds abstractly and by convention. Letters, like phonemes, represent a class of sounds that make a distinctive contribution to meaning. But unlike phonemes, letters are metarepresentations; they designate a sound by assigning it a place in a system of signs. The metarepresentational nature of these signs is what makes grasping the relation between sound and sign difficult and leads some children to abandon the attempt to map letters to sound, reverting to the strategy of recognizing words on the basis of the visual patterns, something observed primarily in poor readers (Share, 2008; Wolf, 2008).

While some children seem to effortlessly grasp how writing maps to speaking, for others it presents a major obstacle and for all children some years are required to learn the practices, the implicit and explicit rules, for sorting out the relation between writing and speech. Part of the problem, as mentioned, is the loose mapping between sounds and letters. The other, the problem of concern here, is that letters are metarepresentations. They are devices for categorizing and thinking about sounds. Stated more boldly, the letters of the alphabet are names for the concepts that represent distinctive sounds.

READING AND PHONOLOGICAL AWARENESS

E. B. Huey (1910, p. 111), the great theorist of reading, insisted that meaning depended upon recognition of a word as a whole, not the single letters, for only the words had meaning. He acknowledged that the practice of writing "tends to increase the consciousness of single letters as they appear in words." What the great Huey did not seem to know was that the central problem in learning to recognize words and letters was not a visual problem but rather the difficulty in finding in one's own speech discrete sounds that letters could represent. This, of course, is in part a result of the "clavichord" effect, the indirect mapping of sound to sign.

Alvin and Isabelle Liberman (Liberman & Shankweiler, 1991) were the first to notice that children with reading difficulties had parallel difficulties with phonology. Prior to their work it was believed that the main problem in learning to read was learning which signs went with which sounds. The Libermans argued that difficulties arose less from distinguishing the visual signs than from isolating the spoken sounds that the signs were to represent. It is now widely agreed that limited phonological knowledge, an inability to hear the subtleties of sound and to think about those sounds, presents a major hurdle to learning to read. Lacking an awareness of discrete sounds, there was little or nothing in the learner's speech for the letters to represent. Vellutino (1979) made the general case that, at least for alphabetic writing systems, reading problems are primarily linguistic rather than visual problems.

But are reading problems to be traced to phonological abilities, namely, those abilities that make up the linguistic competence of speakers, or are they, as I suggest, metaphonological abilities, the ability to think about phonemes so as to represent them in a new medium? Clearly, the implicit knowledge of the phonology is a necessary ingredient but not a sufficient one. Metaphonological knowledge is what allows one to isolate phonemes, identify them and associate them with letters of the alphabet. This metaphonological knowledge, commonly referred to as phonological awareness, makes phonological knowledge explicit. It involves a metarepresentational shift from *use* to *mention*, a shift in level of discourse that itself may be confusing. Downing (1984) pointed out the confusion generated in children learning to read if they have not yet recognized the shift from talking about things to talking about the words and sounds for things. Language, including its phonology, tends to be transparent to its users; a conceptual shift is required to shift attention from meaning to the underlying form that expresses that meaning.

IMPLICIT PHONOLOGY

It is astonishing how readily most children succeed in learning a first language given the complexity of the phonology and syntax of language. So much so that traditional theories of learning are completely inadequate to explain language learning. Chomsky (1980) cited the "poverty of the stimulus" as an argument for the innateness of language and the uniqueness of a brain that could learn so much from so little. A precocious sensitivity to the sound patterns of language is indicated by the fact that even before they become speakers infants adjust their babbling to the phonological distinctions of the mother tongue they are exposed to. Yet as Jackendoff pointed out, much of phonological knowledge is unconscious even as it is being acquired implicitly in social routines with adults. Only under special circumstances may such implicit processes be made explicit and brought into consciousness as objects of thought. Learning an alphabet is one such circumstance. One hears the tune, not the notes the tune is composed of; learning to read is learning the notes.

Representing sounds by letters of the alphabet reorganizes those sounds into discrete categories. The sounds now represented are no longer identical to phonological structure but are rather the sounds identified with the letters. Phonological awareness is the awareness of those sounds picked out, and metarepresented by the letters of the alphabet. With more letters one may hear more sounds. The concept *letter* links a visual sign to a detectable property of speech. The inventory of letters becomes the inventory of spoken sounds, allowing one to think about those properties, classifying them as vowels or consonants, for example. Phonological awareness is not some flood of consciousness that comes over one but rather the awareness of those specific properties of language that new concepts disclose and make available to further talk and thought.

This is not to deny that there is some sensitivity to the sound properties implicit in the practice of speaking before one acquires a metalanguage. Infants respond well to meaningless verbal routines, to rhyme and rhythm, and they monitor anomalies in social routines including linguistic ones (Grieve, 1990; Tunmer, Pratt & Herriman, 1984). On the other hand, there is wide agreement that a series of changes occur in children's awareness of certain properties of language in the preschool years and especially as they learn to read (Treiman & Zukowsky, 1991). This new awareness goes under several descriptions including reflexive awareness, explicit awareness, metalinguistic awareness and the like. What is involved is the invention of concepts *for* and knowledge *about* those properties of language implicit in speech that are made explicit in the writing system.

PHONOLOGICAL AWARENESS

Phonological awareness is typically measured by asking learners to delete a phoneme from a spoken word: /f/ from "fish" or /a/ from "about," to ask which words start with the same sound, to ask for words that rhyme, to count the syllables in a word, to find words that have the same ending and the like. Such tasks are metarepresentational in that they query not the things but the words for things, not the sounds cars make but the sounds in the word "car." Word awareness and phonological awareness are intertwined in such tasks.

There is a high and well-known correlation between success in learning to read and phonological awareness (Lundberg, Olofsson & Wall, 1980). That correlation is used to justify reading programs that emphasize the teaching of phonics (Adams, Treiman & Pressley, 1998; Bradley & Bryant, 1983). Valtin (2014) has re-analyzed some of this data to show that phonological awareness is indistinguishable from reading ability and therefore should not be seen as a pre-reading skill so much as a symptom of reading competence. Phonological awareness is an important aspect of learning to read in that it provides guidance to the reader as to the sound of the word one is attempting to recognize. But it is at the same time an index of the subtle change in one's orientation to language as one learns to read. There is a conceptual shift from the meanings expressed in the language to the properties of the language that give rise to those meanings. It is this consciousness of language that is one of the legacies of literacy. Tests of phonological awareness are one among many research and diagnostic tasks that have provoked much dispute, and I return to this issue in Chapter 11.

Phonological awareness is sometimes thought to be a developmental rather than an acquired competence and has led researchers to describe its development in terms of an age-dependent series of stages beginning around age 3. However, the developmental claim was clearly ruled out by the findings of Morais, Alegria and Content (1987), who compared the metaphonological abilities of two groups of normal adults from a remote Portuguese fishing village, half of whom had been exposed to an alphabet as children although they never became routine readers, the other half with no exposure to the alphabet. Only those who had been exposed to the alphabet were able as adults to succeed on such tasks. Read, Zhang, Nie and Ding (1986) compared adult Chinese readers who had been taught to read an alphabetic script, *pinyin*, with those of another group who read only Chinese characters. Again, those exposed to an alphabet could perform well on tasks measuring phonological awareness. Awareness of the phonology of the language, then, is less a developmental competence than a consequence of literacy and training with an alphabet. Hence, we may conclude that learning to read and write with an alphabet makes explicit aspects of language that are present but implicit in speaking. In making them explicit, literacy brings consciousness to language.

Nonetheless, there may be developmental constraints on learning to represent sounds by letters in that such learning is a metarepresentational achievement. Representations of representations may in principle be more complex and mentally demanding. Developmental considerations would help to explain why the teaching of reading is usually postponed until about the age of 5 or 6 years, about the time that children acquire other metarepresentational competencies including the theory of mind. Furthermore, the onset of formal schooling, that is, schooling directed to the acquisition of basic skills, is almost universally begun about the age of 6 years.

USES OF THE DISCOVERY OF PHONOLOGY

Learning the alphabet is instrumental to functions other than learning to read and write and where it serves as a cognitive tool rather than as an aspect of consciousness of language. Alphabetization is too common and too pervasive in the modern world to require extended comment. Post boxes, catalogs, directories, indexes, libraries, bureaucracies and even classroom roll-calls are based on and listed in alphabetical order, the order memorized as the ABCs.

Historian Elting Morrison (1966) tells the story of the most powerful officer in the US Army who had never commanded a troop in the field in war or peace. Nonetheless he became a Major General in the US Army. This was because he had invented a card index. As a young officer he had been assigned to the Bureau of Pensions. Every day the bureau received dozens of requests for information regarding the eligibility of servicemen for a pension, requests that took some six months to fill. One year after Lieutenant Ainsworth, the future General, took over the job, an answer could be provided within 24 hours. The instrument of this revolution was the card index. By 1905 he was a General in the War Department responsible for all the paperwork, the records and correspondence that went through the army.

Thus the alphabet is a tool of the mind useful for classifying knowledge as an aid to carrying out the world's work. Furthermore, it provides a scheme for organizing and thinking about one's own knowledge about language and the world. No small thing, it allows one to play Scrabble! But the primary significance of the invention of the alphabet was not that it serves as a useful tool but rather that, like all full writing systems, it produces a new consciousness of language.

The discovery of the phoneme is perhaps the clearest case of an implicit feature of language that, without an alphabetic writing system, may have remained buried under layers of meaning and the more conspicuous auditory properties of speech such as syllables and rhymes. These are features that remain part of the implicit knowledge of persons in non-alphabetic cultures but are part of the consciousness of everyone who can read.

Learning an alphabet throws some light on the issue of the social construction of knowledge. Clearly the alphabet is a social construction, evolved over a long period of time and acquired by children by deliberate instruction. Reading, as is often pointed out, is not a natural activity (Wolf, 2008). Because it is a social construction some have concluded that there is no fact of the matter, that we are restricted to the postmodern world of discourse. But the invention of the alphabet is not only a social construction, a social and discursive convenience. Rather the alphabet provides a set of concepts that reveal, make explicit, what was actually there all along, albeit in a somewhat different form, awaiting discovery. The history of writing was in this way a voyage of discovery and children's learning to read and write should be a chance to relive that voyage. That the alphabet is not the true or final theory of phonology does not distract from the fact that it reveals something that was previously unknown about language.[1]

[1] A minor technical point. My earlier claim (1994) that written signs represented spoken ones led to the charge of technological determinism. I should have said that the concept of *letter* both defines what will count as a visual sign and what will count as a spoken sound.

SUMMING UP

The minimal contrastive units of sound that make up the phonology of a language are discriminated in learning that language. As we saw, some phonological distinctions are learned even before infants manage comprehensible speech. But, as I have argued, that knowledge remains implicit and largely or wholly out of consciousness. The invention of the alphabet was contingent on finding those minimal units of sound that the written letters could be assigned to. Sounds become objects of thought by means of the concepts acquired in learning the letters of the alphabet. Learning to read an alphabet requires that one learn to analyze the stream of speech into the units represented by those letters. Finding those sounds, distinguishing them, thinking about them and assigning them to written signs is a metarepresentational task such that the letters invented are representations of the sounds implicit in speech. Learning to read and write creates a new consciousness of this aspect of language. Once learned the alphabet creates a phonological illusion that the only sounds heard are those represented by spelling, thus overlooking the variable sounds associated with plural *s*.

The development of phonological awareness provides an important model or precedent for thinking about how other properties of language, in particular words and sentences, come to be objects of thought. In these cases too, it will be argued, the consciousness of these important properties of language are a product of the invention and mastery of concepts for referring to aspects of speech suited to a writing system and expressed in a metalanguage. Because words and sentences are embodiments of meaning, turning them into objects of thought has profound significance as they help to reveal the very roots of rationality. That is our next task.

7 The Discovery of Words and Thinking about Words

Teacher: *"Use your own words"*
Student: *"I don't know any other words"*

Surely it is an oxymoron to say that fluent speakers of a language do not know what a word is. Words are the basic constituents of communicative speech, so it is difficult to imagine how speakers could use words if they don't know what words are and what they mean. The claim of this chapter is that speakers of a language ordinarily think *with* words rather than *about* words. Semantic structure, like phonological and syntactic structure, is unconscious. What one is conscious of is what the words are about, namely, what the words refer to and what the speaker means to convey in using them. While such a claim may seem odd, it is in fact a fundamental assumption of modern linguistic theory as formulated in the writings of Saussure and Jacobson. They claimed that the linguistic structures used in producing and understanding language are unconscious, revealed only through scientific study: "Structural linguistics shifts from the study of conscious linguistic phenomena to the study of their unconscious infrastructure" (Levi-Strauss, 1963, p. 33). The claim that the underlying structure or infrastructure of language is unconscious is just another way of saying that language is largely transparent to its object. But, one may argue, surely speakers are conscious of the meaning. As we shall see, the *meaning* of "meaning" is the problem.

There are three questions that must be addressed. The first is to make clear what is meant by saying that linguistic structure is unconscious and transparent to its object. Second, if we can establish that language is transparent, how does such transparent knowledge come to be an explicit object of thought? And third, how are reading and literacy implicated in creating this consciousness?

TRANSPARENCY

First we must show that the knowledge of linguistic form is, in fact, implicit and unconscious. As mentioned earlier, consciousness does not clearly distinguish sentient creatures from sapient creatures. For this reason I relied on the implicit–explicit distinction. To make something explicit is to make it into the subject of discourse, something that one could talk or think about, what I earlier called *sapient* consciousness. So what are the conditions under which aspects of language, specifically words, become something to talk about?

Literate speakers tend to take their own introspective powers as universal and express incredulity at the claim that someone may not know what a word is or what a word means (Halverson, 1991). But consider Charles Dickens's universally reviled pedagogue, Gradgrind, who insisted that Sissy Jupe, "girl number twenty" whose father was a horse trainer, did not know the meaning of the word "horse":

> "Girl number twenty unable to define a horse!" said Mr. Gradgrind, for the general behoof of all the little pitchers. "Girl number twenty possessed of no facts, in reference to one of the commonest of animals! Some boy's definition of a horse. Bitzer, yours."
>
> ...
>
> "Bitzer," said Thomas Gradgrind. "Your definition of a horse."
>
> "Quadruped. Graminivorous. Forty teeth, namely twenty-four grinders, four eye-teeth, and twelve incisive. Sheds coat in the spring; in marshy countries, sheds hoofs, too. Hoofs hard, but requiring to be shod with iron. Age known by marks in mouth." Thus (and much more) Bitzer.
>
> "Now girl number twenty," said Mr. Gradgrind. "You know what a horse is."
>
> (Charles Dickens, *Hard Times*)

Of course our sympathies run with Sissy Jupe, who clearly knew what a horse was and knew how to use the word "horse" to refer to her father's animals. Thus we may be inclined to dismiss Gradgrind's claim that Sissy only "now knows what a horse is." More correctly, Gradgrind could have said "You now know the meaning of the word 'horse'." The difference between knowing how to use a word to refer to a horse and knowing the meaning of the word "horse" is subtle and puzzled philosophers until the 19th century. And puzzles most of us to this day.

Words occupy a precarious place in linguistic theory, halfway, I would say, between orality and literacy. There is no consensus on defining what a word is other than it stands alone in a dictionary – that alone should convince one that word is a literate artifact, a product of writing. Rather than taking words as the units of meaning, linguists talk instead of *morphemes*, units of the semantic system that can serve as the root or base of words such as *un/believe/able*. *Word* is used only as a shorthand. Jackendoff (2002) put words at the interface between syntactic structures and semantic structures. Words have a phonemic form and express a meaning and they do so with grammatical tags tied to them, "belief" is a noun, "believe" is a transitive verb and so on. At the same time words make a distinctive contribution to the meaning of the sentences in which they occur. Sentences are used to make statements that are true or false and promises that are sincere or false and so on. The contribution the word makes to that truth or falsity of the sentence in which it occurs is what defines its meaning.

All of this linguistic structure is implicit in the practice of speaking but is made explicit by linguists and pedagogues. The concept *word* may be defined in terms of the conventions of writing and printing – a piece of language that is easily recognizable in speech and visually distinguishable in writing. This is the sort of compromise we saw in the invention of the alphabet, where convenience for easy reading, writing and thinking help to shape and define the units. The fact that a word is both a piece of writing and a piece of speech engenders the mistaken belief that words and the concept of *word* are objects of awareness to all speakers rather than, as I am suggesting, concepts invented to make the implicit and unconscious processes of speaking into conscious objects of knowledge. Even when a word is singled out, it tends to be treated as transparent to what it represents in its context of use, just as Sissy Jupe did.

Philosophers, too, have added importantly to the concept of meaning. Augustine claimed that the meaning of a word was given by pointing to its bearer, what is called the referential theory of meaning. Locke (1690/1961) claimed that words were associated not with things but with ideas, which in turn were faint copies or representations of things. Modern philosophy of language began when Frege (Dummett, 1993), a 19th-century logician, distinguished meaning into two parts, the *sense* of a term and the *reference*, the thing, event or idea referred to. Frege described *sense* as "the mode of presentation" of the referent; or, as I once argued, the way or manner of referring to a referent (Olson, 1970). This distinction accounts for the fact that two statements referring to the same object may have different senses, as first argued by Frege (Dummett, 1993). *Sense* is that aspect of meaning that inheres in the language across uses and thus may be singled out as *sentence meaning* as opposed to *speaker's meaning* (Grice, 1989) and allows one to distinguish what *it* means from what *he* means by it, a distinction I showed was late to develop and that, I argued, was associated with literacy (Olson, 1977).

Frege advanced his distinction to make a logical point, namely, that the same reference (and truth value) could be designated by different expressions. He pointed out that the expressions "The Morning Star" and "The Evening Star" have the same reference, the planet Venus. But the two expressions have different *senses* or semantic meanings. Thus it is informative to say, indeed it was a major astronomical discovery, that "The Morning Star is the Evening Star." Frege's contribution was to bring into our consciousness something that was implicit in language, namely, the *sense* of an expression. The reference of the expression had been explicit and conscious all along and in fact dominated the discussion of meaning prior to Frege. The *sense* of a word or expression is that which makes its way into a modern dictionary, while the discussion of the *reference* of the word makes its way into the encyclopedia.

Frege disclosed a previously undetected property of language, namely, that words had a *sense* apart from the referent they pointed to. Learners acquire the *sense* of a word as part of the implicit and unconscious meaning of a word.[1] Children take the first step to making such knowledge explicit, something to think about, when they acquire the concept of a word but master it more fully when they begin to think about synonymy and paraphrase, and to "use other words" to express the same or similar meaning.

Following Frege, we may say that linguistic meaning is the set of largely implicit rules for designating the referent. In my own earlier work I argued that meaning was the referent in context (Olson, 1970). What I should have said was that linguistic meaning, what Frege called *sense*, is what is left when the reference, the thing or event referred to, is canceled out. Thus even adults may fail to notice that two meanings can take the same referent and the identical meaning can refer to different referents. To refer to the simple example I used at the time, "The white one" and "The little one" may refer to the same block of wood but in different contexts of alternatives. But I overlooked the fact that the same expression, "The little one," has a constant *sense* that may be used to refer to an entirely different object in a different context. What permits these diverse functions is the unconscious semantic or linguistic meaning, the *sense*. To claim as some writers do (Wells, 1999) that the meaning of a text is what the reader brings to it overlooks the fact that some readers may simply identify the reference of an expression, while others attend to the *sense* of a word or expression. The latter, as we shall see, is important for reading critically. Fregean sense is the set of conventions that one acquires in becoming a member of a speech community but that

[1] I italicize the word "sense" throughout this chapter to indicate its Fregean use.

ordinarily remains out of consciousness and therefore transparent. Pre-literate consciousness falls on the object or state referred to, the reference; some training is required to bring the *sense* into consciousness. When these implicit linguistic conventions or norms are made explicit by means of a metalanguage, they provide a standard against which any interpretation may be measured and one can enter into debates about meaning, as did Alice and Humpty Dumpty.

Vygotsky took a step in the Fregean direction, if imperfectly, by distinguishing ordinary from scientific concepts and by distinguishing conventional meanings of words, as given, for example, in the dictionary, from personal, contextual meanings, which, unfortunately, he called the sense, thereby reversing Frege's usage. "Sense emerges when conventional meanings are brought into concrete practical activity by individuals in the service of specific motives and goals" (Lantolf & Poehner, 2014). Sense is "a dynamic fluid and complex whole, which … changes in different minds and situations" (Vygotsky, 1986, p. 245). Vygotsky's *sense* is perhaps better described as contextual meaning or *use*, whereas his dictionary meanings, more precisely his "scientific concepts," as equivalent to Frege's *sense*.

Fodor criticized Vygotsky's claim about the transparency of language on just this point. Vygotsky claimed that for the child the meaning of a term was the object or event described: "the word to the child is an integral part of the object" (1986, pp. 222–224). Again, for a child "the meaning of a word is a complex of concrete objects connected by a factual tie." Only later in development, Vygotsky claimed, does "signification independent of meaning, and meaning independent of reference appear."

In the first volume of the journal *Cognition*, Fodor pronounced Vygotsky's claims about word meaning as vacuous by showing that if Vygotsky were correct, the meaning of such expressions as "Churchill is the Prime Minister of Britain" would be tautologies as both the subject and the predicate refer to the same person. He pointed out that such expressions are not tautologies but rather convey important information graspable by even the youngest children and in fact are important for learning a language. Therefore, Vygotsky was wrong in claiming that for the child the meaning was the referent or reference of the expression.

Admittedly Vygotsky's claim was too broad, just as Fodor's rejection is too categorical. What Vygotsky could more correctly claim, and this I believe is closer to his intention, is that children, like many adults, are conscious of the meanings expressed in language in terms of the objects referred to rather than the implicit properties of the linguistic form used for expressing them, the Fregean *sense*. What Vygotsky was claiming was that, as Piaget had shown, pre-reading children apparently lacked the ability to think about a word as a conceptual object with a meaning as distinguished from its use in pointing to a referent. That is, they lacked the concept *word*. *Word* is a *metalinguistic* concept that, no less than the concept *phoneme*, makes explicit what had otherwise remained implicit in the social practice of speaking. What words are about, their reference, is normally the object of consciousness and is incorrectly adopted as the meaning of the expression. The *sense* independent of its reference remains implicit and unrecognized as such by children. Words as objects of discourse are brought into consciousness, it is argued, largely through alphabetic writing, a historical achievement as well as a developmental one. That discovery enables one to talk about the length of words, to form the lists of words and, importantly, to talk of the similarity of their meanings. But an adequate account of that semantic structure brought with the concept of word, the *sense*, remained puzzling until Frege.

Bernstein (2010) pointed out that the "linguistic turn" in philosophy, the turn associated with Frege, Wittgenstein, Brandom and others, brought a clear distinction between talking and talking about talk, between using words and the metalinguistic concept of word. As mentioned, although traditional philosophy distinguished ordinary from philosophical uses of terms, it lacked the use–mention distinction, that is, the language–metalanguage distinction (Kneale & Kneale, 1984). Earlier philosophers, in discussing words such as "justice," assumed they were talking about reality, later ones about correct usage of a word. Frege inspired philosophers to distinguish semantic meaning, *sense*, from reference. What is to be added is that acquiring the concept of word is critical to making this distinction.

THE HISTORY OF CONSCIOUSNESS OF WORDS

The analysis of a spoken utterance into a string of discrete words is difficult for a number of reasons. First, not all languages are readily carved into identifiable constituents comparable to those found in modern printed English. Pinker (1994, pp. 120–121) pointed out that in Kivunjo, a Bantu language, the verb "Naikimlyiia" (stripped of its accent marks) means "He is eating it for her"; composed of eight parts combining a variety of prefixes and suffixes, it builds an entire sentence out of a single complex verb. Clearly "word" is not a conspicuous entity in Kivunjo.

Second, words were not identified with lexical items in antiquity. Havelock (1982, p. 289) argued that Homer, an oral poet, thought not with words but with phrases such as "the wine-dark sea." Even when word came to be isolated in writing, the Greek word *logos*, usually translated as "word," was at first used to refer not to a single word but rather to a saying or to speech generally. Even in Biblical times "word" meant not a single word but a saying, just as in our times we say "I give you my word." Beowulf speaks of an orator's "word hoard," an expression usually translated as "vocabulary"; however, it is much more likely that it referred to one's stock of sayings than to individual words.

Leiper (2013, p. 6) re-examined pre-5th-century BC Greek writings for evidence of cognitive change that came with writing. She concluded that consciousness of language developed only as the Greeks became literate and only then were they capable of letter and word identification. In the Latin West words became distinct visible entities in written texts only in the 11th century; until then expressions had been written in *Scripta continua*. Segmenting a continuous text into discrete words was introduced primarily to facilitate silent reading (Saenger, 1982). But segmenting an utterance into discrete words was critical to the development of the ability to think about words.

Even when words were isolated in writing, their significance for thinking was slow to be recognized. J. P. Small, a noted archeologist, commented: "in classical antiquity, the 'value' of the word as a tool to organize and retrieve other words simply was not understood" (1993, personal communication; 1997). She illustrates her claim by showing that Pliny's *Natural History* lacked any scheme for organizing information around words rather than the things described. Consequently, Pliny's table of contents was essentially the whole book. Small concludes: "The realization of what your language is like comes after you try to model it in another medium [such as writing] ... Every concept, like that of word, takes an incredibly long time to develop, master, and finally become so taken for granted that it is not even noticed" (1993, personal communication).

Anthropologists have explored the concept of word in some pre-literate societies. The findings of Himmelmann (2006) are typical and will have to serve as a sample of a rich and somewhat divided anthropological literature. He notes that whereas literate native speakers have relatively clear ideas about wordhood given by the conventions of print, in many non-literate societies, although speakers may be able to segment utterances into form-meaning pairings of word-like sizes, the "consistency with which such segmentation is performed ... varies greatly between individual speakers and speech communities" (pp. 254–255). Earlier, Scribner and Cole (1981) had found that those familiar with a syllabic script could easily break utterances into syllables yet were unable to break them into words; they lacked the concept of *word.*

Relative to non-Western languages, English is readily segmented into words, many of which can be represented by a visually distinctive group of letters. As Small noted, the very visibility of words seems to have altered our cognitive practices, including making word lists, dictionaries and organized bodies of knowledge.

LITERACY AND CONSCIOUSNESS OF THE *SENSE* OF WORDS

Words become objects of thought primarily when children learn to read. Word awareness was first studied by Piaget and his colleagues (Papandropoulou & Sinclair, 1974), who showed that pre-operational children lacked a concept of *word*. When 5- and 6-year-old children were asked for a long word they would accept "train" because trains are long but reject "caterpillar" because caterpillars are tiny. Piaget treated the acquisition of the concept *word* as a developmental phenomenon as it reliably developed around the age of 6 in all the Swiss children! Others would see this development as a consequence of learning to read, although most acknowledge that development may be a necessary condition if not a sufficient one.

Even in a literate culture, pre-reading children are sometimes surprised to discover that they are actually speaking words. One parent reported an English-speaking child learning to speak French who attempted to display her newly acquired competence to her grandmother by saying, "Grandma, do you know how to say 'horse' in French?" The grandmother, playing along with the game, said she did not. The child then volunteered "Cheval." This was followed by a pause, after which the child asked, "How do you say 'horse' in English?" (Jane Wakefield, personal communication).

Although word awareness appears in most children at about age 6, just as Piaget's group noticed, it is a special achievement tied primarily to learning to read and write. Reid (1960) discovered that children's earliest concept of a word was as a unit of print where words are clearly distinguished by spaces, rather than as an elementary constituent of speech. Francis (1973) found that only half of the 50 children entering school correctly responded to her request to "tell me a word." Downing (1984) pointed out how pedagogical discourse could be confusing if children had yet to learn the distinction between words and things.

The fact that children lack a metarepresentational concept *word* does not imply a complete lack of awareness of language. Children as young as 2 years have been shown to make corrections to the phonological, lexical and syntactic forms of own and others' utterances; they ask questions about the meaning of words, what things are called, they generalize rules and so on in the course of learning a language (see Grieve, 1990; Tunmer, Pratt & Herriman, 1984). Their efforts are directed at understanding others and remedying misunderstanding. Although names are early recognized as words, words such as "of" and "in" are treated as separate words only when children become readers (Tunmer & Bowey, 1984). Homer (2009) has summarized this research on word awareness and concluded that consciousness of words as possible objects of thought is largely indistinguishable from consciousness of the written word. Although children can be taught to divide utterances into words at an earlier age (Karmiloff-Smith, 1992), the skill is greatly enhanced through the pedagogical practices of the school that call attention to words, how they are spelled and what they refer to. Even then discourse about words pertains primarily to their reference, that is, to what the words refer to or are about rather than to their meaning, that is, their Fregean *sense*.

Although the word "word" is added to the lexicon of children in learning to read, it is of course not restricted to references to print; it is soon applied to oral language to become an important part of linguistic competence quite divorced from its origins in learning to read. Once words are recognized as words, they become potential objects of thought in that one can ask about their length, their sounds, their meanings, their relation to other words and their contribution to the meanings of the sentences they occur in. Furthermore, the concept of word metarepresents and makes explicit an aspect of linguistic structure that had previously been implicit in their ordinary usage, namely, the *sense* of a term.

THINKING ABOUT WORDS, THEIR MEANING AND THEIR *SENSE*

The discovery of words as objects to recognize, refer to and talk about merely sets the stage, as mentioned, for thinking about words, their correct pronunciation, their meanings and their relations to other words. The transformation from thinking about things to thinking about words is a major preoccupation of literacy training and a major contribution to children's intellectual development. Yet it is not always clear that what is important in thinking about words is not what they refer to but rather their Fregean *sense*. It is the consciousness of the *sense* of a term that allows for judgments of similarity of meaning, of synonymy, antonymy and hyponymy.

There is an abundance of evidence for the claim that literate education is in part learning to think about words and meanings, much of it provided by Vygotsky and his associates. Luria (1976, pp. 57–58) showed schooled and unschooled subjects a series of drawings of familiar objects and asked them to find the item that did not belong. One set included *hammer, saw, log, hatchet*. Those who had not been to school had difficulty coming up with the superordinate term "tool" and using it to exclude "log," claiming that the other items all went with log "to build anything." Even teaching unschooled subjects to classify objects into categories proved difficult. Shown an ax and a sickle and having to choose a similar item from among a *saw, log, ear of grain*, some insisted on pairing the sickle with grain and the ax with the log and so on. What Luria's results show is that this shift is not a developmental change that occurs with age, but rather one that occurs with the study of language and literacy. But what had children learned? They had learned to distinguish the reference of the terms from the *sense* of the terms, for it is their *sense* that gives the terms equivalence and their relations to other words.

Many of these findings were replicated in a variety of traditional and modern societies by Bruner and his colleagues (Bruner, Olver & Greenfield, 1966). Thus in one study (Olver & Hornsby, 1966) children ranging from 6 to 18 years of age were asked to tell how different items are alike, beginning: "how are banana and peach alike?" *Potato* was added, then asking: "How is potato different from banana and peach?" And then: "How are banana, peach and potato alike?" Whereas 6-year-olds tended to say "a banana is yellow, and a peach is red and yellow" and so on, older children tended to say "they are something to eat" or "They are all food."

Such results are often interpreted as indicating a shift to thinking more abstractly. However, it is more than that. Whereas the younger children's answers are about the objects mentioned, the older children's answers are about the semantic relations among the words, their *senses*. With literate schooling the discourse begins to shift from discourse about objects to discourse about the language, primarily words, their meanings and their links to other words.

The emancipation of words from their referents is also seen in children's response to word association tests. One such task was useful for distinguishing two forms of aphasia, one with word finding, a "paradigmatic" disorder, the other with relating words grammatically, a "syntagmatic" disorder. Syntagmatic associations are those that link words grammatically, "cold–winter," whereas paradigmatic ones draw on words from the same grammatical class, "cold–hot." Later research revealed a "syntagmatic" to "paradigmatic" shift that occurred in children around the age of 7. Cronin (2002) reported a developmental study that showed that as children became more skilled at reading, they produced more paradigmatic associations. This is just what we would expect if the shift is primarily one from thinking about the reference of terms to thinking about the semantic relations among words, their *sense.*

The link between literacy and this special consciousness of the *sense* of a term has long escaped not only all pre-reading children but also most literate adults and even the psychologists who study them. Carl Jung, Freud's student and later rival, invented the "Word association test" as a means of examining subjects' unconscious feelings and beliefs. The test was applied to hundreds of subjects. To his surprise, the major differences he discovered were not those between men and women or between the young and the old or between the disturbed and the sane. Rather the primary differences were those between educated and non-educated subjects, those he took to be subnormal. Normal, reasonably educated subjects, given a word such as "glass" responded with "iron," words from the same syntactic and semantic class. Indeed they were instructed to do so and they readily complied. The uneducated, on the other hand, told stories, offered explanations, provided paraphrases and the like. Jung correctly concluded that these uneducated subjects "are not accustomed to deal with single words, but only know them in connexions [*sic*] as symbols with a meaning" (Jung, 1918/1969, p. 183). These responses are of the same form as those obtained from young children and, as I mentioned, from Sissy Jupe. Roy Harris (2009, p. 40) has stressed just this point: "Literacy produces a mind-set in which words are treated as context-free items with context-free meanings." Those meanings consist of their *senses* rather than their usual referents.

Word association tests, then, provide evidence of a person's ability to think about words as opposed to think about the things represented by the words. Thinking about words is to think about their *sense* rather than their reference. The *sense* of the words is captured in their relations to other words, whether in terms of their form class, their synonyms, their antonyms, or their place in the lexical hierarchy. Knowing words as a speaker or even isolating words from within a sentence is therefore different from thinking about words; only the latter is metalinguistic and associated with literacy and education. Such knowledge has become the prototypical standard for the measurement, some say the mismeasurement, of intelligence.

Doherty and Perner (1998) provided a convincing example of younger children's inability to think about even familiar words independently of their referents. Four- to six-year-old children were first pretested to determine that they were able to correctly associate two more or less synonymous words such as "bunny" and "rabbit" with a picture of a rabbit. The experimental task required the children to name the picture using the word alternative to that used by the experimenter. Thus, if the experimenter said "rabbit," the child was to say "bunny." Children found this task more or less impossible until about the age of 7. Again this suggests that children acquire the ability to think about the words as words in relation to each other, that is as synonyms, only later in their development, arguably as they learn to read. This observation fits nicely with the Robinson, Goelman and Olson (1983) finding that children until this age had difficulty distinguishing what was said from what was meant, that is, of distinguishing the ambiguity of a word or sentence from the misinterpretations assigned by a listener.

Consciousness of words, that is, the ability to think about the *sense* of words is essential in distinguishing verbatim repetition from paraphrase, paraphrase from quotation, what was said from what was meant, to define words, to arrange them in terms of synonymy, antonymy, hyponymy and to derive their logical entailments. Ayer (1936) called these entailments "analytic" or logical truths, distinguishing them from "synthetic" empirical truths. Analytic truths are true by definition, that is, knowledge that could be derived by logical necessity; a horse is necessarily a quadruped, as Gradgrind insisted. Analytic truths and logical inferences depend upon the *sense* of words rather than their referents. Creating a definition is the attempt to recapture *sense* thereby creating analytic truths. Quine (1960) was later to show that the distinction between analytic and synthetic statements, though useful, is not absolute. Definitions can evolve in the light of new knowledge.

Educators since Dewey have been wary of "book knowledge" or purely "verbal" knowledge, by which they meant memorized verbal formulas. Words are worth learning only when they are seen by the learner to carry a meaning about the world and later when words themselves find a place in the space of reasons. But one result of downplaying book learning has been to reduce the study of words to the study of things with a corresponding failure to distinguish between vocabulary growth and metalinguistic knowledge. Knowledge *of* words in contexts is linguistic knowledge; knowledge *about* words is metalinguistic knowledge. Both are important. Metalinguistic knowledge, we may recall, is thinking about words in terms of their *senses* captured in definitions and in their relations to other words as in synonymy, antonymy and entailment. Metalinguistic knowledge is essential to critical thinking, whereas learning words, broadening one's vocabulary, is primarily broadening one's knowledge about the world. Children pick up some dozen words a day over their entire childhood, a process that accelerates if they become readers. But learning to think about words is a peculiarly literate competence, advanced through learning to read and through the study of words, their definitions and the implicational relations to other words. To think about words is to think about thinking, the foundation of rationality.

CONCLUSION

Learning a language is a universal human achievement; thinking about language is a product of and fostered by literacy. Learning a language involves acquiring the phonological, syntactical and semantic competencies that remain unconscious and implicit in speaking. In regard to phonology, as we saw, children detect slight but significant differences in sound patterns of the language from an early age but the system of phonological knowledge remains implicit and unconscious. Learning the alphabet turns those sounds into objects that one can talk and think about. In this chapter, I have made the parallel argument, namely, that semantic knowledge is similarly an unconscious and implicit aspect of one's knowledge of language. To justify this claim it was necessary to distinguish the *sense* of an expression from its *reference*. Learning a language is learning to bring one's experiences into a common conscious understanding. But in talking about experiences of the world they are also acquiring an implicit and unconscious semantic system, an abstract, semantic space or network of similarities, differences and hierarchical relations among words. All of this implicit linguistic knowledge, this Fregean *sense*, is acquired in learning to speak. What the metalanguage does is make explicit this implicit knowledge such that one can talk about words, their sounds, their grammatical roles and their relations to other words as synonyms, antonyms and hyponyms that make up the *sense* of a word. When children do acquire the concept of a synonym they are bringing into consciousness the semantic relations that were previously an implicit and unconscious part of their linguistic competence. Ironically, they are becoming conscious of something they knew all along. Children are sometimes surprised to find, once informed about *opposites*, how easily they can produce them.

It should not be necessary at this point to remind the reader that this specialized knowledge *about* words is secondary to competence with the ordinary use of words in common speech. That vernacular or ordinary linguistic competence is what makes us human in the sense that it makes thought possible. But what is implicit in ordinary conversational language becomes explicit when one acquires the appropriate metalanguage for talking about words and meanings. Literacy provides that vocabulary and schooling the opportunity for an extended reflection on the properties and uses of that metalinguistic vocabulary for critical, reflective thinking. This reflective vocabulary is greatly elaborated when we turn to the sentences, the topic of the next chapter.

8 Sentences and Logic

Galileo's laws of falling bodies hold only in a vacuum. (Anonymous)

To a literate adult nothing is more obvious than that one speaks in sentences, that a sentence is an expression of a complete thought, and that it is the smallest unit of language that may be judged as true or false. To us sentences may be long or short, meaningful or meaningless, grammatical or ungrammatical. However, our literate intuitions mislead. Although every speaker has an implicit grammar that can generate sentences, the concept of a sentence is not universal. In this chapter I advance the theory that, like the concept of word, *sentence* is a metalinguistic concept that becomes explicit only with writing and that is useful for referring to and talking about written text.

A sentence is a grammatical form with a meaning. But while the meaning expressed is the focus of shared consciousness, the linguistic form, the grammar employed in generating the sentence, remains implicit in speaking. That is, speakers have no conscious knowledge of the fact that when they change the grammatical subject from "he" to "they" they automatically changed the verb form from "is" to "are" to achieve subject–verb agreement. The argument of this chapter is that the concept of a sentence allows one to make explicit the previously implicit knowledge of some of these properties of speech, including the grammar and the linguistic or semantic meaning of sentences. Thinking about sentences, thereby bringing aspects of grammar and semantics into consciousness, I suggested, is both a legacy of writing and reading and the means to a certain kind of rationality.

Just as a special kind of learning is required to distinguish words from the things and events they refer to, so too special learning is required to distinguish sentences from the meanings they convey in their ordinary contextual use. And just as the separation of words from their objects was the starting point for philosophy, so too the isolation of sentences from their use in meaningful utterances was the starting point for the study of logic and formal rationality. Thinking about sentences apart from utterances begins with the metarepresentational concept of *sentence*.

In producing and understanding ordinary contextually appropriate utterances one draws appropriate inferences from what was said. But the underlying structure and processes involved are largely out of awareness. The metalinguistic concept of a sentence brings these underlying structures into consciousness as objects with particular properties such as *clear* or *ambiguous*, *grammatical* or *ungrammatical* and, importantly, as *implied* or *entailed*. Such inferences are justified by appeal to wording rather than to belief.

As with words, sentences are difficult to detect by children and others unacquainted with writing in that they are buried deeply within understandable utterances. In an appropriate context, on hearing "The cat is hungry" one becomes aware of the hungry cat. With the concept of *sentence* one can ask if it has four words, is grammatical or ambiguous and whether it implies other sentences, judgments that may require one to set aside all thoughts about the cat.

It takes considerable linguistic training to consider the grammar of an expression independently of its meaning. Linguist Victoria Fromkin used the expression "Bird house black" as a prompt to encourage students to think about grammar. Most students interpret the expression to mean "black bird house." However, linguists prefer the interpretation that "'bird house' must be adjectival, a kind of black," because the grammar of the English noun phrase requires that the final word of a phrase be a noun with the preceding words serving as modifiers. Perhaps, one could think, a kind of paint for bird-houses. As long as grammatical knowledge is unconscious it cannot be strictly applied, so one ends up with a plausible meaning "black bird house." But, literate persons, in possession of an explicit knowledge of grammar, may impose the rules of grammar on even an awkward phrase. To think about the grammar is therefore a learned form of competence. Although to be a speaker is to know a grammar, thinking about the grammar requires a metarepresentational concept of *sentence*.

A sentence is a unit of language fundamental to any grammatical analysis. But it is only indirectly related to the constituents of actual speech. As Chafe (1985) pointed out, conversational speech is composed of phrases and clauses of limited length suited to the discourse of which it is part. On the other hand, a sentence is a well-defined unit of written language. Sentences have one or more clauses, each with a subject and a predicate, as well as beginning with a capital and ending with a period. Fromkin, Rodman and Hymes (2007) point out that while speech allows wide dialectal variation, writing has a rather strict definition of a sentence, a fact not always honored by beginning or even advanced writers. That written standard may flow back into speaking, sometimes with an easily ridiculed effect – recall Martin Joos's Miss Fiditch who would rather parse than eat or James Joyce's Miss Equitone whose speech was as flat as a string of letters.

Not only are sentences embedded in utterances, utterances themselves are ordinarily embedded in the *pragmatics* of conversational discourse. Grice (1989) claimed that conversation was organized in terms of a Cooperative Principle elaborated in four "maxims": quantity, quality, relation and manner. Quantity requires that one provide the correct information; Quality, that it not be misleading; Relation that it be relevant; and Manner that it serve the general purposes of the conversation. Although designed for analyzing the pragmatics of conversation, the maxims are also broadly applicable to all uses of language, written or oral. The Quantity maxim carries the obligation to tell the truth. The Quality maxim appears in literary theory as the dramatic principle referred to as "Chekhov's gun," so-called because, as Chekhov pointed out, "if there is a gun in the first act, you may be certain that it will be used in the third." That is, every element in the expression must be necessary and irreplaceable. The Cooperative Principle creates a certain trust in the speaker or writer. That trust is not always warranted, as we shall see when we turn to "test questions" (Chapter 10).

In sum, a sentence is an abstract linguistic object only indirectly related to the actual speaking practices of persons. The metalinguistic concept of *sentence* turns this constituent of speech into an object to which one may assign a grammar, a meaning and a set of logical relations linking it to other sentences. As with words, sentences are visually distinctive in modern writing and printing and provide a useful visual model for children in acquiring the concepts *word* and *sentence.* Once acquired such concepts may be recognized as applicable to speech as well as to writing, in both cases providing objects that one may comment on and think about.

Distinguishing sentences from the contexts in which they are normally embedded is sometimes described as decontextualization. How it is achieved remains unstated. The concept of metarepresentation is intended to make clear that decontextualization is a product of representing a structure, as a *sentence*, as an object to think about. The metarepresentation of a sentence relies on a meaning–use distinction in that a piece of language is lifted from its ordinary use, allowing it to be considered as an object in its own right with its own properties, as we saw earlier in the discussion of words. Quotation is a primary means of metarepresentation that opens up expressions to revision and reinterpretation (Olson & Oatley, 2014). Thinking about the properties of a sentence turns out to be important to modern conceptions of rationality and indeed to the philosophy of language.

CONSCIOUSNESS OF SENTENCES

Vygotsky's claim that language is largely transparent entails that one attends to and talks about the intentions shared and the events described while the linguistic forms employed remain out of consciousness. How then are such structures acquired? As we saw in an earlier chapter, some suggest that language learning itself is unconscious, others that although learning requires conscious attention, once learned these structures become automatic and unconscious. Still others claim that they are innate. No matter how they are acquired, every speaker of a language possesses implicit knowledge of a grammar that permits him or her to understand and generate sentences, even if that knowledge is unconscious. Karanth and Suchitra (1993) found that non-literate subjects were unable to distinguish grammatical from ungrammatical sentences; they based their judgments on meaning, not form. To think about that grammatical form requires the acquisition of the metarepresentational concept *sentence*. Equipped with the concept one is invited to think about and comment on the sentence as *long*, *short*, *well-formed*, *ambiguous*, *relevant*, *run-on*, *periodic*, *simple*, *complex*, as composed of *subjects* and *predicates*. More importantly, it allows one to think about the logical relations between sentences such as *implying* or *contradicting* each other, as well as their place in an argument or extended text as *premise*, *topic sentence* or *concluding statement*. The more controversial claim is that such concepts are acquired and elaborated primarily in the context of reading, writing and thinking about written text (Olson, 1977). Although all language is implicitly logical in that the meaning of any utterance is in part what can be inferred from it, the logic of ordinary language remains largely implicit in speaking rather than itself being an object of thought. Thus special means, primarily concepts, are required to bring these structures into consciousness, that is, to turn them into objects of thought and discourse.

As with words, there is considerable evidence that the ability to think about sentences as objects is both a cultural-historical achievement and that the ability is associated with literacy and schooling.

DISCOVERING SENTENCES

While for some purposes it is important to distinguish sentences that we may judge as grammatical or ungrammatical from statements that we may judge as true or false, in what follows, unless necessary, I shall refer to both as sentences.

Roy Harris (2009) advanced the claim that Aristotle's theory of language and his invention of logic were based not on oral utterances but on abstracted written sentences. Aristotle in *On Interpretation* developed the formal logical formulas known as *modus ponens* and *modus tollens* that set out the laws of valid inference. As evidence for his argument, Harris notes that Aristotle used purely logical formulas that could be applied to any utterance: "If A then B" and "A" one may correctly infer "B," but "If A then B" and "B" one may not correctly infer "A," although the unsuspecting often make such invalid inferences. The important point, however, is that the rules of logic were developed to characterize the linguistic/logical form of sentences rather than to explain the practical procedures involved in the production and understanding of ordinary, contextually appropriate spoken utterances. Once developed the rules may be applied to ordinary utterances, sometimes revealing that practical inferences are invalid.

R. Harris, citing Kneale and Kneale (1984), points out that Aristotle never made the use–mention distinction. Consequently, in talking about his formulaic sentences Aristotle assumed he was talking about ordinary speech. This failure to distinguish language from metalanguage has led generations of scholars to assume that the rules of logic are the rules for thinking while continuing to fault thinkers if their reasoning does not follow the canons of logic. Had Aristotle and his followers recognized that the rules of logic are metarepresentational rules, abstract rules for criticizing and evaluating arguments, rather than the laws of thought, much confusion could have been avoided. This point goes some distance in explaining the relation between System One and System Two processes discussed earlier and that I return to in Chapter 10.

Of course, the rules derived for valid inference are useful for evaluating ordinary arguments. But when recognized as rules for criticizing thought, that is, for evaluating inferences as *valid* or *invalid*, it becomes clear that these are rules available primarily to the initiated, those who have learned to think about sentences as objects, divorced from pragmatic context. Equipped with the metalinguistic concept *sentence* one may ask not only about the grammatical form of the sentence but also about the logical relations within and between sentences. If there are laws of thought they will have to be found in ordinary pragmatic discourse and practical action.

Children learn what a sentence is, that is, they acquire the concept *sentence*, when they learn to read. Even young children know that questions require answers, commands compliance, ordinary assertions understanding. Whereas "What did you say?" is understood by the youngest children, the teacher's request to "Say it in your own words" or to "Use complete sentences" falls, initially, on deaf ears because, as mentioned earlier, utterances are not necessarily sentences. Learning where to position a capital letter and insert a period are important parts of learning to write that help to define a sentence. Learning what sentences are and how to refer to them, talk about them and shape them effectively makes up essentially the entire Language Arts Curriculum of the early school years. Children learn to distinguish "what *it* said" in a text from "what *he* said" in reference to an actual speaker. Further, they learn to distinguish "what *he* said" from "what *he* meant" in order to understand the difference between misunderstanding and ambiguity.

LEARNING TO THINK ABOUT SENTENCES

Four independent lines of evidence show that subjects attend to the assumed meaning of an expression rather than to the grammatical properties of sentences and the semantic properties of the words composing them. This evidence further indicates that children in becoming literate come to pay increasing attention to the linguistic form in addition to the primary intended meaning of sentences.

First, some of our early research (Robinson, Goelman & Olson, 1983) showed that first-grade children were unable to distinguish the ambiguity of a sentence from the misunderstandings that it generated. Elizabeth Robinson, one of the authors, had discovered that given instructions that were incomplete, younger children, rather than noting that incompleteness, blamed the listener for failing to comply with what the task required. At about the same time I (Olson, 1975) had found that children of that age often failed to distinguish what they had actually *said* from what they had *meant* to say. Putting these two lines of argument together led Robinson, Goelman and Olson to conduct a study to see if these two explanations were equivalent, namely, that listener blaming was the consequence of failure to recognize the ambiguity of a speaker's sentence. Indeed they were; children given an ambiguous command faulted the listener when a response error occurred rather than pointing to the ambiguity of the sentence expressing the command. To illustrate, told "Give me the red block," when there were two red blocks available but only one met the speaker's requirements, resulting in the listener picking the unintended red block, children attributed the error to a failure on the part of the listener rather than to the ambiguity of the sentence produced by the speaker. By the second grade children almost without exception pointed to the inadequacy of the sentence, saying, for example, "You only said 'the red one' when there were two red ones" or "You should have said 'Little red one'." Subsequent studies (Lee, Torrance & Olson, 2001) showed that young children accepted as "what they had said" if it was a true paraphrase, again suggesting a conflation of what was *said* and what was *meant*, an inability to think about a sentence as an object. Even when they actually remember the speaker's words, they may fail to recognize its ambiguity.

Second, Margaret Donaldson (1978, p. 70) showed that some of the difficulties children had in solving Piaget's developmental tasks hinged importantly on the wording of the expressions used in the task. When the tasks were redescribed in a way that was comprehensible to the child, the difficulties often disappeared. Success in most cases came only when children began, as she said, "to pay scrupulous attention to the very wording of the task," again suggesting that younger children attended to meanings rather than sentences employed.[1]

Third, distinguishing what is actually stated in a text from the interpretations and implications drawn is a competence that is only slowly acquired. Harris (2000) and Hjelmquist and Hedelin (199) found that even 2- and 3-year-old children could on occasion justify an answer by appealing to the very words used by the questioner. But by 6 years of age, Harris reports, in answering questions children routinely "refer back to the wording of the premises" (2000, p. 110). Remembering what was said is critical to grasping the said–meant distinction that appears around 6 years of age. So although the process begins before schooling, it is fostered by the "analytic orientation" to language taught both by educated parents and in the school, resulting in the ability to treat a sentence as an object for reflection. As we shall see, the difficulty is not in children's inability to remember what was said so much as an inability to recognize it as having some property such as being ambiguous or entailing another sentence by virtue of its meaning, what I earlier called "analyticity."

Fourth, the ability to think about sentences as objects that have been lifted from their ordinary contexts of use is a learned rather than a developmental achievement. While children are quite capable users of a language, they attend more to the contextual meaning conveyed rather than abstracting the sentence, metarepresenting it and examining its properties. One exemplary study, although cited in many contexts for many purposes, may serve to show that this is not simply a developmental phenomenon but a cultural-historical one associated with literacy. Luria (1976), in collaboration with Vygotsky, conducted a series of studies in Uzbekistan, an area undergoing rapid social change under the collectivization programs

1 Although Donaldson and I agree on the importance of attention to the very words, it is not clear that Donaldson would endorse my further claim that that attention derived from and was enhanced by reading.

of the Soviet government in the early 1930s. Luria was able to give a series of psychological tests, including classification and reasoning tests, to a group of traditional non-literate farmers and to a comparable group from the same villages who had some formal schooling. The least literate tended to treat tasks in a concrete, context-bound way, whereas those more educated treated them in a more formal, logical way, just as Vygotsky's theories had suggested. Just what the educated subjects had learned, however, remains controversial. The responses of the uneducated subjects provide the critical clue. In a typical, widely cited example, subjects were told the following story:

> In the far North, where there is snow, all the bears are white. Novaya Zemlya is in the Far North and there is always snow there. What color are the bears there?
>
> Literate subjects, of course, answered "White". The non-literate subjects tended to reply with some variant of: "I don't know ... there are different sorts of bears". (Luria, 1976, pp. 108–109).

Luria called such responses failures to infer from the syllogism in that untutored subjects give insufficient weight to what we call the major premise "All the bears are white" and in particular the quantifier "all." However, what Luria thought of as a premise may be seen by his non-literate subject as an informal statement that he is reluctant to agree with. Hence, while it is a failure of logic it is not necessarily a failure of reasoning. The subject treated the task as a linguistic rather than a metalinguistic task in that he failed to treat the *sentence* as a premise for the argument. Thinking about sentences as objects apart from their contextual meaning and use is, therefore, a metalinguistic orientation to language promoted by schooling. Cole (1996) showed that uneducated subjects could be taught this form of thought, although they continued to be reluctant to treat counterfactual statements as premises. Furthermore, the quantifier used in the premise tends to be problematic. Although even young children can apply the concept to small collections of objects, Leslie and Gelman (2012) found that children tended to drop the quantifier in reporting generic statements.

These results for sentences are strikingly similar to those reported earlier for phonemes and words. Recall that Portuguese subjects unfamiliar with the alphabet had difficulties with phoneme segmentation. And recall Jung's discovery that naive uneducated subjects had difficulties on the "word association test," where they told stories, recalled events and the like rather than responding to the word as a word. We may conclude that sentences, like phonemes and words, are objects created by metarepresentational concepts sponsored and elaborated through literacy.

THE ONTOLOGY OF SENTENCES

If words and sentences abstracted from their contexts of use are not universally recognized, are sentences real things in the world or are they artifacts, abstract entities created by grammarians and philosophers as Harris (2009), Linell (2005), Wertsch (1991) and others have suggested? Clearly, people can produce grammatical utterances without knowing they speak in sentences. Sentences are implicit in the utterance of such speech acts as assertions, statements, questions, promises made to persons about things or states of affairs in the world that may be true or false, believed or denied.

But what is said, promised, asked can be metarepresented by putting that content in quotation marks. Speech is reported by means of such metalinguistic complement-taking verbs as *say*, *ask* and *tell* that turn "what is said" into a distinctive object of consciousness. The concept *sentence* is special in that it allows one to treat an expression as mentioned rather than used and to comment on it as grammatical, as a premise, as entailed by an earlier sentence and so on. This lexicon is greatly elaborated in literate discourse to include such concepts as *statement*, *claim*, *assertion*, *suggestion*, *inference* or *conclusion*, concepts important for critical thought.

Consider, for example, Franz Kafka's (1946) "A Little Fable." "'Oh!' said the mouse. 'The world is getting smaller every day'." In possession of the appropriate metalinguistic concepts one could characterize the mouse's utterance as a *claim, a grievance, an allegation*, thereby indicating how the reader understood the utterance. These concepts are all metalinguistic in that they are ways of saying something about something said.

Once it is isolated as an object of thought, one can ask a further set of questions about a statement, whether it is an *inference* or an *assumption*, for example. If an assumption it must be acknowledged, if an inference it must be valid, if a conclusion it must follow from the evidence. Such reflections on language are made possible by metarepresentational concepts beginning with *sentence*, concepts applicable to entities isolated, often, by and for writing.

So, we are left with a question. Are such abstracted structures as sentences and statements – mentioned rather than used – real objects or merely theoretical fictions? Much theoretical and pedagogical dispute hangs on the answer to this question. Those who take sentences to be real, cognitive scientists among them, make judgments about the intellectual competence and mental processes of persons on the basis of their responses to such abstracted sentences, as we saw in the studies by Luria, Kahneman and others. The contextualists, Vygotskians among them, deny that responses to decontextualized words and sentences are indicative of the cognitive abilities of subjects in part because such decontextualized objects are cultural artifacts. Further, they join a growing body of critics who question the validity of testing in general and high-stakes testing in particular that rely on such decontextualized expressions. Wertsch (1991, p. 59), for example, follows Bakhtin in urging the study of language in its concrete contexts of use rather than studying words and sentences that "belong to nobody and are addressed to nobody." And Gigerenzer (1991) criticized Kahneman for basing his conclusions about human rationality on "textbook" examples, problems that occur only in artificial situations. Clearly, language is a social practice in which the pragmatic functions such as making statements or asking questions are primary over the semantic relations among words and sentences. So, again, what is the status of invented objects such as words and sentences? And what inferences are to be drawn about human competence from their judgments about such artificial statements formulated as "test questions"?

I take my lead from the epigraph to this chapter: "Galileo's laws of falling bodies hold only in a vacuum." My suggestion is that abstract linguistic objects such as words and sentences are best seen as laboratory objects, separated from ordinary natural use so that their underlying lawful relations can be studied and perhaps revealed. They are the sorts of objects that Hacking (1983) in his account of laboratory science has described as "hybred" objects, objects created only in the laboratory but yet designed to reveal fundamental truths about nature. The physicist Weinberg, too, pointed out that some of the entities postulated by physicists "exist only in the laboratory." The same is true of sentences; they are creations resulting from lifting expressions from their normal contextual use. Yet, when abstracted from discourse their study may reveal fundamental properties of language and thought and thus of the nature of human competence. Recall that Aristotle's study of sentences out of context allowed him to abstract the rules of logic, even if those rules have a doubtful role in reasoning. Similarly, logicians' examination of the logical connectives provide us with the rules of inference and developmental psychologists reveal orderly stages of mastery. Thus, tasks that rely on the grasp of metarepresentational concepts *words* and *sentences*, even if they are artificial, allow scientists to work out the properties and uses of the semantic relations honored implicitly in speech. One cannot entertain the thought that two words are synonymous without the concept of a word and one cannot entertain the thought that two sentences are paraphrases of each other without the concept of a sentence, even if these relations commonly occur in ordinary speech. Consciousness of these relations are legacies, I suggest, of writing and literacy.

But at the same time it must be remembered that the truths and laws discovered in the laboratory hold only "in a vacuum." When what is learned about sentences is applied to real life, pragmatic conditions apply. This point turns out to be crucial when we examine the sentences used in testing generally and in judgments of rationality in particular. The rules strictly hold only for the sentences abstracted away from ordinary discourse. In actual use in discourse, other considerations may come into play. Sentences as laboratory objects assume what are called *ceteris paribus* conditions, that is, those other unmentioned conditions that are assumed as "being equal." In real discourse one cannot make such an assumption about either a specific word or sentence as their meanings are affected by the actual context and pragmatics of utterance.

All abstract rules and principles regardless of the domain, including moral, legal, scientific and religious domains, are derived from laboratory objects. The formal principles derived from the study of laboratory objects – including strict definition and logical implication – may be applied back into local context, sometimes with the effect of making statements clear, as we shall see when we discuss written prose. More generally, these rules apply primarily as a framework for evaluations and a way of appraising thinking, argument and judgment. At the same time, failing to recognize the special hybred nature of sentences abstracted from their normal context of use may lead one to draw unwarranted conclusions about the thinking of persons and may result in serious miscommunication with learners who mistake, for example, long words with long things.

Although all speakers of a language have the ability to state, imply, hint, insist on things or to deny, explain, wonder, suspect and so on, what they may lack and what metarepresentational concepts may provide is an explicit way of characterizing statements in these ways. These concepts are metarepresentational and designed for talking about talk. They are devices for explicating what was implicit in speech. And writing, I have claimed, is instrumental in this process of making explicit.

LOGICAL CONNECTIVES IN AND BETWEEN SENTENCES

Not only is an explicit syllogistic logic a part of a literate tradition in that the laws of logic are derived from *mentioned* rather than *used* sentences, the logical connectives linking sentences that are common in ordinary language play a double role when they are adopted to play a role in extended logical thought. Their meanings become more formal when a metarepresentational stance is applied to them, that is, when we make them objects of thought, as did President Clinton famously, when he was reported to have said "That depends upon what the meaning of 'is' is."

The common logical connectives "and," "or," "not," "is" and the quantifier "all" are ubiquitous in the ordinary conversational language of even young pre-school children. Yet they also play a critical role in systematic thinking and in formal problem-solving tasks on which these same young children often fail. What appears to be a logical failure, however, may often be shown to be a pragmatically appropriate answer to a somewhat different question.

The relational terms including "and," "or" and "not" have a wide range of uses in ordinary discourse. "And" sometimes means "and then," sometimes "in order to," sometimes "only if" and the like. "Or" is commonly used disjunctively to indicate mutually exclusive alternatives such as "Soup or juice?" when asked by the waiter, sometimes appositionally to indicate alternative wordings such as "formal or logical." Only when "strictly speaking," that is, in educated, literate discourse where the intended meaning falls on the precise meaning of the words employed, does the meaning become more focused and explicitly logical. Only in such discourse can "and" come to be treated as synonymous with "plus" such that "A and B" is equivalent to "B and A." In ordinary discourse the terms are not easily reordered: "Love and marriage" is not equivalent to "Marriage and love." By the same argument it is only in formal literate discourse that "or" acquires a sufficiently definitive meaning to allow it to be used in contexts that violate its ordinary pragmatic use, primarily that of contrasting mutually exclusive alternatives. It is this more formal educated meaning of "or" that is tested by Piaget's (1962) somewhat misleading question commonly failed by primary school children. Given a collection of three rabbits and two ducks, the children are then asked: "Are there more rabbits or animals?" They answer "more rabbits," interpreting the question as "rabbits or ducks." Donaldson (1978) challenged Piaget's claims along just these lines by showing that when the questions made "human sense," what I called pragmatic, children could often solve them.

The meaning and uses of the copula "is" are even more diverse.[2] The meaning of the copula became the focus of debate in the Early Modern period in the discussions of the Eucharist (see Olson, 1994, p. 29; Caines, 2009). The diverse uses of the various conjugations of the verb "to be" range from God's "Let there be light," to Jesus' "This is my body," to Aristotle's "All men are mortal," to Levy-Bruhl's "Corn is deer," to Descartes' "I think therefore I am," to the mathematician's "Two and two are four," to the cognitive scientist's "A robin *is a* bird" and to our own "You are my sunshine." The linking verb serves diverse functions but takes quite precise meanings when metarepresented as a word in the specialized disciplines of logic and mathematics as well as in formal reasoning tasks (see Chapter 10).

This diversity of meanings and uses of connective terms is admirably suited to the diversity of their pragmatic functions. Grice was the first to point out this discrepancy between formal or semantic meaning and informal pragmatic meaning of these connectives. In his William James lectures delivered in 1967, Grice (1989, p. 22) noted the differences between two philosophical stances "in regard to such words as *not, and, or, if,* and *all.*" Some saw these concepts as lacking in logical rigor and preferred the formal notations, including "$\wedge$," "$\vee$," "$\neg$," only roughly translated as "and," "or" and "not."

[2] Joseph Heath pointed out that the copula "is" was a feature of Aristotelian logic but does not appear in Fregean, that is, modern logic.

Others, like Grice himself, found ordinary language concepts logically adequate but governed by the pragmatics of conversational discourse. The pragmatics of ordinary conversational language is regulated by the Cooperative Principle that require that one be attuned to the purpose of the discourse and the needs of the listener.

Thus, in parallel to the logician's formal implications, Grice offered the less formal, yet clearly rational, concept of implicatures, meanings that though not stated explicitly nonetheless adequately and conventionally convey an intention. The Cooperative Principle allows one to *imply* without actually stating and to *allude* without claiming and so on. These two logics, one important to logical thought and discourse, the other to conversational and narrative discourse, may come into conflict (Olson, 2012). In a pragmatic or narrative context one assumes a cooperative stance, that is, that the information provided would be relevant and not misleading. So children in response to the question "Are there more rabbits or animals?" are not being irrational when they say "ducks" rather than "animals," because in normal cooperative conversational discourse "or" is used primarily to contrast mutually exclusive alternatives, namely ducks and rabbits, members of the same superordinate class, not to contrast a superordinate with a subordinate. Only careful attention to the connective allows it to override the pragmatic context. Logical reasoning depends upon what Grice called "sentence meaning," as opposed to the more pragmatic "speaker's meaning." The sentence meaning is isolated through treating words as objects with precise definitions and sentences as having precise logical relations to each other. This is the metalinguistic orientation I have attributed to literate uses of language.

By the middle school years children do come to say that there are more animals than rabbits and they do make judgments that adults agree are more logical. Children's performance on a variety of logical reasoning tasks improved with age (and schooling). Piaget explained logical development as the product of the child's own efforts toward equilibration, a more or less coherent picture of the world. Vygotsky, on the other hand, argued that logical development was in part the product of a culture of literacy and schooling. Although all normal humans learn a language and are thereby inducted into "the space of reasons," there is a kind of reasoning that is historical and cultural and that may be distinguished as "formal" or "rational." Thinking and reasoning *about* words and sentences is a peculiarly metalinguistic activity sponsored through reading, writing and schooling in the meanings of words.

Experimental studies of young children's judgments about the correct use of "or" and of "scalars" such as modals (might vs. must) and quantifiers (some/all) have shown an orderly sequence of stages of development (Braine & Rumain, 1981; Noveck, 2001). Later studies revealed the importance of pragmatic considerations. Thus, Papafragou and Musolino (2003) reported that younger children accepted the description "Some elephants have trunks," whereas older children and adults reject it, preferring "All elephants have trunks." That is, older subjects appear to treat "some" as implying "not all" and so reject it. The standard interpretation of such data (Crain & Khlentzos, 2010; Levinson, 1983) is that children correctly understand logical terms including the quantifier "all" but that the pragmatics of the situation overwhelm the semantics. Alternatively, it may be argued that the formal, metarepresentational meaning of "all" comes to prevail over the more familiar pragmatic contexts of interpretation only with literacy and schooling; only with "scrupulous attention" to the wording does the formal or logical meaning of "all" come to predominate (Donaldson, 1978). Leslie and Gelman (2012) found that the recall of statements quantified by "all" tend to lose the quantifier and are recalled as generic statements. They acknowledge that the importance of the quantifier comes to be recognized with age and schooling. While age may be a necessary condition it is not a sufficient one for learning such structures; learning the metarepresentational concepts for thinking about words and their contrastive meanings appears to be required as well. This conclusion fits well with Luria's finding that for one untrained in attending to wording, "'All' the bears" need not necessarily mean "all."

REASONING WITH SENTENCES

In the discussion of children's acquisition of the concept of *word*, it was reported that unschooled adults tend to talk not about the word, its synonyms, antonyms and its grammatical class, but rather about the object or event denoted by the word. They tended to think about reference rather than meaning. A similar pattern emerges when unschooled adults are confronted with sentences in reasoning tasks. Rather than confining interpretation to the text (Olson, 1977), they reason around the text, inventing speculative interpretations. Reasoning tasks are peculiar in that they do not call for actual practical reasoning in a lived context but rather reasoning about imagined worlds stipulated by sentences. Such sentences are what I have referred to as "laboratory objects." This topic is of such significance that I devote an entire later chapter, Chapter 10, to "test questions," the most common form of laboratory objects.

THE TWO LANGUAGES OF THOUGHT

Grice's distinction between the two logics with their distinctive orientations to language and meaning is important for three reasons. First, it provides a linguistic basis for the distinction between ordinary pragmatic uses of language and the more formal, rational or logical uses of language. Second, the pragmatic orientation to language is what justifies John Locke's claim that "one does not need the syllogism to be reasonable." Luria's untutored peasants are not unreasonable; indeed they provide an abundance of reasons, even if they overlook the logical implications of "all." Third, educators should be aware that children bring this pragmatic orientation to language; to learn the more formal uses of language they must bring their implicit knowledge of language into consciousness through learning the appropriate metalanguage. And finally, it highlights the importance of formal rationality in modern life.

J. Heath (2014) pointed out the obvious gaps in political reasoning about such topics as gun laws, vaccination and climate change. He cited the case of Governor Rick Perry of Texas who, in response to the worst drought in a century, declared three official "Days of prayer for rain," all the while keeping the oil wells pumping and refineries glowing. When it comes to the cultivation of rationality, Heath says "there can be no substitute for formal education" (p. 312).

A formal language shaped in reference to a metalanguage provides standards for both use and appraisal. Such language has been described as a specific written register (Biber, 1986, 2009) and as the Classical Style (Turner & Thomas, 2011) that will be considered in the next chapter. This use of language is taught and monitored in school contexts where the conventions of meaning and use become explicitly normative, subject to training and enforcement. The resulting register of language is clearly not a normal way of speaking. Through historical time and in the service of particular goals – the administration of justice or the resolution of philosophical disputes – modern Western languages have developed the norms and standards for appraising the lexical and syntactic structures that make up this written register. These resources are particularly appropriate to the written academic discourse that requires "a scrupulous attention to language in its own right" (Donaldson, 1978, p. 70) and that Snow and Uccelli (2009) and others find characteristic of the language of the school and that Halliday (1985) has found to be representative of scientific discourse.

Written texts that meet these normative standards are not simply spoken ones written down. Unlike informal oral utterances, written text "depends on no cues other than linguistic cues; it is addressed to no one in particular, its author is essentially anonymous, and its meaning is primarily that represented by the sentence meaning" (Olson, 1977). We have been misled, says R. Harris, into thinking that spoken language is "a fixed code for the formulation of propositions" (2009, p. 86), whereas texts in the written register are shaped to serve that function. Harris called such texts "unsponsored" and understanding them requires a subtle but important shift in thinking about language. This shift, long a matter of literacy and education, has only recently been recognized in the philosophy of language as "the linguistic turn," the shift in emphasis from the discussion of whiteness of snow to the discussion of the truth of "Snow is white" (Olson & Astington, 2013; Quine, 1960). This discourse is designed to facilitate judgments of *truth* and *validity.* Truth itself is a metarepresentational concept that sets a standard in terms of which any statement may be judged.

The language for thinking about thinking is just that evolved for talking about texts, a language that continues to develop through the school and university years. Olson and Astington (1990) presented university undergraduates a series of multiple-choice items such as the following:

> It's Adam's birthday tomorrow. Barbara is just sneaking out of the house to buy a present for him when he sees her and asks her where she is going. Barbara says: "We're out of milk. I'm going to the store" (choose the correct verb from amongst the following four alternatives): Barbara *means, concedes, asserts, implies* that she is going to buy milk.

Only half of the undergraduates chose the correct verb "implies"; the majority chose "asserts," a finding the authors interpret as a failure to distinguish between what is said, the sentence meaning, and what is meant, the presumed intended speaker's meaning.

The things that can be *claimed* can also be *doubted, conjectured, inferred* and the like. In their book about laboratory life, Latour and Woolgar (1986) found that ideas first floated in a laboratory were noted as *hunches* and *guesses*, as they gathered shape they became *hypotheses*, as they accumulated evidence they became *theories* or *claims* and, if successful, ended their lives as *conclusions*. The metalanguage for talking about statements and beliefs is therefore an epistemology, a set of concepts for thinking about knowing.[3]

In sum, we have two languages for thinking, the first, a vernacular everyday language that depends heavily on context and on the Gricean conversational maxims. Such language is a universal possession of the linguistic mind and, as Locke pointed out, makes all human beings conscious and *reasonable.* The second, a language subject to the explicit norms and standards for appraising the choice of words and the logical relations among sentences, produces a language that is not only reasonable but indeed *rational.*

SENTENCE AS A METAREPRESENTATIONAL OBJECT

It may be useful to review just what is involved in a metalinguistic concept such as *word* or *sentence.* The underlying linguistic form of an expression is the unconscious means one uses to produce a shared conversational meaning, what the expression is about. The metarepresentational concept of a sentence is a tool that allows one to explore that unconscious grammatical and semantic structure – to make it an object of attention and to examine its implicit properties and formalize them into rules and definitions. Those properties include, for words, their *sense,* and for sentences, their logical or sentence meanings. These properties, when isolated, provide a norm or standard for judgments of correctness, thus allowing subjects in experiments to calculate the logical rather than pragmatic answers to questions. In rejecting the statement "Some elephants have trunks," children have come to appreciate that the very word "some" implies "not all" and so reject the statement. The younger children thinking only of the reference, the elephant with the trunk, accept it.

[3] E. D. Hirsch (1987), whose listing of what every child needs to learn has become a model for the Core Curriculum, completely overlooks the concepts critical to metacognitive thought such as *assume, infer, conclude* and *hypothesize.* It appears to sponsor a school for traditional knowledge acquisition rather than a school for thinking.

REASONING ABOUT THE WORLD AND REASONING ABOUT THE LANGUAGE

In this chapter I have examined the evidence indicating that there is a special form of reasoning that depends critically on thinking *about* as opposed to thinking *with* sentences. Thinking about the language is made possible by the acquisition of a metalanguage for referring to aspects of language such as *words, sentences* and *statements*, thus allowing one to comment on them. In ordinary language the Cooperative Principle insures a focus on the shared object of discourse, the reference. But in some schooled contexts and especially in the context of reasoning it is insufficient to attend only to the most plausible message and one must attend as well to the linguistic forms and their formal meanings in order to decide on an appropriate interpretation. In thinking about a horse one may retrieve all one knows about a horse, but in thinking about the word "horse" one may be required rather to think about the place of the word in a network of similarities and differences and thus to construct synonyms and hyponyms. Instead of thinking only about her father's horse, Sissy Jupe has to learn to think of the meaning of the word horse and its definition as a domesticated quadruped. And instead of thinking about elephants, on hearing "some elephants" children may think about the word "some" and its relations to other words such as "not all."

A metalanguage is not the exclusive possession of the literate. As mentioned earlier, G. H. Mead (1934) pointed out that all language contains a metalanguage consisting of variations on *ask, say* and *tell*. Feldman (1991) showed that this was also true of the language of the Ilongot, a traditional rural group of dry-land farmers in the Philippines. Speakers distinguish between "straight" and "crooked" speech as well as use hedges such as "kind of" and "maybe" and ways of referring to utterances such as "tell," "say," "hear," "call," "speak," "command," "promise" and the like. Jackendoff (2002, p. 255) draws attention to "relational vocabulary" such as *wonder if* and *suppose that* that allows thoughts to be "attended to, focused on, modified, and remembered." These verbs fall into the class of *saying* and *thinking* discussed earlier. The metarepresentational concepts associated with literacy are those that were invented for referring to the properties of language that may be used to justify an interpretation. *Word* and *sentence* are primary examples of metalinguistic concepts that have allowed the detection of aspects of meaning and of logical form that once brought into consciousness can be used as a literate standard for the assessment of any expression.

The frontier between the metalinguistic resources of ordinary oral language untainted by literacy and those elaborated or sponsored by literacy is not well defined in the existing literature. Some would despair of the project. Part of the problem is that any distinction invented for analysis of written texts may readily apply to spoken utterances, as we saw for the concept of word.

Four criteria may be suggested that serve to distinguish the metalinguistic concepts associated with literacy. First, they have evolved with writing and are most readily applied to written text. Second, they require a literate education for their mastery. Third, they explicitly refer to properties that are implicit and unconscious but necessarily present in some form in spoken language. Finally, a literate metalanguage refers to pieces of language primarily by means of abstract nouns designating objects on which one can comment. Into this class fall such concepts as *phonemes*, *words* and *sentences* as well as *statements*, *propositions*, *beliefs* and *theories* and the ways for characterizing them as *clear*, *valid* or *true*.

Even then, what the metalanguage brings into consciousness is something that was already present, if only implicitly, in the language. Words do have *sense* or there would be nothing to make explicit and sentences are logically related or they would have no use in argument. But when made explicit they may come to serve as a basis for deriving norms for appraisal as well as conceptual tools for thinking.

Peter Carruthers (2007, p. 206) makes just this point. He noted that most people:

> are bad at reasoning about reasoning – at identifying mistakes in reasoning, at theorizing about standards of good reasoning, and at improving their own and others' reasoning. Yet this is precisely the competence that the self-monitoring model predicts we should have.
>
> One of the defining features of human civilizations, in fact, is that they contain socially-transmitted bodies of belief about the ways in which one should reason.
>
> And these bodies of belief have to be laboriously acquired through processes of formal education. (They include the canons of good scientific method, developed piecemeal over the last five centuries or so, as well as principles of validity, codified in systems of logic.) Insofar as we have any competence in evaluating and improving reasoning, therefore, this isn't a natural competence, but a [deliberately] socially transmitted one. (Emphasis added)

These are the metacognitive resources that are to be elaborated and taught as part of our literate tradition. How they are taught and learned is our next concern.

9 Prose and Rational Argument

In olden days, a glimpse of stocking
Was looked on as something shocking.
But now, God knows,
Anything goes.
Good authors too who once knew better words
Now only use four-letter words
Writing prose.
Anything goes. (Cole Porter)

Not so! Not anything goes, in prose. Prose has rules that, while not as rigid as those of ragtime, nonetheless define a peculiar, special, historically evolved form of discourse that is more or less synonymous with the culture of writing. That form is the result of a focused consciousness of the words and sentences that make up the specific written register (Biber, 1986, 2009) that I shall refer to simply as written prose. This form of language serves the major intellectual activities of a modern society ranging from science to literature to government. But it is a form of language that arises from a metarepresentational consciousness of language, of treating prose as itself an object.

WRITING CLASSICAL PROSE

We may think that prose is the proprietary language of the classroom. But in fact the prominence of prose as the object of study in the classroom is a reflection of the overwhelming uses of prose in ordinary life in a modern bureaucratic society. Prose is the language of bureaucracy (D. Smith, 1990), the language of memo (Gillory, 2004), of record and report, as well as policy and law and a variety of vital social functions. Hoffman and Murphy (2005, p. 3) note: "The rising literacy that always accompanies trade and technology created an expanded reading public hungry for stories of people like themselves in prose like that of the newspapers, journals, and scientific treatises that had come to dominate the new technology of print."

Although written prose has taken somewhat different forms or genres and serves diverse functions, there is a basic style of prose that is not merely one genre among others but basic to most if not all of them. This style of prose has been set out by literary theorists Turner and Thomas (2011) in an admirable book, *Clear and Simple as the Truth: Writing Classic Prose*. The usefulness of what they call the Classical style "is manifest" (2011, p. 11) in that it is almost universally adopted for scientific, literary, bureaucratic and academic purposes. And yet, they note, the Classical style lies beyond the competence of most secondary school graduates and many university graduates. Turner and Thomas attribute the poor quality of writing to the fact that writing is taught either as self-expression or as a body of skills rather than as an intellectual activity, a form of thinking. Poor writing is fostered by the assumption that prose is merely preserved talk.

The Classical style, the authors suggest, is exemplified in such writers as Descartes and Jane Austen.[1] The Classical style takes for granted two of the features that modern enlightened readers now find objectionable, the assumption that language is transparent to the reality it describes and, second, that it can reveal object truths. Further, the Classical style even denies it is a style; it takes itself to be a naked, natural way of speaking. Turner and Thomas treat these objections as shared conceits – secrets writers know and share, but don't admit and take as granted by their readers. Writers of the Classical style treat it as the written version of plain and simple telling of the truth. While to modern readers these are "conceits," they

[1] Keith Oatley suggests that Austen's ironic style tends to make the shared "conceit" between writer and reader explicit, as if the writer and reader winked at each other.

were once held as achievable goals by the inventors of style in the 17th century. I shall regard the Classical style as the set of norms and standards for evaluating prose in a way similar to those norms that regulate the meaning of words and the logical properties of sentences. Thus prose is a critical, metalinguistic concept that articulates the norms and standards for much of written language and, subsequently, for careful speech.

Although the origins of prose may be traced to Plato it has been refined over time into the Classical style. Turner and Thomas point out that the Classical style is suited to the "pursuit of truth for its own sake" (2011, p. 76), it offers a "disinterested expression of unconditional truth" (p. 12), it assumes an equality and "symmetry between writer and reader" (p. 46) and it assumes that language is adequate and "sufficient for any thought" (p. 60). The Classical prose writer does not attempt to persuade but rather to "offer the reader an unobstructed view" (p. 60) of the plain truth that the author had seen or discovered. Nothing is to be assumed and "every word counts" (p. 36). These features constitute a set of norms or standards, known to the writer, in terms of which every word, sentence and paragraph may be critically evaluated (p. 72). The Classical style, then, is norm-driven. Note that these norms are less for generating text than for setting the standard for evaluating and talking about text. Like logic, they are honored as ideals to aspire to rather than simply as unreflective practices.

Several of these features derive from Grice's conversational maxims. Yet writing Classical prose is not a natural activity but requires deliberate effort to acquire (Turner & Thomas, 2011, p. 10). Plain style, the more natural style of ordinary oral discourse, resembles the Classical style but is uncritical, lacking the awareness of any principle of validation. Confusing Plain style with Classical style is responsible, Turner and Thomas suggest, for the poor quality of writing and the teaching of writing in America. Monsieur Jourdain, Molière's bourgeois gentleman, discovered, late in life, that he had always been speaking prose. This is, of course, a small joke. Classical style is not Plain style but rather a specialized use of language in which, contrary to the song, not anything goes. If Classical style has a "voice," it is not your own voice. It depends on voice lessons.

Hence, across the diversity of uses of writing there are distinctive features of the classical style of prose, what I refer to as written prose, that make it not only a useful tool but a medium for abstract, reflective thought. Several of these features indicate why prose as a metalinguistic concept is uniquely associated with literacy.

RECOGNIZING CLASSICAL PROSE

The most conspicuous fact about prose in the Classical style is that it is written, indeed composed, to be read rather than to be heard. It assumes the possibility of an individual, solitary, unknown reader who can mull over a text at his or her leisure and who assumes he or she could have written that or a similar text themselves.

Second, written prose has several linguistic features peculiar to writing that have been exploited in literature. Banfield (1993, p. 357) pointed out that written literary composition "frees language from the speech act"; promises, warnings, threats are understood but are not complied with. In written literature no *you* exists, the *I* may not be the speaker/writer and the *now* may be co-temporal with the past.

Third, prose hides the presence of the writer, to "direct the readers gaze to something in the world" (Turner & Thomas, 2011). This shared "gaze" at the world makes author and reader equals in that the truth arrived at is not at the whim or the authority of the author but relies on a view of reality shared with the reader. In this way prose is uniquely democratic. Hiding the author gives prose a "view from nowhere" (Nagel, 1986), an attempt at an objective perspective that belongs to no one in particular and yet is shared to a large extent by writer and reader. A historian of science (Shapin, 1985) described how 17th-century scientists wrote in such a way as to treat readers as "virtual witnesses" to what they themselves had seen, for example, through a telescope.

Fourth, although invisible, the writer must "stand entirely behind the thought she represents" (Turner & Thomas, 2011, p. 72) and accept individual responsibility for the text, knowing that readers will hold the writer accountable. Recall that these features are best seen as normative, as ideals or goals against which prose writing in the Classical style may be judged by self and others.

A fifth feature arises from the first. Against Alexander Pope's advice that "the sound must seem an echo to the sense," the appeal is to come from the defined meanings of terms and the logical form of the statements. In fact this principle became explicit in 17th-century science when the Royal Society of London called for a mathematical plainness of language and a rigorous pruning of "amplification, digression and swellings of style" (Spratt, 1667/1966, p. 371). The language used was to be the equivalent of open, direct speech but now achieved in writing. This is not a small achievement and modern writers still need to be taught to write "clear and simple as the truth."

Sixth, prose bears a strong similarity to ordinary, direct speech with which it is easily confused, as did Molière's M. Jourdain. But prose does take its model from plain speech in that, as in a conversation, the speaker is just one among equals. Even Plato, who would exclude poets from his Republic because of their promiscuous use of language, used the direct quotation of the plain speech of Socrates as the model for the language of prose: "Then ... isn't the definition of justice, speaking the truth and giving back what one takes?" (Bloom, 1968, p. 7). Classical prose directs attention to the very words and their meanings.

Seventh, the meaning of written prose depends on the precise meanings of words and sentences such as "All men are mortal" or "Snow is white," such that if abstracted from speaker and from immediate context and examined in their own rights they would still convey a meaning from which logical implications may be drawn.

The eighth feature is captured in the notion of extended. The significance of written prose is that a single line of argument may be developed and examined for coherence and validity over a length of discourse that is impossible to manage without writing. In the simplest case one can examine the first sentence of a piece of prose to see if it logically entails the concluding sentence that occurs hundreds of lines later. Its extended nature is why it is chosen, as in the essays of Montaigne, as the medium for "gathering one's thoughts" on a topic. Prose, whether a paragraph, an essay or a book, is a medium for "monologue"; even when the content represents diverse viewpoints it does so from a single standpoint.

The ninth feature comes from its fixity as an object both in the sense that it is preserved across time and therefore available to new generations of readers, but equally importantly in that it is open to rereading, reinterpretation, rewriting and revision so long as those rereadings can be justified by appeal to the text. Prose, like oral argument, invites criticism but in addition invites the invention of a language of criticism.

The concept of prose is metarepresentational in the same way that the concepts of word and sentence are. The concept of prose is normative in that it allows us to evaluate any text or document in terms of the standards of Classical prose. Classical prose, while pretending to simply disclose reality, does so by a self-consciousness of the norms and standards of critical discourse that make it Classical. These norms are expressed by such critical concepts as *clarity, simplicity, directness,* as well *sameness of meaning, definition, paraphrase, topic sentence, contradiction, argument, inference, proof* and many others. This, of course, is the language of critical thinking, the language of rationality.

THE INVENTION OF PROSE

Writing is the basic or default medium of prose. Historical evidence indicates that a writing system was a necessary condition for the invention of extended prose discourse. Havelock (1982) was among the first to notice the change in writing style that evolved in the classical Greek period around the 5th century BC. Prior to its invention, one of the earliest uses of Greek writing was for the transcription of orally composed poetry, specifically *The Iliad* and *The Odyssey*. While writing continued to be used for writing Greek poetry and drama, the important cultural shift came with "the invention of fluent prose" (1982, p. 87). Extended prose discourse, produced and composed in writing and designed to be read rather than heard, marked a turning point in the relation between oral and written discourse. Whereas earlier writing recorded the sayings of the gods or the vows and laws of kings, prose could be written in the first person, it could preserve important information without being poetic and memorable, it could impose order on arguments and it could be extended into longer discourses.

This theme has been greatly elaborated by Goldhill (2002), who unhesitatingly attributes the intellectual achievements of the Greeks to "the invention of prose." Prose is an invention in that this register of language replaced verse as the primary medium of significant speech in the 5th century BC. Verse, until then, predominated because it was memorable and because its exotic style carried prestige and authority. With the invention of prose, weighty words were increasingly organized in terms of continuous strings of coherent statements. He writes: "Prose is the medium in which the intellectual revolution of the [Greek] enlightenment is enacted ... After the fifth century [BC] almost all serious philosophy, history, medicine, mathematics, theology – the sciences of authority – are conducted solely in prose" (Goldhill, 2002, p. 4). Again, "prose becomes the medium for authoritative expression" (p. 5).

Goldhill finds Greek prose to be distinctive from earlier forms of discourse in four ways. First, whereas poetry relied on a "muse" as source of inspiration, prose was strictly man-made, the product of an authoring writer. Man was represented as an agent in the world who was the creator not merely the conveyor of cultural truths. Second, such prose was marked by a new consciousness of language and its uses, resulting in the study of rhetoric – how to design speech to achieve particular effects (Goldhill, 2002, p. 66). Third, prose relied on a certain standardization of the meanings of terms such as truth and justice as well as the rules of valid argument. Fourth, prose discourse tended to focus on certain modes of explanation, especially the causes of happenings, the reasons for action and responsibilities for outcomes, all posed in a naturalist, as opposed to mythical, framework. Prose was the medium for "the unwavering pursuit of truth through logical argument" (p. 82).

The language of prose took shape in the writings of Plato in his account and defense of philosophical thought, that is, the attempt to arrive at abstract and defensible concepts of such matters as truth, justice and beauty. But whereas Plato and his teacher Socrates expressed their thoughts as open questions, his pupil Aristotle (born 384 BC) and his students were the ones to systematize the rules and norms for prose – the importance of defining terms, working out the rules of logic and combining statements to form valid arguments. Goldhill (2002, p. 104) writes:

> Where the success and privilege of *logos* [the word] once depended on a persuasive performance for an audience in a context, argument now is to have a decontextualized, impersonal framing, and its own, internal rules of success … [A]uthority now exists in the relation between sentences, and not in the relation between speaker and audience, abstract, formal argument is now *to speak for itself*.

Harris (2009) noted this property calling prose "authorless text," while I (Olson, 1977) described it as "autonomous," as relying heavily on the sense of the expressions and the meaning in the text. It is the argument itself that is to be persuasive, not the voice and authority of the speaker. Thus knowledge came to be distinguished from the knower; truth from the wise man (Havelock, 1982, p. 290). Like Havelock, Goldhill shows that the rules governing prose were worked out in a particular social context and in the service of social and political goals. Once developed, new goals such as the pursuit of truth for its own sake came into view.

The relation between prose, a linguistic form, and writing, a technology for representing those forms in a material object, is complex in that prose may be either written or performed orally. But even when performed orally it is informed by the practices and norms devised for written prose discourse. Whether spoken or written, it is "the new language of prose – its writing, delivery, and interpretation [that] is absolutely fundamental ... to the intellectual revolution of the 5th c. [BC] enlightenment" (Goldhill, 2002, p. 79).

Leiper (2013, p. 318) examined the evolution of prose in 5th-century-BC Greece in terms of the training given to students in composing original, extended written prose *euboulia*, good careful reasoned arguments. Extended "serially reasoned" prose writing was an important part of Sophistic education. "Thinking for writing" prose requires sustained reasoning within a fixed framework in which *pro* and *con* arguments, arguments from probability and necessity, were to be pulled together to form a *logos* that could stand as a rational approach to any posed problem. "The development of extended discursive argument necessitated the use of prose writing" (p. 320), in part because the written artifact allowed rereading, revision and criticism.

In the hands of these early Greek writers, then, narrative prose became history, argumentative prose became philosophy and descriptive prose became science, three branches of thought heavily dependent upon writing prose in what became the Classical style.

The story was repeated when classical Greek and Roman writing was revived in the Renaissance. Literary theorists trace the reinvention of modern prose writing to Boccaccio's (1313–1375) *Decameron*. Acocella (2013) pointed out that whereas earlier writing tended to be written both in verse and with a simple associative syntactic style, described as *paratactic*, AthenBthenCthenD, Boccaccio's syntax involves subordinate clauses linked by such verbs as *because, even though* and *previously*: "This is the kind of sentence structure that was handed down to us by Latin, and that Western people, whether or not they ever studied Latin recognize as their own" (p. 81). Literary theorists are more interested in the invention of genre than in the invention of modes of thought, but Acocella acknowledges that Boccaccio's prosaic style is "more intelligent." Formal rationality is simply the name for thinking that runs in those prosaic grooves.

The norms for modern academic writing are now sufficiently standardized that they can be demonstrated empirically. Douglas Biber (2009) isolated a "written register" by examining some 20 million words of written texts from four registers: conversation, fiction, newspapers and academic prose. The differences he found derive largely from the conditions of production and reception. Freed from interruption and from time and space constraints, writers have freedom to exploit logical complexity of content and complex grammatical structure in the creation of a text. Opportunities for rewriting allow the text to be revised to meet the metalinguistic standards of Classical written prose. Consequently, written prose has become the medium of choice for critical, reflective thought.

LEARNING TO WRITE CLASSICAL PROSE

If extended written prose was the most important genre of discourse invented by the Greeks and revived in the Renaissance, it is no surprise that teaching students to write prose was a major preoccupation of both Sophistic and Renaissance schools and that the teaching of academic or expository prose is the primary goal of the writing programs in modern schools. Contemporary research on writing confirms that the major obstacles facing learners are just those features that make expository prose in the Classical style distinctive from ordinary speech. First, beginning writers have the problem of choosing a discourse stance. For first-person narratives, that choice presents itself as a familiar conversational stance. For Classical expository prose, on the other hand, the writer must create a detached impersonal stance, shareable with the reader. Second, there is the problem of choosing a topic and announcing it with a topic sentence that has sufficient precision to serve as the criterion for deciding what is relevant or irrelevant to the entire text. Third, the text must carry a greater informational density through precise vocabulary and elaborate noun phrases than does ordinary speech. It is as if every word costs the writer and the text has to yield a good level of return for the reader's effort. This is often achieved through rewriting and editing. Fourth, the causal, logical or evidential relations between the statements as well as their relation to the topic must be clear and explicit. This requires that the "and then ..." or "and another idea," the structures common to oral discourse, give way to "because," "caused by," "a symptom of," "it follows from" of written prose. Finally, the text is to reach a conclusion that satisfies the expectations set up by the original topic sentence.

Experimental studies of students learning to write have shown that the features characterizing prose are just those that novice writers are learning to negotiate (Berman & Ravid, 2009) and that learners are actually taught in a course on academic writing (Snow & Uccelli, 2009). These comparisons between oral and written discourse show, among other things, that oral discourse tends to be dominated by paratactic syntactic forms: "and then," whereas those written, by the same subjects, tended to rely much more heavily on subordination, "because," "in order to," thereby expressing the causal and logical links between clauses and sentences. Kuhn (2015) has examined students' epistemological development in terms of the metaknowledge that students acquire in dialogue and in essay writing. In both cases difficulties arose primarily in linking claims to evidence, in evaluating the validity of arguments and in relating arguments to each other. Rather than explicitly indicating the relation between claims and evidence, students simply offer "unanchored additions" by adding "here's another thing" rather than spelling out the relation contrastively, "on the other hand," or deductively, "because" or "it follows." Whereas oral dialogue tended to lead children to draw on their own experiences, written essays tended to lead them to draw on shared, documented information. She concluded that "socially mediated metacognitive talk about thinking may be a key factor" in collaborative activity as well as a key component in learning to write prose.

Kuhn's findings are upheld by the recent Twelfth Grade NAEP Assessment in the United States that showed that the two primary factors separating advanced readers from others was, first, the ability to critically evaluate the arguments presented in a text, and second, the ability to evaluate evidence (National Center for Educational Statistics, 2010). That is, to reason successfully, students have to learn to metarepresent statements as evidence for or against a theory or a claim and arguments as valid or invalid. Kuhn argued that oral argumentation is vital to mastering written prose.

Higher-order concepts for managing prose are slow to develop. Hass and Flower (1988) discovered that many able readers were able to identify words, locate information in a text and recall particular contents. Yet they often provide a paraphrase when asked to analyze, summarize when asked to criticize and retell when asked to interpret. These metalinguistic concepts are devices for thinking about statements in relation to the more general purpose of a piece of prose. Thinking begins when one distinguishes a belief from the reasons for believing it, which, in turn, are to be examined in their own right. The metalinguistic distinctions between beliefs, claims and theories and the evidence that supports them is the beginning of critical thought. Linking them together makes Classical prose.

Research on the teaching of academic writing has shown the complexity of the concepts involved in understanding and criticizing written prose. Macbeth (2006) studied the difficulties international undergraduates had in grasping such concepts as *main idea*. Such concepts have no role in ordinary oral discourse and are as mystifying to young adults as the concept of *phoneme* is to prereading children. The concepts are metarepresentational, marking the step from discourse into talking about discourse. Such talk requires the mastery of a new and alien set of concepts, the language of criticism. These concepts are in part, as Murphy (1990) suggests, indexical, at first exemplified rather than defined. They become defined and subject to reflection when they enter into a network of contrasting alternatives such as *topic, main idea, assumption, argument, evidence* and *validity.* This metalanguage does not constitute the rules for writing, which must indeed be learned through practice and discourse, but a critical framework for thinking about that writing, a specialized normative language acquired through talk and teaching.

Writing permits, indeed invites, revising one's ideas (Hayes & Flower, 1980). Revision, as Bereiter and Scardamalia (1987) pointed out, involves the process of adjusting content to fit the rhetorical form, that is, the conventions of a genre. Furthermore, the written medium allows time and space to consider the adequacy of the message, the possibility of ambiguity, and to anticipate the possible objections of the reader. Revision depends on these critical metarepresentational concepts.

Marcel Proust (1982) captured the relation between form and content in his perspicacious statement about "good poets [for whom] ... the tyranny of rhyme forces [them] into the discovery of their finest lines" (p. 25). Interpreted, this means that historically evolved forms or genre, whether poetry or prose, provide categories with precise criteria into which thoughts may be inserted; reorganizing the thought so that it meets the criterion may generate ideas that otherwise would never have come to mind. To do this, of course, one must be conscious of the standards involved and the objects to which they apply.

TESTING PROSE WRITING

The concept of written tests and "test questions" is so much a genre of writing that I shall consider it separately in the next chapter. Here I consider testing only in regard to learning to write prose. Just as tests are designed to examine learners' mastery of phonemes, words and sentences, so tests have been designed to test students' mastery of prose. Comprehension of prose is assessed primarily through multiple-choice tests. Here is a practice item from the Scholastic

Achievement Test (SAT), a test widely used for college admission that requires one to choose the correct word to fill the blank:

> With the 1969 film *The Learning Tree*, Gordon Parks proved what a truly ______ artist he was: he not only directed the film and composed its musical score, but also adapted its screenplay from his own novel.

Subjects are to choose between: complacent, protean, lauded, clairvoyant and harried. "Versatile" would have been far more appropriate, but in the attempt to use "real" text, test-makers had quoted an excerpt from a published work by an established author from which the "correct" answer, "protean," was derived.

Here is another practice item from the SAT website:

> *Choose the word or set of words that, when inserted in the sentence, **best** fits the meaning of the sentence as a whole.*
>
> Observing the newspaper's tradition of ______ attention to accuracy, the reporter ______ every statement made by her informant.
>
> - (A) scrupulous ... verified
> - (B) lax ... challenged
> - (C) sporadic ... corroborated
> - (D) systematic ... bungled
> - (E) inordinate ... exaggerated

Again, I would have preferred "indifferent ... distorted" but (A) would do! Such tests are widely criticized in part because they allow little scope for thinking and originality. As a result students are also asked to compose a piece of writing on demand in a testing context. This change added new urgency to the teaching of prose writing that has now become part of the Common Core Curriculum.

A widely used program for the teaching of prose writing has been designed by Calkins (2006) and her associates as part of the

Columbia University Writing Workshop. The program is designed to teach students the conventions of prose writing that will help them succeed on the writing section of the Scholastic Aptitude Test.

To perform well on these written assessments, students are taught to interpret the prompts that test designers use to define the kind of writing expected. Common prompts ask students to argue, persuade, give reasons or take a position on a topic. A typical assignment for the SAT may be "Do you believe that what does not kill you makes you stronger? Write an essay supporting your point of view. Use texts, experiences and observations to support your position."

Students are taught to make their essay interesting by beginning with a "hook," a catchy phrase or observation, and use it to articulate the "framing idea" for the text. Then they are encouraged to write two or three paragraphs advancing their idea and supporting it with evidence from the literature or from personal experience. And finally they are encouraged to restate the thesis as a kind of conclusion. As we noted earlier, concepts such as main idea, claims, evidence, conclusion are complex metarepresentational concepts that, while important, are difficult to master.

Educators knowing precisely what the test requires can train students specifically to succeed on them. Knowing what the test requires also allows "test-prep" mills to rack up significant gains for their clients. This closed loop clearly undermines the validity of the test. The writing assignment that was intended to give students scope to develop their thinking may have, in fact, been reduced to a learned formula. Yet learning the formula may serve as a tool for organizing thinking.

As Proctor (2002) has noted, much prose is written to be marked, not written to be read. It is a far cry from the high purpose that Francis Bacon envisioned for using writing to "question the natural world." "Scientists," Bacon said, "should each observe and record their observations, writing them up in short prose pieces that would then be read, retested, and built upon by other scientists" (Proctor, 2002, p. 173). Bacon's chain, linking hypothesis, observation and reasoning, is a model not only for scientific thought but also for critical reflective thinking. Thinking about knowledge in terms of hypotheses and supporting evidence is what some cognitive scientists have attempted to explain by postulating a special recursive loop that turns beliefs into objects of reflection (Shallice, 1988). Writing prose is just such a medium for thinking and rethinking. Rethinking is by definition recursive; metalinguistic concepts for talking about text provide a promising account of just what rethinking involves. To use writing only for display rather than as a means for advancing understanding is an unfortunate consequence of test-centered accountability.

Written prose is the product of a kind of consciousness of language that includes the ability to think about words and sentences as objects but also to think about the statements made in terms of their roles as *claims, reasons* and *evidence* in the formulation of an argument or the presentation of a point of view. Even children use evidence and give reasons. What they have yet to learn is a set of concepts for thinking about evidence and reasons. Such concepts are not merely words but carry as part of their meaning the explicit rules for their use. Thus, prose as a metarepresentational concept draws attention to the standards to be met if a piece of writing is to be counted as prose. The cognitive distinctions involved in learning to write and read Classical prose are just those required for thinking reflectively and critically. And that prose is a legacy of writing and a literate tradition.

This analytical, reflective use of language is acquired over years of reading and writing prose texts. Again, learning to write prose in the Classical style is an exercise in reflective thinking. It is reflective in the sense that the norms and standards for Classical prose serve as criteria for creating and evaluating any belief or argument, oral or written.

A final word. The "conceits" appropriate for writing Classical prose must at some point be acknowledged as conceits. The rules for writing and reading do not make up a true and defensible epistemology nor an adequate account of how we think. Yet they are central to all serious academic writing, including that of this author. What recent writers refer to, somewhat dismissively, as Modernism is the failure to recognize that those conceits are principles of writing; recognizing them as conceits is characteristic of Postmodernism. There is, I have argued, no access to knowledge about nature without concepts and concepts are man-made. Similarly, there is no access to the meaning of a text without the appropriate concepts and those concepts must be brought by the reader. One cannot see words without the concept of word. Consequently, the assumption that "the meaning is in the text" (Olson, 1977), while a useful admonition to developing writers, is misleading if taken as an account of the relation between texts and their meanings. Even the best Classical prose is not self-interpreting but relies on the knowledge of the reader, which in turn is sustained by the institutional practices of the "textual community." Nonetheless the rules of the Classical style are those that are honored in serious academic writing even while acknowledging that "plain and simple as the truth" is more an aspiration than an achievable goal. The challenge in teaching the Language Arts is to respect texts as authoritative and yet open to interpretation and criticism without yielding to the appeal of an "anything goes" relativism.

10 The Testing of Rationality and the Rationality of Testing

We have confused reason with literacy and rationalism with a single technology. (McLuhan, 1964, p. 15)

The written artifacts that we examined in the previous chapters – words, sentences, prose – require a metarepresentational stance to language that is most fully exemplified in psychological research and educational assessments, namely, verbal test questions. Written tests, reviled by some and deemed essential by others, form a special genre or register of language on which the account developed in the preceding chapters may throw some new light.

The dubious legacy of written tests derives from the fact that they, like the words and sentences of which they are composed, are literary artifacts. They are based not on language that is *used* but language that is *mentioned*; language that is bracketed as if by quotation marks and that, consequently, calls for a special strategy or rule for interpretation. Recognizing test questions as artifacts may help to explain both their usefulness and the ways in which they mislead.

TESTS FOR RATIONALITY ARE TESTS FOR METAREPRESENTATIONAL ATTITUDE TO LANGUAGE

The very evidence that I have used in the previous chapters to justify the claim that words and sentences are literate metarepresentational objects also serves as evidence that the mastery of these metarepresentational objects defines a higher level of rationality. Judging a sentence to be ambiguous is an indication of a developing metarepresentational competence associated with literacy. But equally, the ability to recognize that ambiguity counts as evidence for the development of reflective thought. The evidence in both cases comes from subjects' answers to questions that have a peculiar linguistic form and call for a special mode of interpretation. It would not be inappropriate to describe this specialized form of written language as a genre, but I shall refer to it simply as the class of *test questions*.

Test questions constitute a fifth type of metarepresentational artifact, after phonemes, words, sentences and prose, that are distinctive of written culture. Although asking questions, like making statements and offering promises, are pervasive in all language, *test questions* are readily distinguished from ordinary questions. Test questions are to real, ordinary questions what Classical prose is to common prose, questions shaped up to meet a set of special conditions. And like Classical prose, test questions require special knowledge and a special metarepresentational approach to language for successfully dealing with them.

First, test questions leave unclear who is asking the questions and the motivation for asking them; they arise seemingly from nowhere and so disrupt rather than extend an ongoing social interaction.

Second, whereas the answers to real questions are, by definition, unknown, those for test questions are known, or at least seriously constrained. Recognizing them as such is essential to answering them.

Third, test questions have a fixed, repeatable form with a fixed, correct and easily scoreable answer that makes them appropriate for a large population of test-takers and experimental subjects. Even when phrased as an open form such as "Discuss," the discussion is to follow a fixed formula, as we saw in the teaching and testing of prose writing.

Fourth, test questions are designed to discriminate among test-takers. A score reveals not an objective standard but only a performance relative to other test-takers. Consequently, minor differences in wording, so long as they discriminate, make up the test. The result is a deviousness and subtlety uncharacteristic of ordinary discourse (Mehan, 1979).

Fifth, test questions assume a fixed interpretation or meaning presumably available to every subject. There is assumed to be a true, correct answer. This meaning of a test question is just that analyzed earlier in our discussion of *word, sentence* and *prose,* namely, the meanings *mentioned* rather than *used,* and in that sense a test question is *metarepresentational.* For only such meanings yield the fixed interpretation that entitles one to assume that *ceteris paribus* conditions, "all things being equal," apply. As we saw earlier, in ordinary discourse such conditions cannot be assumed. In ordinary discourse, context is critical – everything and everyone is always potentially relevant; in ordinary discourse, cooperation and rationality are the implicit norms – make your contributions to the discourse true, helpful, relevant in such a way that a mutual understanding may be achieved. With test questions, meaning is reduced to that of sentence meaning, the meanings taken as conventional in the language-using public rather than the local conditions of the speaker and listener. (I earlier identified this conventional meaning in terms of Fregean *sense.*)

As we saw in the analysis of sentences, test questions take the form of a quotation. If we recall Luria's test given to Siberian peasants, when the experimenter said "Ivan saw a bear," there is, in fact, no Ivan and there is no bear. The test question requires a shift in orientation from using language to thinking about language, a shift sponsored in large part, I argued, by writing and literacy.

This artificial detached quality is what gives test questions their analytical advantages. They are "pure" objects analogous to Galileo's objects falling in a vacuum. They allow one to sort out abstract qualities that are difficult if not impossible to pick out in their natural environment. Test questions allowed the discovery that most pre-school children think "train" is a long word and that "some elephants have trunks" is perfectly acceptable, or that "The man has no hat," though true, may be affirmed with a negation, "No (he doesn't have a hat)." And test questions reveal that even adult subjects are more likely to judge an argument as valid if they happen to agree with the conclusion. I traced the difficulties with and the ultimate success with such test questions to the necessity of adopting a critical or metarepresentational stance to the statements that made up the test questions. Thus, test questions yield important information about the language and about the development of intellectual competencies.

As in all the sciences, problems occur when the laws derived in the laboratory are extrapolated into the real environment; the environments stipulated in test questions may not match those of the real world or they may hold only in a specialized world or in a specialized intellectual mode of discourse.

There is a deep irony here. In the search for universal properties of human reason, the invention of test questions has allowed us to uncover a specialized competence associated with a relatively modern technology, the written word. Moreover, the ordinary pragmatic linguistic competence, including sensitivity to the Gricean maxims, may result in errors that are taken as a sign of irrationality. So who is rational and what is rationality? We may sort our conflicting claims by a closer analysis of the relation between test questions and real ones.

Test questions are not simply algebraic calculi from which answers can be generated (although they approach that). The sentences that are presented as test questions could have been appropriately expressed at some imaginable place and time. In fact, some theories of reasoning (Johnson-Laird, 2006; Oatley, 2015) claim that this is in fact how thinkers solve theoretical problems, namely, by creating a mental model. Rather than building upon a shared preexisting context as in the normal case, readers are required to imaginatively construct a world that hews to the properties delineated in the test question. Hence, it is not quite correct to call such expressions "decontextualized." Rather test questions should be seen as metarepresentational objects, pieces of language lifted from the context of ordinary discourse to become the objects of imagination, reflection, criticism and analysis. Just as a word is an object that can be plucked out of a sentence and defined, so too a test sentence or question is an object plucked from some imagined discourse that calls for some particular and distinctive analysis. Test questions, as suggested earlier, put language into quotation marks, thereby creating a world in which the rules of logic serve as norms for judging the validity of the reasoning.

As metarepresentations, rather than representations, test questions, and written texts generally, call for special interpretive strategies. That analysis relies on specific conventional, indeed definitional, meanings of the terms and the logical relations between words and between sentences. Test questions call for "scrupulous attention," as Donaldson recommended, or "paying attention," as Kahneman suggested. But they require in addition some knowledge that test questions are not ordinary questions but rather abstracted objects calling for analysis. Here is where metalinguistic concepts of *word* and its *senses* as well as the concept of *sentence* and its *entailments* come into view.

The peculiarity of test questions arises from the fact that the more or less universal cooperative conversational rules appropriate for the interpretation of an expression conflict with the norms and standards for abstracted word and sentence meaning. Recall Luria's unlettered subject who, when told (out of the blue) "All the bears in Novaya Zemlya are white," refused to draw any necessary inference. He was unable to metarepresent the utterance as a *premise* in which every word counts, and hence he failed the task. But the Cooperative Principle would ordinarily have prevented Luria from offering the statement as a premise to a listener who has no understanding of the metalinguistic concept of a *premise* or the special demands of test questions. The statement is out of line with the expectancies and competencies of the listener. While the test is useful for determining if the subject has the concept of a premise, it is quite misleading if used as a test of reasoning ability more generally.

The distinction between language and metalanguage has some overlap with what Kahneman (2011) and Stanovich (2009) called System One and System Two thinking. But whereas those writers attempted to describe a vast range of cognitive functions in terms of two quite general categories, I have attempted only to distinguish ordinary (fast) uses of language in thinking from the reflective thinking that depends upon some sophistication with a particular set of metalinguistic distinctions. Moreover, the fast uses of linguistic resources, I argued, are discontinuous with the habits and expectancies of non-verbal animals. Fast, System One actions of humans rest on a network of concepts in "the space of reasons" that subjects may appeal to when asked to justify their actions and accept their responsibilities, even if the evaluation of these reasons is inadequate.

TESTING RATIONALITY AS METAREPRESENTATION

Here are some examples of the test questions used for analyzing the literacy levels of children as well as for judging the rationality of persons:

1. This from a test of metalinguistic (phonological) awareness: *What does "blate" say?* These are non-words, but if learners know the metalinguistic rules including those about long and short vowels (even if they cannot state the rule), they will be able to provide a suitable pronunciation. Alternatively, if they recognize the non-word as similar to a known word such as "plate," they may succeed without knowledge of the vowel rule. What is noteworthy is that the task requires that the linguistic form be treated as an object out of context. Put another way, the language is *mentioned* rather than *used*.
2. This from the study of cognitive development. One may recall Piaget's misleading question, *Are there more ducks or animals?*, given three ducks and two rabbits. Children assuming the Gricean Quality maxim may take the questioner to have meant ducks or rabbits. A metalinguistic ability to think about the precise meaning of "or" may enable them to apply it to this unexpected pairing.

3. Test questions are common in the study of children's language and reading comprehension. Beal (1990) read stories that implied but did not state an important fact. One story read:

   Cindy's family went to the beach. Cindy made a sand castle. The waves were big that day. Her sand castle got smashed. Her father helped her make another one.

   The children were then asked if the story "said" the waves smashed the sand castle or if they had "figured it out." Only 9- and 10-year-olds correctly answered that they had "figured it out." Beal correctly concluded: "Once the child has interpreted the text, its words literally appear to represent his or her interpretation. The child cannot then clearly identify the inferences and assumptions that were made in order to understand it" (1990, p. 1022). What the younger children have yet to learn is a metalinguistic distinction between what is asserted and what is merely implied, between what was said and what was meant. The correct answer, that the story did not say so, violates the Gricean Cooperative Principle in that the story invites the inference. Children are less likely to accept what was implied as what was said if they have a written record to consult (Olson, 1994, pp. 124 ff.).
4. Tests also use prose to test the reading comprehension of students by means of decontextualized sentences that call for a metarepresentational analysis:

   Mr. D., 31, moonlights as an engineer in the film industry, occasionally driving three and a half hours to Manhattan to pay the bills.

   Why does he drive three-and-a-half hours?
   Most subjects tend, not unreasonably, to reply "To pay the bills," whereas the correct answer is to work in the film industry. He works in the film industry to pay the bills. A comma after "Manhattan" may have helped to mark out the embedded clause but close reading and rereading is required to determine the appropriate subject.
5. The following sentence from the *New York Times* (September 27, 2015), a paper known for its "high" literate standards, is a suitable model for "test" questions:

Efforts to develop and deploy vaccines against Ebola and other infectious diseases ravaging these animals could grind to a halt.
What could grind to a halt?

The less skilled reader is less likely to scan back through the stacked embedded clauses to find the subject of the sentence. That reader is likely to consider "animals" or "diseases" or "vaccines" before they find, if they do, "efforts." The ability to do so would be scored as indicating both a high level of reading comprehension and, in another context, a high level of rationality. "Efforts" is the kind of deverbalized noun that Halliday (1985) found to be distinctive of written scientific discourse.

6. A simpler version of this kind of question, adapted for younger children, comes from Uccelli et al.'s (2014) test of literate language proficiency:

   "The sheep the girl looked at is running." Who is running?

   Younger children tend to pick as subject the noun nearest the verb "running."

7. Consider the following item drawn from tests of critical thinking and which is taken as evidence of rationality:

   Take two apples from three applies. How many apples do you have?

   The pragmatic meaning derived on the basis of the Cooperative Principle would lead one to assign the question to the familiar category of subtraction and thus to say "One." But careful attention to the linguistic form allows one to note the imperative "You took two" so, necessarily, you have two. We note in passing the similarity between this item and the interpretation of "bird house black" discussed earlier.

8. Another test question:

   A farmer had 27 cows and all but 8 died. How many does the farmer have left?

   The pragmatic meaning leading to the incorrect answer "19" is triggered by the misleading expression "have left."

9. Another test item made famous by Rokeach, who hoped thereby to define a trait called authoritarianism, and which Stanovich (2009) adopts as a test of rationality:

   You have two coins. Together they add up to 30 cents. One of them is not a nickel. What are they?

   The solution depends on noticing that "one of them is not a nickel" does not disallow the possibility that "the other one is." Such solutions depend on the ability to lift the expressions from their context in order to construct a strict interpretation. This metalinguistic competence is enhanced, I suggested, by literacy. Indeed, Rokeach's reliance on such questions confuses metarepresentational thought with authoritarianism. Stanovich's (2009) suggestion that success on such items is correlated with self-control seems more promising. But if this is the case, self-control should be seen as the result of learning how to read in a linguistically critical way.
10. Or consider another of the questions used by both Kahneman and Stanovich to assess rationality:

    A ball and a bat cost $1.10. The bat costs $1.00 more than the ball. How much does the ball cost?

    Here one easily falls prey to placing insufficient weight on "more than."
11. Kahneman's famous "Linda" problem, on which he based his claim about irrationality, is subject to the same analysis. Subjects were told:

    Linda is thirty-one years old, single, outspoken, and very bright. She majored in philosophy. As a student, she was deeply concerned with issues of discrimination and social justice, and also participated in antinuclear demonstrations.

    Subjects were then asked: "Which alternative is more probable? 1) Linda is a bank teller, or 2) Linda is a bank teller and is active in the feminist movement."

Subjects overwhelmingly choose (2), ignoring the mathematical fact that (2) is a subset of (1) and therefore, strictly speaking, less probable. When this is pointed out, most subjects are willing to revise their conclusion. However, Kahneman draws two strong and questionable inferences from this finding: first, that subjects have an unconscious bias in reasoning, what he calls the "conjunction fallacy"; and second that they are, therefore, irrational. However, both inferences are doubtful. If subjects honor the Gricean maxims discussed earlier, they will not discount the facts about Linda as irrelevant to their conclusion. Furthermore, the existence of the "conjunction fallacy" is questionable in that it disappears if the choice options are simply rearranged. If asked "Which is more probable" that (1) Linda is active in the feminist movement, or (2) Linda is active in the feminist movement and a bank teller, subjects choose (1), thereby showing that what has been called the "conjunction fallacy" is little more than an artifact produced by the peculiarity of a "test question" that violates the Gricean maxims. Crupi and Tentori (2016) have recently provided a probabilistic model that coincides with the Gricean account offered here. Presumably it is to honor the Gricean maxims that Kahneman's subjects frequently treat "probable" as if it were a synonym of "plausible" or "likely" (Gigerenzer, Todd & the ABC Research Group, 1999; Kahneman, 2011).

The fact that adult subjects routinely fail such test questions leads Stanovich (2009) to propose a distinctive mental process or ability separate from more general intelligence that he defines as rationality. Clearly a person's answers on such test questions fail to meet the criteria for success. But can one infer from this that the person failing to make the correct judgment is irrational? Only if test questions are valid measures of mental competence required to handle real problems. Test questions, recall, measure competence in an artificial "laboratory" world. Thus, while test questions are useful empirical tools for examining mental processes they may be invalid tools for judging human rationality. This is the conclusion drawn by anthropologists for a century; test questions are tied to specific literate cultural practices. If human competence is a matter of reasoning in real-world contexts, very much a pragmatic competence, performance on such questions is not a valid indicator of such competence.

On the other hand, if competence is judged as relevant to a somewhat specialized linguistic environment such as the university, such tests may be valid. Such test questions find their place in the SAT because they predict success at university, suggesting an overlap in what test questions require and what academic success requires. This is the competence Stanovich defines as rational. Being reasonable and being literate in the sense of possessing knowledge of definitions and logic, the first dependent upon language, the second on metalanguage, are worth distinguishing, and Stanovich's findings may be interpreted as evidence for this distinction.

But what then is the status of competence with laboratory objects? First, like any laboratory-created objects, they may tell us something about underlying processes, in this case the processes involved in judging and criticizing statements. Second, such tests demonstrate that an important form of human competence derives not only from the ability to use language but also from the ability to think about certain properties of language at the expense of others. Third, such tests point us to aspects of knowledge that are worth learning and teaching and that are appropriately assigned to educational programs. Fourth, they alert us to the importance of the entire history of literacy with its explosion of talk about talk. Reading and criticizing texts, long the concern of the language arts, is not only an acquaintance with literature but also, I have argued, an avenue to a critical, reflective mind and a particular use of language.

The critical competencies required to deal with test questions, even if they violate the Gricean maxims, may be usefully applied to ordinary thinking. The concepts essential for thinking about precise meanings of terms and logical relations among them provide a norm or standard against which ordinary talk and action may be evaluated. Such evaluations are what we mean by critical thinking. Test questions are a means for teasing out these norms and standards. Teaching people to recognize and honor them is important to serious discourse about issues such as climate change and health sciences and, indeed, in everyday life. Hence, the importance of education.

On the other hand, judgments based on responses to test questions may be quite misleading if they are taken as representing language use rather than language about language, that is as metarepresentational objects. First, a lack of metarepresentational competence may be taken as a lack of linguistic competence, as we saw in the case of Sissy Jupe. Second, failure may be taken as a lack of mental ability rather than unfamiliarity with literate practices, as we saw in the case of Ivan and the white bears. Third, the converse of the second, poor performance may fail to alert teachers to the importance of making a distinction between talking about things and talking about words for things, a metarepresentational stance new to some learners and a common impediment to learning to read. Finally, test questions involving hypothetical cases that, while useful for exploring general principles, are of limited value for deciding specific cases where a multitude of contextual factors may be relevant. Ordinary use of language is, as we say, situated in a particular context.

The use of test questions as tools for investigating human thinking has become common in the social sciences more generally. Judgments about human morality are based on subject's reactions to decontextualized statements, what I have called laboratory objects. The so-called "Trolley problem," a typical test question, is widely assumed to say something important about moral judgment in the real world. What such tasks may provide is an opportunity to articulate the ethical principles useful for judging actions, but are largely irrelevant to actual moral decisions in which an unlimited number of factors may be relevant. In fact, the Canadian Supreme Court raised concerns about the appropriateness of basing judgments on "hypothetical cases" that lacked common sense. Hypothetical cases, like test questions, assume *ceteris paribus* conditions that can never be met in making real decisions. At best they help to articulate ethical principles.

As I mentioned in the chapter on metarepresentation, Kahneman's (2011) *Thinking Fast and Slow* demonstrates the conflict that sometimes arises between everyday thinking and reflective thinking. As well as acknowledging the "marvels" of intuitive thought, much of which occurs outside of consciousness, Kahneman documents how such intuitions often bias and interfere with more rational or logical judgments. His goal is to "introduce a language for thinking and talking about the mind" (p. 12). And although Kahneman suggests that reflective thinking, what he calls System Two, "requires a richer vocabulary than is available in everyday language" (p. 3), his account leaves unaddressed the special metalinguistic nature of reflective thinking, that is, of thinking about thinking that depends in large part on education and literacy. To that end, I first distinguished language use from metalanguage, and second, described the kind of discourse that evolves when that metalinguistic knowledge comes to influence ordinary language, namely, logical prose and reflective thinking.

LANGUAGE AND METALANGUAGE IN THE THEORY OF THINKING

I have distinguished two orientations to language: one as a means of thinking (representing) and communicating about the world, the other a means of metarepresenting and hence reflecting on the language used. The first generates reasons for action and thought, the second for reasoning about those reasons. If we choose, we may call the first "reasonable" and define the latter, following Stanovich (2009), as "rational." It is this second metarepresentational competence that is examined in test questions and that I have associated with literacy.

An increased respect for the reasonableness of all human beings is not a call to return to the Sissy Jupes of the world or to

Luria's Uzbek peasant as models of human rationality, but it is a call to include them in the class of thinking, reasoning creatures. But at the same time it is a call to provide access to a literate education that would provide the critical concepts for thinking about thinking and access to a modern document-based culture.

PART IV The Implications and Uses of Metarepresentational Language

11 The Psychology and Pedagogy of Reading

Literacy development at every level pivots on the ability to treat language itself as not merely an instrument, but an object *of thought, analysis, and reflection.* (Adams, Treiman & Pressley, 1998, p. 277)

If we are justified in the claim that reading brings a new consciousness of language and if that consciousness is the route to rationality, it is necessary to examine just how reading gives rise to such consciousness. And further, to ask how that consciousness of language relates to learning to read and to becoming a skilled and then a critical reader.

Although important advances have been made both in understanding the underlying cognitive processes involved in reading and in the forms of pedagogy appropriate for its development, two of the issues we have discussed may throw new light on the study of reading and learning to read. The first is the relation between language and metalanguage, the second between conscious and unconscious knowledge. They turn out to be related in that the metalinguistic concepts acquired in learning to read are just those that make the unconscious linguistic practices into conscious knowledge. Having established these links we may then go on to ask how such knowledge allows us to evaluate the diverse claims about learning to read in terms of more general principles including the agency of the learner, the relation of mind to world and the nature of norms and standards for judging success.

LEARNING A SCRIPT

The invention of writing brought language into consciousness, that is, turned aspects of language into objects of thought, without the intention to do so, by the creation of a script that could represent the implicit and largely unconscious aspects of speech including discrete *sounds*, *words* and *sentences*. But the consequence of this achievement may be read in two quite different ways, ways that distinguish quite different understandings of what is involved in reading and in learning to read. In fact the debates about reading and learning to read involve either the assertion or the denial of the importance of consciousness of language in reading and learning to read and, consequently, of the importance of learning metalinguistic concepts for referring to aspects of language. Those who assert the importance of such knowledge claim that learners must grasp the metalinguistic relations between properties of speech and those of writing – letters representing sounds, written words representing spoken words and so on – as preconditions for literacy. Deniers assert that the use of visual signs is sufficiently analogous to the uses of speech sounds that the processes underlying their use remains unconscious in learning to read just as they are in learning to speak. As long as attention is focused on the meaning, they suggest, the underlying semantic and grammatical structures will be acquired while remaining implicit and unconscious.

Although no one writer is clearly identifiable with any position on this series of issues, in order to examine the current discourse on reading and learning to read, the so-called reading wars, we may return to our basic distinction between using language and thinking about language, the second, as we said, is metarepresentational. To most literacy practitioners, both perspectives are completely compelling and they support a "balanced" approach rather than a showdown. The unfortunate consequence is a muddle.

THE PLACE OF METAREPRESENTATIONAL KNOWLEDGE IN TWO PERSPECTIVES ON READING

Reading as a social practice. This perspective implies that reading, like speaking, depends upon implicit, unconscious processes and furthermore that what is implicit is better left implicit if the goal of reading is that of understanding. Noted reading theorist Frank Smith, in his hugely influential book *Understanding Reading* (1971, 2012), argued that all language learning, including learning to read, is based on understanding, not on the drill and practice of subskills. The brain, he suggested, takes care of sorting out the grammar involved so long as one focuses on understanding what is being said or read. Only part of the learning process is conscious, namely the meaning or content of what is said or written. The analysis of linguistic form that gives rise to this understanding occurs below the level of awareness; calling attention to it could be distracting. Smith points to clear analogies in domains other than reading that involve unconscious processes, including the fact that we easily recognize a familiar face but how we do so remains out of awareness. My example was that we recognize when we correctly whistle a tune but we have little or no idea of how we achieve it. Indeed, the study of eye movements of readers shows the haphazard gathering of information in leading up to judgment; one scans until one can make a judgment. What they are scanning for in the attempt to understand is, Smith says, information. But what information? Presumably those visual features that indicate the implicit linguistic structures identified by Saussure and Chomsky. But in Smith's view, just as the processes remain implicit and unconscious in speaking, they remain implicit and unconscious in reading and learning to read. The reader's concern, the focus of attention, is on the meaning of the word or story. Only in grasping the meaning are the lexical and grammatical properties of the expression resolved.

Another authority on the teaching and learning of languages, Stephen Krashen (1989), summarized a wide range of evidence to justify his claim that we do not acquire language when we speak it, nor when errors are corrected. Nor, as everyone agrees, is it the result of learning and memorizing the rules of grammar. Rather, Krashen argues, we acquire language when we understand it, when we understand what people tell us and when we understand what we read. The knowledge of the language remains implicit and unconscious. Knowledge of the grammar develops as one encounters more comprehensible input. The entire process of language acquisition is "subconscious"; while it is happening, the acquirer is not aware it is happening nor of the rules that have been acquired: "this knowledge is represented subconsciously in the brain" (Krashen, 1989).

The linguistic knowledge represented subconsciously in the brain is just the knowledge that Saussure and modern linguists succeeded in making explicit, but which is implicit in the ability to talk. Once explicit, the grammar and vocabulary may be taught to other would-be linguists but not, Krashen suggests, as a method of learning to talk or to read. Thus Krashen, like Smith, is led to his well-known opposition to basic skills training as a method of teaching reading. For the purposes of reading and learning to read such knowledge is better left implicit. The teacher's concern with rules, norms and standards expressed in terms of "Basic Skills" are seen as irrelevant, indeed, distracting. Metalinguistic knowledge plays no clear role in this account. Finally, as the learner is responsible for "bringing the meaning" to the text, there is little concern for what authorities may insist is to be found in the world or in the text; standards of correctness are set aside while the agency and creative efforts of the learner are encouraged.

Reading as a metalinguistic competence. This second and predominant perspective grants that sharing an understanding or grasping a meaning is critical to language learning and further that the grammatical structures involved are implicit and unconscious in speaking. But this perspective denies that this is equally true of reading or learning to read. Ventris deciphered Linear B, they may point out, only when he recognized it as a representation of spoken Greek. Children learn to read, this perspective implies, only when they recognize the script as a representation of their own spoken language, that is, when they recognize that visual signs indicate aspects of sounds heard, words spoken, sentences expressed or speech acts made. Visual search for indications of these structures continues until a comprehensible meaning emerges.

This second perspective tends to be aligned with the so-called Basic Skills approach to learning to read, as exemplified in the Common Core Curriculum, and is defended primarily by experimental psychologists (Carroll, Snowling, Stevenson & Hulme, 2003; Dehaene, 2009; Rayner, Foorman, Perfetti, Pesetsky & Seidenberg, 2001) who have used a variety of experimental tasks to examine underlying processes in phoneme, word and sentence recognition, as well as to pinpoint the problems that pose significant hurdles to all learners in learning to read. It is also defended by studies showing that learning to read is in large part a phonological problem rather than a visual learning problem, and that the phonological problem is of a special kind, namely, the ability to think about the phonology in a special, metarepresentational way. This metarepresentational way is described as phonological awareness or, alternatively, as grasping the alphabetic principle. Beginning readers must achieve the "cognitive insight" into the relations between sounds and meanings (Downing & Valtin, 1984).

The metalinguistic perspective on reading dominates educational policy in the United States, United Kingdom and Canada. That policy adopts a Standards Based Assessment (SBA) model designed to turn the research findings summarized by the National Reading Panel (2000) into a specific set of achievable outcomes. The National Reading Panel had concluded that the most conspicuous dimensions of reading success and failure were phonological awareness (the ability to analyze oral words into discrete syllables and phonemes), phonetics (the ability to sound out unknown words), fluent word recognition, vocabulary and the ability to summarize, paraphrase or otherwise express in words one's understanding. The recommended pedagogy is designed to advance knowledge of letter names, letter–sound pairings, vocabulary, fluency and comprehension. Grade-level standards can be set for each and, indeed, the Common Core

Standards Initiative (www.corestandards.org) sets these out as the foundation for literacy development and is widely adopted as a form of "best practice."

The most general recommendation of the Panel, in fact, was to insist on the importance of a deep immersion in a culture of reading, including being read to, attending to written signs and above all talking about language, all of which may be described as an introduction to the social practice of reading. Yet, there is a striking indifference to meaning in the formulation of the standards set out in the Common Core. Thus teachers are urged to teach children (and they will be tested on this) the rules for long and short vowel sounds in nonsense words apart from the use of these vowels in distinguishing well-known words such as "win" and "wine" or "don" and "done" (whoops – one should read this as /doan/ if the rule about long vowels were inviolate). The Common Core assumes that learning and knowing the rules, the metalinguistic knowledge, is prerequisite to and hence the only way to arrive at a meaning. Consequently, there is a focus on arriving at the correct answer, the correct sound, the correct meaning and in learning the standards and norms for making such judgments.

From this perspective, the first problem in understanding reading and learning to read is distinguishing language in use from the metalanguage. The second is recognizing that the metarepresentations represent something that exists implicitly in the primary language (for example, discovering phonemes). And the third is to apply this metalinguistic knowledge to the printed word: "'B-i-r-d' says 'bird'." When one can do this, they have acquired the Basic Skills. But as we saw in Chapter 4, mapping sounds to signs is not a simple matter.

Both perspectives on reading acknowledge that linguistic competence is just the ability to understand and produce utterances. While the meaning, specifically the reference or the content, of the utterance is acknowledged to be conscious, the underlying linguistic processes and structures involved in speaking and listening, all agree, remain largely unconscious. This is just what Vygotsky had claimed in saying that language was transparent and further that reading made language opaque. This opacity was the result, I argued, of acquiring such metalinguistic concepts as *letters* and *words* that link visual forms to constituents of speech. The reading wars are about whether or not such opacity is necessary for reading and learning to read.

Recall that both Smith and Krashen had argued that in learning to read, as in learning to talk, the meaning was conscious but the processes involved in arriving at that meaning were unconscious and implicit. Indeed, the unconscious learning of underlying forms is seen as the consequence of grasping a meaning. However, if that were true children would know no more about words and phonemes when they learn to read than they do when they learn to speak. But as we saw in Chapters 5 through 8, children in learning to read do acquire concepts like *word* and some knowledge of the phonological sounds represented by the letters. Readers, unlike non-readers, can break utterances into word-like units, they can delete phonemes from words and words from sentences, and solve a large variety of metalinguistic tasks. It follows that learning to read, unlike learning to speak, results in metalinguistic knowledge that makes some of these underlying processes explicit. On this point Smith and Krashen are clearly wrong. On the other hand, they are clearly right in distinguishing the practice of reading, as the practice of finding meaning in a text, from the metarepresentational discourse about sounds, words, sentences and the like. So we are driven back to the question of the relation between reading and talk about reading.

METALINGUISTICS IN ITS PLACE

Metarepresentational knowledge is knowledge *about* reading, not the processes actually *used* in reading. Metarepresentational concepts provide a normative frame for judging utterances and actions; they are insufficient for generating behavior including reading behavior. Thus it is important not to confuse the processes involved in assigning a meaning to a text, actual reading, from the metarepresentational commentary on that process, including letter–sound pairing, rules of spelling, correctness of pronunciation.

As we saw in the discussion of reasoning, logic is a metalanguage for talking about reasoning. It provides the criteria or norms for judging the validity of reasoning, not the actual practices involved in ordinary reasoning. So, too, for the metalinguistics of reading. Metalinguistic concepts highlight what to look for in order to distinguish correct from incorrect judgments; they are largely norm-driven and critical. At best they highlight basic rules and principles to be honored, not actual practices, many of which remain implicit. Metarepresentational concepts take linguistic processes off-line so as to make comments about them such as "Caterpillar is a long word" or "C-a-t spells cat." Hence, we may conclude that Basic Skills are in fact metarepresentational skills, not reading skills. They are understandings that must be in place if one is to read.

Metarepresentational talk is primarily the domain of the parents and teachers, such as when they point out, say, that the name printed on the door of a child's room says "Jane," that "b" says "buh" or that there is a difference between "hop" and "hope" or that "cheval" means "horse." The richness of this metarepresentational talk in homes, including that around shared book reading, is one of the features that distinguish early from delayed readers (Aram, Fine & Ziv, 2013). This metarepresentational understanding is essential, indeed invariably involved in learning to read. On the other hand, as metarepresentational talk is *about* reading, some aspects of the actual reading processes, those involved in combining different sources of information, for example, may become and remain implicit, just as Smith and Krashen argued. Reading is not the systematic application of metarepresentational rules; rules are for judging, not for acting. Nonetheless, they are acquired by all readers, as shown by their success on metalinguistic tasks. Once acquired, the processes involved in generating a sentence or in assigning a meaning are largely automatic and invisible whether in listening or reading.

A huge body of reading research has been devoted to examining such implicit processes, including those involved in taking the letter *s* as a phoneme or a morpheme (Nunez & Bryant, 2009). Dehaene (2009, p. 219), who studies the brain processes involved in word recognition, points out that most of these processes are unconscious: "Our brain takes each string apart, then recomposes it into a hierarchy of letters, bigrams, syllables, and morphemes. Effortless reading simply serves to show that these decomposition and recomposition states have become entirely automatic and unconscious." Metalinguistic concepts make explicit such states and processes by entering them into the "space of reasons," as something to learn and to think about. Metalinguistic talk may be seen either as a basic precondition for reading or as consequence of learning to read. This, as we shall see, is a false opposition.

THE USES OF METALANGUAGE IN READING AND LEARNING TO READ

The more specific question is whether and when metalinguistic talk about written forms such as letters, words, sentences is appropriate, and more specifically, whether and how such concepts play out in the process of reading and learning to read. To learn to read is to grasp concepts relating the acoustic space of spoken language to the visual space of printed symbols. Knowledge of those printed symbols is to know, to be conscious of, the properties of speech that those symbols represent. Hence, learning to read is the route to that consciousness. Thus some metalinguistic concepts may be necessary conditions for learning to read but not sufficient ones.[1] Much more is required before one becomes a skilled reader. In order to acquire the metarepresentational concept of *word* as both a piece of writing and a piece of speech, the learner must be able to find something in each medium to treat as equivalent. We know which metarepresentational concepts

[1] I am indebted to Marilyn Jaeger Adams for this suggestion.

are at play in learning to read, as these are the concepts that every reader has acquired. These are the concepts summarized as linguistic awareness. Furthermore, comprehension failure and mistakes in reading are readily traced to the lack of such concepts. Teachers are correctly advised to direct beginning readers to the features of writing that are related to those of speech. This is part of the understanding that makes learning possible.

This allows us an escape from what looks like a dilemma. Learning to read is not only mastering the practice of reading, it is learning, at the same time, a set of metalinguistic concepts for thinking and talking about reading. This is the metalanguage shared by parent and child or teacher and child as they talk about what the child is seeing and what is to be seen in the text before her. This metalanguage is so common as to escape notice, but is involved in every exchange between the child faced by a text and a parent or teacher who is suggesting and monitoring the practices – "That says 'dog'." "Says" here is the metalinguistic verb borrowed from everyday language. The metalanguage develops into a literate metalanguage when concepts like *letter* and *word* are introduced to explicitly link properties of speech to properties of the written script. Such metalanguage provides the rules and norms for correct usage (e.g., "That's not a word").

But it is important to remember that these concepts are *about* language and reading, they do not constitute the processes, largely implicit and unconscious and increasingly automatic, that readers implement in finding a meaning in a text. Put simply, while metalinguistic concepts tell readers what to look for, reading is the practical competence in finding and aligning these features to produce a meaning. The more concepts available, the more one can see in a text.

Renate Valtin (2014) criticized the skills-based approach to teaching literacy by arguing that it is impossible to demonstrate a causal relation between phonological awareness and learning to read. In a re-analysis of earlier studies that had claimed that ability on phonemic tasks predicted reading ability, she reported that those children successful in the phonemic tasks were already readers when entering school and that preschool reading ability correlated more highly with later reading achievement than did the ability to reverse phonemes. She urged that metalinguistic knowledge be viewed within a framework of written language acquisition. She concluded that an isolated training of letters and sounds outside the context of reading and writing does not lead children to grasp the *function* of letters and sounds (let alone phonemes). Learning, she suggests, depends upon "emerging insights" into what those letters are for. And she recommends a program in the preschool years that focuses on oral language development and on the functions of written language in stories, instructions, lists and other contexts. As I argued above, "emerging insights" are precisely those represented by metalinguistic concepts. An important part of pre-school and early school education involves talking to children *about* language. Reading begins when they can equally talk about text, including words, their sounds, their uses and their meanings. That is the foundation on which literacy learning is based.

GENERAL PERSPECTIVES ON READING AND LEARNING TO READ

Although arguments about reading tend to focus on questions of process and pedagogy, the debate about the role of metalinguistic concepts in reading and learning to read draws on three more general and abstract problems, namely, the agency problem, the mind–world problem and the practice vs. norms problem. Consider them in turn.

Agency. The agency problem is that of whether or not one is conscious of and responsible for what one is doing. One view, deriving from the Pragmatists, is that the learner, not the teacher and not the learner's brain, is responsible for learning; learning is a species of thinking. While the learner may be held accountable for his or her learning, it is the learner who is seen as the responsible agent. Alternatively, if the learning process is automatic and unavailable to consciousness, the learner's agency and responsibility for meeting norms and standards disappears.

Many cognitive scientists, including the distinguished neuroscientist Dehaene, treat the reader as synonymous with basic cognitive functions implemented in the brain, thus identifying the intentions of the agent with the functioning of his or her brain. Recall how he described word recognition: "Our brain takes each string apart, then recomposes it into a hierarchy of letters, bigrams, syllables, and morphemes" (Dehaene, 2009, p. 219); that is, the brain is the agent and the processes are automatic. But he goes on to suggest that teachers "must aim to lay down an efficient neuronal hierarchy, so that a child can recognize letters and phonemes and easily turn them into speech sounds." These are brain processes that are installed in the learner through teaching. But whereas teaching is here treated as an intentional activity, that is, something the teacher is trying to do, learning is regarded as a mechanical process carried out by the learner's brain.

Although the link between brain and behavior is a profound problem, in the case of learning to read, agency is a matter of what the learner can do, take responsibility for and be held accountable in terms of. These, of course, are the processes that are conscious and that depend on concepts and that govern underlying processes. The more elaborated the concepts, the more of the reading process is brought into consciousness. Some of this underlying structure has to be brought into consciousness in order to learn to read, but once acquired runs on automatically just as Dehaene claimed. What Dehaene overlooks, I suggest, is that learners, too, are agents who can be held accountable for learning the rules. Recognizing that the learner is the agent of his or her learning is fundamental to all progressive models of teaching and learning.

Concepts and the mind–world problem. Concepts are offered as the solution to the mind–world problem, that is, the problem of what is given in the world and what is invented by the mind. Rephrased, the question is whether the meaning come from the mind of the reader or from the structures in the text. Some, sympathetic to postmodernism, assume that the reader is a "meaning maker" who advances hypotheses and confirms or rejects them by scanning for evidence and adjusting it to fit his or her expectations. Others take the world and the text as given and assume that the reader is a "meaning finder" who responds to properties, letters and words given by the text. In fact, this reading puzzle is a particular case of the "myth of the given" discussed in Chapter 3.

Taking either the mind or the world as "given" is a species of cognitive fundamentalism. I appealed earlier (Chapter 3) to Sellars' attempt to avoid such fundamentalisms by advancing a more appropriate theory of concepts. That theory insisted that concepts are not free inventions but cognitive structures that permit one to see what is already there; neither mind nor world is primary. This is precisely what I argued in regard to the concept of *word*. Humans invented the concept but the concept allowed them to see that their speech was already composed of words or word-like structures and conversely that some of those visible marks could be seen as words. Monsieur Jourdain was at least partly right: he was speaking prose all along, he just had not recognized it as such. Neither word nor object came first; the concept is acquired only when one finds a pattern in the world that can serve as the meaning of the concept.

Thus we may resolve the dilemma about the role of metalinguistic awareness of phonemes and words in learning to read. The concepts of *words* and *letters* neither precede nor follow the knowledge of the sounds they represent. To construct the concept of a letter is to treat the sounds of speech in a certain way. The concept makes explicit what was implicit in the practice of speaking. Other concepts capture relations among the letters themselves, so-called orthographic rules. Thus basic skills are neither pre-reading nor post-reading skills, neither causes or consequences of reading, but metarepresentations that make explicit what is involved in the processes of speaking and reading. Teaching such concepts is necessary when they have not already been picked up from the literate talk of adults. While there may be some dispute as to whether sound–symbol relations are better discovered than taught, there is no question that they must be learned and it is the teacher's responsibility to hold the learner accountable for that learning.

Approaching concepts this way allows us to offer a minor correction to Vygotsky's claim that scientific concepts precede experience. Rather one should say that concepts become concepts only when they allow one to see the world in a particular way. If the learner can find nothing in the implicit practices of speaking to which the concept *word* is to refer, the concept cannot be acquired and it remains a verbalism. As the New Pragmatists insisted, there is no knowledge without concepts and, further, that concepts reveal what in some sense was already there. The concept of *word* is not a pure invention but something that allows one to see what was there all along. Now we may better understand why word games play such an important part in learning to read: they bring words into consciousness.

Norms and rules. The normative problem is concerned with the correctness of these practices. Because reading is often a private activity it is easy to overlook the fact that reading, both recognizing words and assigning meanings, is a normative activity – there are standards of correctness that are to be met if one is to succeed. Some of these norms are acquired by imitation or invention and remain implicit. But the metalanguage makes these norms explicit so they can serve as standards for judgment and criticism. Such normative judgments become more prominent in educational discourse in that the school is not only an instrument of human development but also an institution designed to pass on the norms and standards of correctness for language use in a literate society. For example, the rules or norms for spelling, such as they are, are less important for generating spelling than for the diagnosis of error; that is, for monitoring spellings in terms of a norm or standard of correctness. These rules should be seen as metarepresentational rather than as the means for generating the spelling of individual words. These norms and standards are neither absolute nor are they to be rigidly applied, but to learn to spell involves the recognition that there are rules for spellings and it is the role of the school to show learners how they may be applied and whether or not they have applied them correctly.

REVISITING BASIC SKILLS

It is a truism that learning is understanding, grasping the meaning or significance of an event, a story or an expression. While a focus on meaning may lead some to overlook the importance of the Basic Skills that make the assignment of meaning possible, the Common Core Curriculum may lead some to ignore the importance of meaning. The Common Core Curriculum treats Basic Skills as the ability to manipulate letters and sounds quite independently of their roles in specifying a meaning. Only those who already have some understanding of what reading is about may see the significance of such activities. But reading is also a matter of understanding the writing system as a comprehensible system of signs with orderly relations to the structures of speech. There are critical understandings that escape many learners, even those from a rich literate environment, and that are sometimes best addressed through just the activities described as Basic Skills. Such training may be essential especially for children who hold completely inappropriate assumptions about reading, have little grasp of how written signs relate to spoken utterances or little grasp of the "alphabetic principle" (Liberman & Shankweiler, 1991). These gaps in knowledge may be detected by tests of Basic Skills and may be addressed by systematic teaching on just those points raised by the National Reading Panel. Furthermore, an exclusive emphasis on the referential meaning, while essential, overlooks the fact that there are systematic properties of language that writing makes explicit, that are comprehensible, that may be talked about and that may call for systematic study and practice.

Once Basic Skills are recognized as metarepresentational skills, their relation to the earlier discussion of "test questions" becomes clear. The Basic Skills are those involved in decontextualized activities that are useful for research into basic processes and may be useful pedagogically but are only indirectly related to actual reading in that they call attention to the language, to isolated sounds and the *sense* of terms, rather than to what the language is about. Again, although this metalanguage is critical to thinking about reading, it is only indirectly involved in the process of reading.

One error in the debate, as Valtin pointed out, is that of taking correlation as causation, seeing reading as the product of Basic Skills. The alternative is to see competence with such skills as phonological awareness as symptoms of reading ability rather than as causes of reading and as a useful diagnostic of difficulties.

The relation between implicit and explicit knowledge may be shown by an analogy. Children in learning to play Hide-and-Seek may acquire the knowledge that only one person at a time is "It" and that who is "It" can shift from one round to the next. Some may discover those rules through play, others by making them explicit through teaching. Whether learned implicitly or explicitly, children must have an understanding of those rules or they are not playing the game. The same is true of reading.

ASSESSING UNDERSTANDING

Understanding is one of those concepts that is so fundamental to learning that it is often assumed rather than analyzed or defined. But if understanding is to provide a basis for the acquisition of both language and literacy it is essential to examine just what understanding entails. Whereas "learning" implies that behavior meets a certain objective criterion, understanding implies that the learning be experienced in a particular personal or subjective way. It entails a feeling of knowing; consequently, understanding is a cognitive emotion. Yet at present there are no explicit criteria even in the brain sciences for identifying the feeling of understanding. Consequently understanding is not useful as an objective standard and we are forced to rely on first-person testimony, "I understand," or some behavioral feature such as compliance with commands or performance on a test.

Understanding, William James claimed, was too vague a concept to earn a place in his *Principles of Psychology* and was better left, he thought, to the tender-minded. The Behaviorists operationalized the concept of understanding by measuring comprehension. Tests of comprehension attempt to provide an objective criterion for understanding; if you passed the test you were said to understand. Cognitive science theories explain understanding as the cognitive state produced when new input is assigned to an existing schema, thereby allowing inference (Moore & Newell, 1973). Wilson and Keil (2000, p. 97) pointed out the important link between explanation and understanding. Understanding is "a cognitive state that remains largely implicit but ... entails prediction, inference and memory." An explanation is the type of speech act that makes the understanding explicit, just as assertions make beliefs explicit. Damasio (2012) described this cognitive state as the subjective feeling of understanding, an emotional response that adults may express as "Ah ha!". Even apes and 3-year-old children, Tomasello claimed, were aware of when they knew and when they did not. Educators recognize in the actions of their students whether or not students "get it": "If they didn't get it, their hands shot up," Steven Katz reported in his classroom studies (Katz, 2001). Thus, the feeling of understanding is a basic and universal emotional response that accompanies the resolution of ambiguity, as Damasio and others suggest. We may be more certain of the status of children's subjective feelings of knowing when they acquire a metalanguage for asking "What?", "Why?" or answering "I don't know," thereby giving explicit form to what previously may have been only a feeling. When the child acquires the metarepresentational concept *understanding* it may be used self-referentially so that the learner can ask or set up a test for their own understanding. This is an essential element of self-control and self-responsibility. The feeling of understanding that learners use to terminate their search for information in reading is important but has yet to be brought into the laboratory.

Although understanding is a cognitive-emotional state internal to a person, that private subjective mental state is an insufficient criterion for understanding, for two reasons. First, this definition leaves unclear the link between understanding and consciousness. Both the feeling of understanding and the belief that one understands are conscious, but only the latter is metarepresentational, something one may say something about. Second, it leaves unspecified the normative standards or criteria to be met; one must be able to distinguish understanding from misunderstanding, a primary concern of the school. The normative standard, that is, the correct understanding, is invested in the teacher who has the task of helping students talk about and revise their understanding to meet the normative standard. Derry (2013, p. 56), we may recall, expressed concern that in their attempt to avoid the authoritarianism that some see in the so-called "transmission" model of teaching, some Vygotskians give a priority to the "the pupils' own conceptions ... over any concern to ensure that the pupils are able to distinguish clearly between correct and incorrect knowledge." She claims that this is the hazard of substituting multiple "voices" for the traditional concern with truth and validity. A clearer metarepresentational concept of understanding is essential to making that distinction: to understand is to understand correctly or justifiably. So here again we see a possible parting of the ways among reading theorists. If one is concerned only with the subjective aspects of meaning, issues of correctness do not arise; if one is concerned with understanding in a more normative sense, attention is more likely to be drawn to those properties of expressions that are true or correct. Schooling, as I argued elsewhere (Olson, 2003), is such a normative enterprise.

A final caveat on the teaching of reading. While the teaching of reading is absolutely critical to a modern society, the specific approach adopted appears to have little bearing on test scores (Cowen, 2003). Far more important is providing comprehensible input and appropriate opportunities for learning. These are matters of setting clear and justifiable goals, providing adequate resources including teaching, monitoring progress and holding children accountable for achieving those goals. Moreover, the major causes of reading failure lie not in pedagogical differences but in macro-social factors such as poverty, home environment, underfunded schools, teacher turnover and the like. Socio-economic status alone accounts for almost half of the variance in achievement scores. Rather than address these major social factors, reformers seek solutions in setting higher, often unachievable standards and then criticizing the schools and teachers for failing to achieve them. This is not to say that teachers have no responsibility for learners' achievements. Rather it is to say that while pedagogy matters, the difference among competing pedagogies may not matter much. It would certainly be a mistake to hope for a simple pedagogical "solution" to the reading "problem."

ASSESSING READING ABILITY

The objective measurement of reading ability by standardized tests provides some evidence of developing competence that may be useful to students, teachers and policy makers. However, standardized tests narrow the conception of reading, thereby limiting the potential significance of test scores, and make research on alternative forms of pedagogy difficult or impossible. They narrow the conception by treating reading and literacy as specific, trainable skills rather than avenues of reflective thought. And they narrow research on alternative pedagogies by constraining pedagogies to those suited to the form and content measured by the standardized assessment. When the form and content of the assessment device is known, pedagogies are easily adapted to the requirements of the assessment such that pedagogy becomes more and more a form of "test-prep," if not in the school then in the private tutorial services available outside the school. As long as North America is in thrall to standardized tests, test-prep and training for the test will hobble educational reform (Olson, 2003).

There is a trade-off in narrowing the curriculum to those skills likely to be assessed by the standardized test. The trade-off is that the gains in levels of achievement of the narrowly defined goals result in a loss in those skills that fall outside the test. This point is interestingly illustrated in the Canada's Council of Ministers of Education (2013) report on the PISA international ranking of the achievement of 15-year-olds. These tests revealed not only a decline in the rankings of Ontario and Canada as a whole among some 65 nations, but more ominously that this decline has been steady over five cycles of testing over a 12-year period.

Warwick Elley of the University of Canterbury in New Zealand, using the above-mentioned PISA data, pointed out that over the past decade Canada, once a banner-bearer in international comparisons, is now one of the big five in steadily declining student achievement over this 12-year period along with England, Australia, New Zealand and the United States (although Sweden seems to be following the same path). These declines are shown graphically in Figure 11.1.

What these countries all share, in addition to falling scores, Elley pointed out, is their adoption of the Standards Based Assessment (SBA) as a model for educational reform, first set out a decade ago in an aspirational US document, *No Child Left Behind.* This SBA reform model, drawn from business, aspires to raise "productivity" through strict accountability, testing with consequences that would eliminate failing teachers and failing schools. Only two other countries out of the 65 in the recent PISA survey – Uruguay and Iceland – showed a declining pattern like these five erstwhile educational leaders. Elley noted that no jurisdiction that followed the SBA model has recorded improvement, a conclusion echoed by Ravitch (2014, p. 25).

The irony is that over the same period that PISA scores were falling, at least three of those jurisdictions, the United States, United Kingdom and Ontario, Canada, made claims about the successful impact of their SBA reforms. Ontario's Education Quality and Accountability Office (EQAO, 2014), using its own tests for the Assessment of Reading, Writing and Mathematics, Primary Division for Ontario, Canada, reported that "Over the past five years, the percentage of

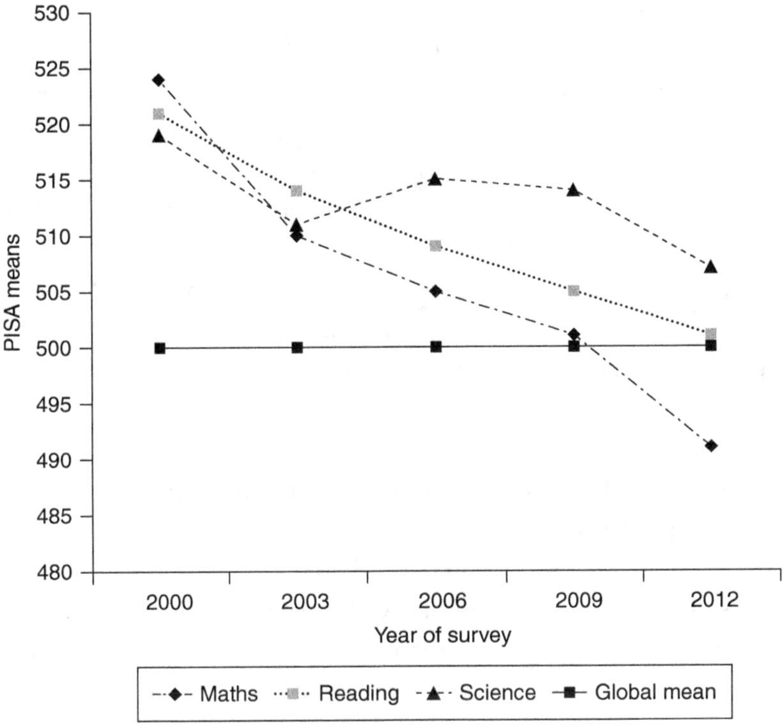

FIGURE 11.1 International comparisons reveal declining school achievement of 15-year-olds in Western countries over the past decade.

students performing at or above the provincial standard in reading has been steadily increasing (from 62% to 70%, an eight-percentage-point increase)." If they are improving dramatically at these earlier ages, why are they falling behind when assessed at age 15? Similar claims were made about the success of the reforms in the United Kingdom (Adonis, 2012) at the same time that the international scores were falling. Until recently similar claims were made for the United States.

Such contradictory findings suggest that SBA may be instrumental in increasing performance on the skills targeted by those tests, but they do so at the expense of the more generalized literacy skills assessed by the PISA tests. Rather than raising standards, the reforms may have succeeded in narrowing the curriculum. And it does so, presumably, because teachers (and test-prep organizations) know what the tests require and they train their students for success on those tests. Indeed, large-scale testing has shown that high school graduates who meet achievement test standards still fail to acquire the ability to evaluate arguments and evidence, the very things that literacy, properly conceived, should promote (National Center for Education Statistics, 2010).

That the SBA model itself is part of the problem is further suggested by the superior performance of Finnish children highlighted in the PISA data. Finnish educator Pasi Sahlberg (2011) points out that contrary to the SBA management models with test-based accountability, Finnish educational policy focuses on the responsibility of all agents, including the teachers and students, for all aspects of the program including curriculum and assessments. Devolved authority and distributed responsibilities contributed both to the welfare of students and job satisfaction of teachers and to enhanced academic achievement.

While some would abjure testing altogether in favor of informal observations, such tests serve an important function in that, as we saw in the discussion of testing, the very test items used for assessing achievement are also useful for diagnostic purposes. Passing or failing test items can alert educators and the learners themselves to the topics or processes that call for additional teaching and practice. Unfortunately large-scale standardized tests such as those employed by PISA and by EQAO allows only ranking of individuals and groups. Tests suitable for detecting specific and local learning problems that may be addressed by the teacher are essential for addressing individual difficulties, but major test-makers show little interest in developing such local resources.[2]

[2] As this book goes to press, President Obama acknowledged that testing in the schools as a means of reform is overdone and called both for limits on testing and for reconsidering their purpose (*New York Times*, October 25, 2015). Canadian educators have yet to recognize the problem.

CRITICAL READING

The aspect of literacy most likely to be underrepresented in strict accountability models of reading is that of reading critically. Critical reading is difficult to assess by means of a test because there is no correct answer! Dewey (1934/2003) distinguished "instrumental" perception (including reading) – in which one achieves some instrumental good by means of looking or reading, say, grasping the sense of a story – from critical perception and reading that involves judgment and requires a clearer conception of the constituent parts and how the parts are related to the whole (p. 310). Northrop Frye (1957, p. 5) is largely responsible for the modern concept of criticism in which he distinguished literature from the science of literature. He wrote: "Criticism is a structure of thought and knowledge existing in its own right, with some measure of independence from the art it deals with" (p. 5). And again: "Art, like nature, has to be distinguished from the systematic study of it, which is criticism" (p. 11). Thus, criticism is metarepresentational in that "literature is not a subject of study, but an object of study" (p. 11). In his early work Frye lamented the lack of a theory of criticism, a systematic science to which one could contribute. Criticism implies a use–mention distinction, that between the object studied and the critical metarepresentation of the object. Critical reading depends on the metarepresentational concepts available to bring to bear on what is read. These are the very concepts we encountered in the discussion of prose writing, namely, concepts such as *topic*, *claim*, *evidence*, *conclusion*, *paraphrase*, *summary* and the like. These are concepts about language that are acquired largely when reading and writing are put to more ambitious goals in content-rich fields such as science and history when reading and writing are harnessed to deliberate and systematic thinking. But they have their origins in the basic concepts about language that become explicit in learning to read.

Although the primary purposes of reading are to gain information and enjoyment, a secondary one is to learn a language for thinking about what is being read; a critical stance applicable not only to literature but to thinking in general, again linking reading and rationality. That is our next topic.

12 The Psychology and Pedagogy of Rationality

Metabeliefs are the means by which normative epistemology exerts leverage on applied thinking, the machinery by which we monitor our own rationality. (Rozeboom, 1972, p. 82)

The ability to think and reason is taken as the hallmark of the human species. Although early humans have intentionally modified stone tools for some 2.6 million years, archeologists now tend to agree that our particular species *homo sapiens* appeared in Africa somewhere between 100,000 and 200,000 years ago. Much later, some 30,000 years ago, they began to shape clay figurines and make images. Only some 5,000 years ago did they invent writing; an invention that is at least associated with the flowering of sapient cultures. "Sapient" means wisdom, the capacity to make informed judgments. So how did sapience evolve? If the biological basis of the human brain evolved little over this period, how are we to explain the dramatic cognitive developments that have occurred during this time? Anthropologist Colin Renfrew (Renfrew, Frith & Malafouris, 2009) calls this the "sapient paradox": why did our "sapient" status take so long to emerge? If brain capacity has not changed, why have indications of increased intelligence, reflectivity, imagination and learning ability characteristic of sapient humans appeared so recently? The alternative to explaining the rise of sapience to the evolution of the brain is the Vygotskian claim for cultural evolution, the long and cumulative processes of inventing, preserving and passing on through teaching the technological achievements of the past. But why the relatively recent surge?

Can the shifts in consciousness associated with written culture elaborated in the previous chapters help to explain the sapient revolution? First, I adopted Brandom's view that sapient consciousness is the ability to say something about something and to give reasons for acting and believing. These are practices associated primarily with elaborately, indeed prolix, verbal cultures. Language, I suggested, is a unique general resource that allows one to say something about something, predication, and then to make that saying the object of further sayings, recursion. Although all natural languages are assumed to have the same expressive powers, these powers are far from equally exploited. Gerd Spittler (1999, personal communication) pointed out the inappropriateness of dubbing cultures without writing as "oral cultures," in that it is members of written cultures that do much of the talking. While humans may have been a verbal species for a hundred thousand years, an increase in sapience may plausibly reflect an increased reliance on and elaboration of verbal culture. Verbal culture is essential for making practices explicit, something to talk and think about and give reasons for. A dramatic elaboration of verbal culture came with the beginnings of literate culture; a cultural tradition built around the creation, storage and reinterpretation of documents and texts.

The second point I hope to have established is the cognitive significance of making language itself explicit, as something to think about. What marked the classical Greek culture was not only its prolixity but its concern with language, including the precise meaning of terms such as justice and the logical structure of argument as indicated, for example, in Aristotelian logic. This was achieved through the invention of a metalanguage, a language for talking about the implicit structures of language as opposed to talking about events in the world. This essentially doubled the number of things to talk about, namely, the world plus the language about the world.

The third point I hope to have established is that the reasons offered to explain thought and action can themselves be subjected to a set of norms that allow one to evaluate the quality of the reasons;

in a word, to reason about reasons. Although all discourse involves inference, representing inferences as inferences allows one to formulate standards for evaluating whether or not inferences are valid. Writing and revising documents and texts provide the possibility of extended arguments that honor the canons of meaning and logic. It is only at this point that thinking and discourse approaches modern standards.

Finally, I hope to have established that there is a form of discourse manifest in test questions, research tasks, academic and scientific texts and in the written register generally that adopt as a norm what I described as a metalinguistic or analytical stance. This stance cancels or subordinates the Gricean Conversational norms suited to personal, contextualized social action, to the formal demands of precise definition and explicit logic. The product is recognized for its intellectual powers including the growth of knowledge and, indeed, its usefulness provided one motivation for its development. But it is not always recognized that because such discourse is metarepresentational and decontextualized, the norms articulated are not directly applicable to informal speech and action. I called this the "laboratory" effect and, while acknowledging its importance, pointed out its inadequacy in accounting for ordinary contextualized speech, thought and action. Primarily, I criticized researchers, test-makers and text writers for failing to acknowledge the difference. Specifically, we literates look down on the Sissy Jupes of the world who know only how to use words rather than how to define them.

On the other hand, I elaborated in some detail how concepts about language expressed in the metalanguage are critical to many of the activities we highly value in a modern literate society, beginning with learning to read and then in learning to write Classical prose. The rules and norms for Classical prose are just those that define formal rationality.

The sapient revolution, then, was less a dramatic step in the evolution of culture generally than an outcome of the creation of a literary and literate culture. Havelock (1989; Logan, 2004) thought so and argued that the invention of the alphabet was important not only because of its ability to represent and to analyze what was said, but also because it allowed the creation of a broad reading public that could change a specialist scribal culture into a more democratic one. So the rise of sapience is not the puzzle; the puzzle is how writing culture changed minds and that, I argued, was through making words and sentences objects of consciousness.

Some further evidence for a linguistic and intellectual awakening comes from a recent reconsideration of Karl Jaspers' mid-20th-century theory of the Axial Age (Jaspers, 1949/2011). Jaspers surveyed the dramatic conceptual shifts that occurred in diverse cultures around the world between the 8th and 3rd centuries BC. This was the period when such figures as Confucius, Buddha, Moses, Zoroaster and Socrates initiated traditions around revered religious and philosophical teachings largely but not exclusively through writing. The Axial Age, modern commentators emphasize, was marked by a kind of discourse and thought premised on the availability of a permanent record that could be considered and reconsidered, and against which current action could be compared. Sapient indeed!

Assman (2012) pointed out that the Axial Age is less a time-bound "age" than a metaphor for a cultural change that occurred somewhat independently in Eastern Mediterranean, Greek, Hebrew, Indian and Chinese cultures. But in each case it involved the creation of institutions for preserving and teaching texts along with new standards for truth and correctness. These changes occurred first in religion and gradually spread to other domains: "The space of writing [puts] a pressure on innovation that is alien to the space of orality" (p. 381). Donald (2012, p. 73), who also takes an evolutionary approach to culture, defended Jaspers' theory by arguing: "The Axial Age might be regarded as the time when humanity went through a major evolutionary step in self-monitoring and supervision that may be described as metacognition. This capacity is really an abstract form of self-awareness for planning action and for conscious self-regulation." We may see it as the birth of a critical faculty.

While language is widely acknowledged as the primary means for forming beliefs and for thinking, writing became a candidate for explaining certain aspects of thought only with the media theorists of the 1960s, including Goody, Havelock, Ong and McLuhan. While their views were quickly assimilated into popular culture, they have been slow to find a place in serious academic thought. McLuhan's aphorism about the medium being the message is just that, an aphorism, but one that hides an important truth. What was required was an account of how just writing something down could change one's mental representation of it, a problem posed by M. Carruthers (1990). In the preceding chapters I have attempted to solve that problem by showing that writing entails a new consciousness of language; what is implicit in speech becomes explicit in learning to read. So let me summarize how a consciousness of language expressed by metalinguistic concepts alters and enlarges the scope of reasoning and the principles of rationality.

THINKING AND REASONING

Thinking and reasoning problems are formulated in language taken off-line in such a way that normal considerations of context, including the Gricean conventions, are suspended. The biases in reasoning demonstrated by Kahneman's and Stanovich's subjects are, I argued, less indications of human irrationality than of the failure of both subject and experimenter to distinguish representational from metarepresentational discourse. While that research demonstrated the variety of human folly, it is equally important in highlighting the special nature of the true or valid solutions to the problems. The "correct" solution cannot simply be assumed but requires explanation. That solution, I argued, depends upon meaning, specifically, the *sense* of the terms and the logical relations among them. This allowed me to conclude that logic is less a means of thinking than a set of norms for how one *ought* to think. Here I followed Jaynes (1976, p. 41), who pointed out: "Logic is the science of the justification of conclusions we have reached by natural reasoning."

Thus the norms and standards of logic that Kahneman describes as System Two are the product of the particular orientation to language I described as metarepresentational. Ordinary thinking, on the other hand, is biased, as Kahneman showed, by seeking confirmation rather than disconfirmation, by being egocentric, by jumping to conclusions, ignoring conflicting evidence, making judgments on the basis of a single case rather than proper sampling, and the like.

Tetlock and Gardner (2014) examined the thinking habits of a large sample of adults and were able to distinguish those who made successful predictions of outcomes from those who were less successful. Successful predictors tended to base their predictions on the available data and they evaluated the data using logic and statistics. These, we may recall, are precisely the habits that the National Center for Educational Statistics (2010) found to be lacking in student writing, namely, the ability to relate claims to evidence and to express the logical relations between statements. Tetlock and Gardner also found, of particular interest to the argument presented here, that good predictors kept records both of evidence and of the success of their predictions.

But again, neither of these research programs makes a clear distinction between reasoning in ordinary language and reasoning about reasoning, the metalinguistic stance to language sponsored by literacy and education. Consequently, they are less theories of thinking than demonstrations of how thinking can go wrong while providing advice on how to avoid errors. My argument has been that reasoning about reasoning depends upon certain critical metalinguistic concepts that bring consciousness to language and are invoked largely by writing and the written tradition. So while all humans use words and give reasons, some exposure to literate discourse is essential to see reasons as "objects" that must meet a set of normative standards, including those of logic, if they are to be seen as valid.

THE EVOLUTION OF REASON AND RATIONALITY

It may be useful to set the account of reasoning and rationality in the more general pragmatic theory of language and mind elaborated to this point. The roles that language and consciousness of language play in the evolution of knowledge and rationality allow us to distinguish three general categories of epistemological development ranging from knowing in the absence of language, knowing through language, and knowing about language, the latter depending upon a consciousness of language first in reading and finally in reasoning.

Prereason: Knowing in the absence of language. As the Pragmatists insisted, all later developments in thinking and reasoning are built upon the practical and social activities of learners. As we have seen, this basic learning prior to learning a language is of two kinds. First, the practical actions shaped to satisfy desires may be described in terms of behavioral rules, the kind of instrumental learning shared with other animals. Even adult humans are heavily reliant on such learning. Jaynes (1976, p. 35) tells of an experiment in which members of a psychology class were asked to compliment any girl at the college wearing red. "Within a week the cafeteria was a blaze of red (and friendliness), and none of the girls was aware of being influenced." In addition there is learning how to participate in practices shared with others in the form of routines, rituals and games of pretense to which human infants are particularly disposed. Infants pay close attention to what others are doing, how they are doing it, what they are trying to do, what they are looking at, and they imitate those actions with some fidelity whether or not they are goal-directed.[1] Imitation, play and pretense are milestones in learning

[1] I observed a group of children playing a kind of wild game that involved a lot of noise and running and I asked one of them what they were doing. She replied that she had no idea, she was, she said, "just trying to get along." In the processes she presumably acquired the implicit rules of the game. This is the implicit social knowledge in practice that is made explicit in learning the rules whether of a game or of a language.

to talk and think (Bateson, 1972; Leslie, 1988), in that such social practices shape the implicit knowledge that is later made explicit in learning a language.

Reason: Knowing through language. To learn a language is to learn a set of procedures for representing in verbal form the knowledge implicit in pre-verbal social practices. Saying something implies that one believes it. Put another way, beliefs are the "sincerity conditions" for saying something. Making beliefs explicit as beliefs is to metarepresent them; an achievement described as acquiring a Theory of Mind, one of the achievements associated with the Axial Age.[2] Concepts of beliefs and desires allow one to provide reasons for those actions. Hence, to be a speaker of a language is to be a reasonable person, that is, one who can give and accept reasons as explanations and justifications for actions. This is the basic and universal form of reasoning, the ability to justify speech and actions by appeal to reasons.

Traditionally beliefs and reasons have been seen as the causes of action. However, actions themselves have multiple complex causes, not always known, that include both situational and internal factors. The extensive literature of biases in reasoning reviewed earlier showed a considerable disconnect between subjects' judgments and valid reasons. People's reasons are often excuses, their beliefs may be false, their reasons invalid, they ignore important information. They may be motivated by desires that they fail to acknowledge or even, as Freud pointed out, deny. Even actions initiated by a reason are attuned to the complexities of situations, not all the properties of which are known to the actor. The finding of Kahneman, Eagleman and others, combined with the earlier conditioning studies reviewed by Jaynes, support the view that it is necessary to distinguish reasons from the causes of action that may be multiple, situational and sometimes outside the reach of consciousness and influenced by desires unacknowledged by the actor.

[2] I initiated a research program that attempted to link the development of an explicit Theory of Mind to the acquisition of literacy. No direct link was established but I continue to harbor such a hunch.

If reasons are not causes, why are they relevant to thinking and acting? As mentioned, reasons are justifications for actions. Giving reasons presumes the acceptance of responsibility for one's actions. Just as language binds one into a speech community, so too the reasons offered must be drawn from those that the community would find acceptable. If an employee is asked "Why are you late?", it is unacceptable to offer as a reason "Because I was sleeping," even if that is the cause. The set of permissible reasons, then, is far more restricted than the multitude of situational considerations that influenced the action and is, at best, a selection of those most relevant and likely to be acceptable to those holding one responsible. Consequently, beliefs and reasons are not the on-line causes of actions so much as they are *about* actions.

Beliefs provide the stock of reasons for characterizing and justifying actions to oneself or to others. They are framed primarily in terms of the agent's beliefs, desires and intentions as these are likely to be understood even if not condoned by others. Actions themselves have multiple complex causes, not always known, that include both situational and internal factors. Reasons, on the other hand, are conscious and they explain and justify those actions. At the same time they cast the actor in the role of a responsible agent, one responsible to others and held accountable by others. Conscious mental life is contained in the language of belief and reason. The ability to express beliefs and provide reasons is presumably intrinsic to all languages, but some societies, those with a tradition of literacy and institutions for advancing that literacy, specialize in this kind of verbal knowledge. Giving reasons, for example, is encouraged in schooling where a persistent directive is "Give reasons for your answers."

Reasons are not, however, irrelevant to action. A conscious reason may set a conscious goal that selects and mobilizes the means, sometimes unconscious, the output of which is compared to the goal. I earlier used the example of attempting to whistle a tune. One has little consciousness of the motions of the mouth and tongue but full consciousness of the sounds produced. Jaynes (1976) provided an even more apposite metaphor for the relation between action and thought. It was the difference, he suggested, between actual driving and back-seat driving. The critical point is that beliefs and reasons are about actions, not their direct causes. But back-seat driving can often determine the action taken.

Making reasons explicit makes them available for others to react to and in this way to improve the reasons and indirectly to change behavior. The result is a body of knowledge acquired through living in a social world that is bought into consciousness through learning a language. Hence, learning a language is an incomparably important achievement or endowment. Once equipped with language, not only may one's actions meet with approval or disapproval but the reasons for those actions may be made public and subject to approval or disapproval. Reasons thus are a normative construal of action. The ability to give reasons is the criterion used to judge that one is a reasonable, that is, a *sapient* person.

REASONS ABOUT REASONS: KNOWING THROUGH A CONSCIOUSNESS OF LANGUAGE

A half-century of research on learning and thinking from Mary Henle (1969) to Kahneman (2011) has demonstrated that actors are not always aware of the internal and situational factors affecting them and that reasoning is affected by biases unacknowledged by subjects. If reasons are not the causes of actions and decisions, it is not surprising that the reasoning even of adults often does not conform to the canons of logic. Reason, as Hume (1739/1978) long ago pointed out, is the slave of the passions, not of truth. What is surprising and unexplained is how reasons ever come to be the causes of action. Why do subjects accept the answers given by logic as preferable to those they a moment earlier had defended? The bigger question, then, is what is the nature of logical reasoning that earns it that special status?

What is lacking in an account of reasoning is a theory explaining why we accept some conclusions as valid. One plausible answer is that just as learning a language involves learning the standards for correct usage, so too the giving of reasons involves learning the standards for acceptable reasons, that is, reasons that stand up to criticism. Even the reasons in ordinary pragmatic discourse meet a certain normative standard in that the reasons may be accepted or rejected by one's community. While every culture has standards for acceptable reasons, those for a modern literate society are distinctive in that they shift the grounds of acceptability from more pragmatic norms to those based on a heightened consciousness of the properties of language, in particular the appeal to the strict definitions of words, the logical relations of sentences and new standards of evidence. Reasoning about reasons on the basis of their linguistic form constitutes a formal rationality.

The relation between the rules of logic and the processes of reasoning simply duplicates the relation between reasons and actions, the relation I described as *use–mention*. Reasons are not the cause of actions nor are the rules of logic the processes of thinking but rather the rules and norms for how one *ought* to think. They provide a standard against which any reasoning may be subjected. Only those who have undergone a rather extensive literary training, including learning to write, have explicit knowledge of these rules and standards.

As we saw, what subjects are actually doing in solving problems has been described by Oatley (2013) and Johnson-Laird (2006) as constructing a mental model of the problem that honors the parameters of the problem while providing concrete situational detail, not unlike that in play in ordinary contextual situations. The answer to the problem and the reasons for holding it are then derived from the mental model. To serve as reasons they must fall within what the community would be willing to accept. Only in more literate contexts would these standards be explicitly linked to linguistic form and monitored. Thus again, how we think is different from the norms for how we ought to think.

Why "ought" we to think that way? Where do these rules come from? Whose rules are they? Clearly those rules serve a social function in advancing knowledge in a modern society. They arise from careful attention to the particular properties implicit in ordinary language use. Definition, as we saw, develops from the metalinguistic operation of setting aside reference while attending to the *sense* of a term. A suitable definition permits valid inference: if it is a horse, it is a quadruped. Statements constructed from well-defined terms imply other statements. Those in turn may be metarepresented as inference, assumptions and the like, the concepts for critical discourse that allow one to see what was, in a sense, already there.

That the normative standards are derived from the implicit properties of spoken language gives some credence to the hypothesis that definition and logic are innate rather than mere social conventions. They are innate in so far as they are already there, implicitly, in an evolved oral language, but they are made explicit and conventional in a particular literate culture.

Persons who make errors on reasoning tasks and on "test questions" are sometimes unfairly judged to be irrational. Real questions are to be interpreted contextually, honoring the Gricean conversational conventions. "Test questions," on the other hand, are "laboratory objects" composed of decontextualized statements that are to be treated metarepresentationally in terms of strict definitions of terms and the canons of logic. In practical reasoning contexts, one cannot assume *ceteris paribus*, that of all things being equal. Reasoning under laboratory conditions assumes *ceteris paribus* and consequently the laws derived, like those of Galileo's for falling objects, hold "only in a vacuum." That, of course, does not mean that such laboratory studies are irrelevant; they help to expose some of the properties involved in making and justifying decisions, the processes and competencies useful in a modern bureaucratic society and that are of urgent concern to the literacy programs of the school.

Here was one of the more important *aperçus* of this inquiry, namely, that one of the more important uses of language, language for reasoning about reasons, like thinking about language, depends upon shifting to a metarepresentational key. Recognizing them as metarepresentational confers two advantages. First, it allows us to clearly distinguish ordinary pragmatic from formal reasoning just as the Two System theory claimed. But in addition it shows the link between them, namely, that formal reasoning depends on making explicit the implicit features of language called on in ordinary, System One thinking. Rather than two discrete systems, one has only a natural language that on occasion may be made explicit as an object of thought. The shift from representation to metarepresentation, while not unique to literacy, is sponsored primarily by literacy. Definitions and logical relations are not only acquired, they are taught and monitored by the community and its institutions and, when successful, they come to alter not only one's writing but also one's speaking habits. Finally, the metarepresentational key introduces an "ought" to thinking, thereby linking rationality to morality.

THE PEDAGOGY OF RATIONALITY

Ordinary thinking is tied up with using language to talk and think about the world and to justify one's beliefs and actions by appeal to reasons. Even children and the uneducated are capable of giving reasons and rejecting ones they don't agree with. Rational thinking, narrowly defined, is thinking about the language used in that thinking. Writing is instrumental in two ways. First, fixing a word or expression in writing makes it available for commentary in a way that oral discourse lacks. As we saw, children in the early school years increasingly justify the answers they give by appeal to the wording of the question. In answering questions about a written text they increasingly turn to written sources. I illustrated the processes involved by reference to early and middle school children's answer to the question "Did the story say that the waves broke the sand castle?" In fact, this is implied by the story and younger children claim that it did. Only after a few years of schooling do they admit that the story had not said so but they had figured it out. Metarepresentational judgments are distinguished by the appeal to the wording of the texts.

But writing is instrumental to thinking in an indirect way, namely, that the concepts for thinking about language are a legacy of writing and the written tradition. Learning a critical language is in a way analogous to learning classical Latin when Latin was the scholarly language of the West. One is introduced to this critical language in part through learning to write Classical prose. The norms for prose are just those essential for formal thinking.

But the concepts useful for thinking critically are not confined to writing and reading. The concepts acquired work their way into oral discourse. Furthermore, reading and writing are surrounded by a penumbra of oral discourse about wording and meaning. Picking out a topic sentence and justifying the choice is part of the oral discourse involved in teaching students to reflect on the language they use in writing.

The pedagogy for rationality is in large part the pedagogy of learning to write Classical prose. The major difficulties in learning to writing Classical prose were just those that the NCES assessments of US 12th-graders found to distinguish successful from unsuccessful writers, namely, the ability to link claims to evidence and the ability to evaluate arguments. Kuhn (2015) reported that skill in oral argumentation is closely related to that of argumentation in writing. In both cases students had difficulties in linking claims to evidence, in evaluating the validity of arguments and in relating arguments to each other. Instead of relating arguments logically by "because" or "it follows," they tended to offer what came to mind by such connectives as "here's another thing." Whereas in oral argumentation about assigned topics students tended to draw on their own experience, in writing essays they drew on shared, documented information. Metacognitive talk is an important aspect of successful pedagogy.

The features of particular importance to this more formal rationality are precise word meanings and precise logical relations, properties I tied to concepts of *words* and *sentences*. The ability to define, as opposed to recognize, words is taken as indicative of advanced levels of intelligence, and the ability to judge a conclusion as invalid is taken as indicative of advanced rationality.

Human rationality was slow to evolve, we may conclude, not because the human brain evolves at a glacial pace but because it depends on the invention, accumulation, teaching and sharing of concepts: first, concepts about the world, and second, sponsored in part by literacy and a literate tradition, concepts about language. These are monumental achievements the implications of which we are only beginning to understand.

DOES A LITERATE RATIONALITY CONSTITUTE A UNIVERSAL STANDARD FOR RATIONALITY?

If, as I have argued, rationality is a product of a special and peculiar metalinguistic understanding of language and mind, one may ask if such rationality provides a universal standard or if it is merely one among many equally useful ways of thinking, one among many "voices of the mind." President Xi of China was recently reported to have claimed that a universal order does not exist. Shaun Breslin, a British scholar and a China expert, has also claimed that the values articulated by the United Nations "are not universal at all, but merely the product of a small number of Western countries' histories, philosophies and developmental trajectories" (*Globe and Mail*, October 3, 2015). This is a view championed by Foucault (1970) with his claim that truths are always expressions of interest.

Certainly the belief in the universality of reason has yielded pride of place to pluralism and with it an assault on the authority of institutions, including scientific and educational ones. Yet it may be possible to justify universal standards for judgments (Heath, 2014). A natural language is the universal possession of the human species. The literate practices I have described, including the definitions of terms and the logical relations among statements, make explicit only what was already implicit in ordinary language. It seems possible that the metalanguage evolved for the clarification and evaluation of meanings and the evaluation of reasons is at least universalizable. If so, language and cultural differences do not rule out the possibility of shared explicit rules and norms for rational discourse in a pluralist society. This, of course, was the aspiration of the Enlightenment.

Many marvel at the uniqueness of literacy and the importance of reading and writing to the development of the mind. Enthusiasm for education is unbounded. Levi-Strauss denied that there was any justification for this enthusiasm. There was, he claimed, no reason for granting such importance to writing. He made that claim, I suggest, because he had no theory of what writing was, of how writing contributed to an altered metarepresentational orientation to language, or of how such an orientation shapes how one thinks. By showing how reading and writing function as intellectual resources, we may have provided such a theory and hence such a reason. Summarizing that theory is the task of the final chapter.

PART V Conclusions

13 Reading, Consciousness and Rationality

> *"If it hadn't been for Miss Clara I might never have known. My whole life might have been wasted. She talked to me. I began to read. It was like being born a second time."* (Jake Blount, a character in McCullers, *The Heart Is a Lonely Hunter*, pp. 127–128)

We have completed our tour of the concepts and consciousness brought into prominence by writing. These concepts are metarepresentational in that they are less about the world than about our ways of representing that world. The concepts of primary concern are those pertaining to *words* and *sentences* as these are the loci for definition and for logic, with their distinctive contributions to reading and rationality. And the result is a theory that is less about writing as a tool or aid for thinking than about what reading and writing does for our speech and hence for our thought. If you missed it, it makes us conscious of some aspects of the language we speak.

The classical scholars who first claimed a causal link between literacy and consciousness, Havelock, Ong, Goody and McLuhan, based their claims on the changes they detected in the forms of discourse – a concern with defining terms and framing arguments in terms of the explicit logical relations that make up written prose – that occurred first in classical Greece and were revived in the West in the late Middle Ages. But the explanatory mechanisms they offered, such as "interiorizing the word," "restructuring consciousness," "eye for ear," "tool use" and the like, while promising, are too vague to serve any serious purpose in the science of mind. Harris (2009) criticized Ong's claim that "reading brings consciousness" by asking "Conscious of what?" Harris's answer, like Vygotsky's, was that

"Writing brings awareness to speech" (p. 183). But, what aspects of speech? Modern Vygotskians such as Wertsch and Roberts attribute this awareness to "the decontextualization of mediational means," but fail to trace the implications of such awareness. Which aspects of language are brought to awareness and just how writing contributes to that awareness are questions that remain unanswered.

To address these questions I offered a linguistic theory of concepts as metarepresentational devices that create new objects, such as words, to which new properties, such as *long word*, *synonym* and the like, could be applied. If, as claimed, these properties already exist in spoken language, why is writing the instrument for making them explicit? Why not just talk about properties of speech? In fact, modern linguists, employing rigorous scientific methods, do just that. However, the concepts of language that entered ordinary discourse with writing were those that the inventors of writing had found useful in devising a usable script, principally signs for sounds, words and sentences and later for discourse markers including paragraphs and quotations. In learning to read one acquires just these concepts, thereby turning these structures into objects of consciousness.

Metarepresentational concepts rely on the *use–mention* distinction, lifting a word or sentence from its normal use and turning it into an object of thought. As such they are subject to a new set of norms or rules for their use. These normative standards may be monitored for correctness by parents and educators, including that dreaded pedagogue Gradgrind. As these concepts are identified with consciousness, we may both honor the classical view that concepts are tied to language and offer a theory of literate concepts that falls within the boundaries of the cognitive sciences. Thus, in this book I aspired to create a space for writing in the cognitive sciences more or less along Vygotskian lines.

A natural language makes thought possible; it is what divides *sentient* beings, a consciousness we share with other animals, from *sapient*, thinking beings. Furthermore, a language introduces one to a consciousness of the world shared with others. The content of language, the grammar of the language and the very fact that it is shared with others all combine to bring this special linguistic consciousness of the world. But the central claim of this book is that reading and writing have an unanticipated and largely unrecognized consequence, namely, that of turning language itself into an object of thought. Mastering the concepts expressed in a metalanguage lies at the core both of learning to read and write and of a distinctive form of rationality.

To understand the implications of writing it was necessary to set aside common prejudices about language. It requires an extended effort for literate readers to acknowledge that the words and sentences they analyze are neither "given" in nature nor available to untutored introspection. Access to them requires the relevant concepts. Our shared literacy bequeaths categories such as *word* and *sentence* that, once learned, make it difficult to imagine a world without words, sentences or, for that matter, logical arguments. The first step, then, in creating a theory about writing and mind is to set such assumptions aside and ask afresh about the origins of such concepts and to recognize that they are not given by nature but are historical inventions rediscovered by every child in learning to read and write.

CONSCIOUSNESS OF LANGUAGE

Although learning a language creates a shared consciousness of the world, a new level of consciousness is achieved through the development of a metalanguage for talking and thinking about language. When thinking is recognized as a linguistic process, the position we discussed in terms of the "linguistic turn" of the New Pragmatists, it becomes clear that the way to advance thinking is through adding a new tier of concepts to the language. Whereas ordinary language allows one to think about the world, the literate metalanguage allows one to think about, that is, to be conscious of, aspects of language that previously were implicit and unconscious in quotidian talk and thought.

Both historical and developmental evidence were presented to show that conscious knowledge *about* certain aspects of the structure of language, in particular *phonemes, words, sentences* and extended logical *prose,* is either non-existent or seriously limited in non-reading and pre-reading individuals and that the invention of, access to and guided practice in writing was instrumental in creating those concepts. Learning to read and write and an extended literate education are essential for the development of this literate consciousness.

To make such claims it was necessary to narrow the concept of *consciousness* to that of making explicit, that is, saying something about something, in this case to say, or at least to be able to say, something about the implicit or unconscious processes involved in ordinary language use. Further, it was necessary to limit the concept of *thinking* to the ability to give reasons and, later, to say something about those reasons. To be conscious of the world is to be able to say something about the world; to be conscious of a *word* is to be able to say something about a word, such as its length, its meaning or its relation to other words. To be conscious of a sentence is to be able to say something about a sentence, such as its truth, its meaning or its logical relation to another sentence. To say something about language is to metarepresent it, to turn it from an object *used* into an object *mentioned,* as if putting it in quotation marks. The acquisition of this metalanguage is important both for learning to read and write and for the development of critical, rational thought. Learning to read and write Classical prose, for example, is an avenue to thinking critically. The art of written discourse becomes an art of thinking (Appleby & Langer, 1987; Oatley, 1996; Oatley & Djikic, 2008).

MAKING KNOWLEDGE ABOUT LANGUAGE EXPLICIT

Speakers of a language have knowledge *of* language but limited knowledge *about* language. So what knowledge is implicit and how does writing make aspects of that language explicit? Linguists including Saussure, Chomsky and Jackendoff point out that the generative structures of language are essentially unconscious. Speakers have no knowledge of how they achieve subject–verb agreement or how they assign suffixes such as "ly" or "ness" to a basic morpheme such as *happy* to turn it into an adverb or a noun. The central argument of this book is, first, that speakers are similarly unaware of the fact that the sounds they produce are composed of a small inventory of phonemes, that utterances they produce are composed of isolatable words and that discourse is composed of logically connected sentences. The second part of the argument is that people acquire knowledge *about* sounds, words, sentences and prose in the context of learning to read and write. Of course, this is not to deny similar knowledge or competence to speakers of an oral language, but only to insist that such knowledge is implicit and largely unconscious. Learning to read and write provides the concepts for bringing language into consciousness. So how does writing bring consciousness to these implicit properties of language?

The translation of language from a time-based temporal structure to a spatial one is the occasion for the discovery and consequently the awareness of certain implicit or underlying features of language. For the inventors of writing systems the problem was to discover properties of speech that could be represented by a limited inventory of visual signs sufficient to convey a meaning. Writing systems are composed of visual patterns arrayed in space to represent sound patterns in the acoustic domain, thus allowing a reader to go back and forth between sounds and signs; to write what was said and to read aloud what was written. The primary obstacle to that translation was the challenge of discovering properties of the spoken utterance that could be represented by visual signs. The concepts mediating them, the concept of word, for example, provide a link between the written sign and a detectable feature of the spoken. Similarly the concept of sentence mediates the relation between components of unsegmented speech and the space inserted between written sentences. The concepts linking the written and the spoken make the previously implicit properties of speech explicit, something to talk about. Such concepts are about language and hence metalinguistic.

Literacy, learning to read and write, is primarily a matter of making the implicit explicit. Making explicit by means of concepts is what makes learning to read a cognitive task; the learner has to discover and grasp the relation between objects in the visual domain and those in the acoustic domain. This involves mastering a set of metarepresentational concepts, some of which come into view only with an extended education. Fluent reading, on the other hand, leaves such metarepresentational knowledge in the background to allow one to focus on the stories told and the meanings conveyed. The metalanguage then serves mainly as a basis for correcting errors.

Metalinguistic concepts create new objects on which one can comment. Once one has the concept *word*, that is, once a word is recognized as a word, it may be compared to other words in terms of physical feature such as length, or semantic features underlying judgments of *synonym*, *antonym* or *hyponym* and the formation of definitions. This involves a shift from the reference of a word, the object in the world that the term refers to in a particular context, to the *sense* of a word, its relation to other words. This is, of course, just the development we saw in children in response to word association tests and in judging synonymy and in giving definitions. And this is why on IQ tests, in answer to the question "How are apples and oranges alike?", the response "They are both round" is given a lower score than the answer "They are both fruit"; the former compares objects, the latter, the word meanings.

THE METALANGUAGE

A metalanguage is simply a language for talking *about* language. There are several metalanguages; grammarians talk of nouns and verbs, logicians of subjects and predicates, discourse theorists talk about genres, literary theorists about poetry and prose. Each of these metalanguages was invented for thinking about properties and uses of language. All metalanguages involve a use–mention distinction; metalanguages lift a structure from its place in normal discourse to make it an object of thought, something that one may say something about. The metalanguage of primary concern here is that derived primarily from writing rather than from speaking. One is introduced to the concept of *word* in learning to read, but the metalanguage is elaborated as one learns to talk about larger structures of language such as sentences and prose. Thus, metalinguistic concepts are important both to reading and rationality. Because these concepts are verbal concepts, they may be applied equally to speaking and to writing.

Equipped with the concept of a *word* one may be led to make the Fregean distinction between meaning as *sense* and meaning as *reference*. It was only by excluding reference that Frege was able to advance the most general laws of language as well as the laws of thought, including those of logical inference and formal definition of terms. The part of meaning that remains after excluding reference, Frege's *sense*, is implicit in speech but may become explicit through the metalanguage for talking about the meanings of words and sentences. What a word means may be contrasted with what one means by a word in the context of an utterance. Without knowing anything about Frege, school children are led into an awareness of Fregean *senses* when they learn to define words and determine the strict implications of sentences. The use–meaning distinction, the language–metalanguage distinction, the reference–sense distinction (and my own earlier say–mean distinction) are largely equivalent ways of explaining why literacy helps to shift one's thinking from thinking about the world to thinking about language.

A metalanguage is not the exclusive possession of the highly literate. All languages contain a metalanguage for talking about some aspects of language. Thus, as Feldman (1991) and others have shown, concepts referring to speech acts such as *ask*, *say*, *tell*, *promise* and mental states such as *to think*, *wonder*, and *know* are more or less universal. But those universal concepts are primarily about reference, not sense. Discourse on *sense* arises only when it is possible to distinguish *sense* from *reference*, "sentence meaning" from "speaker's meaning" and meaning as *mentioned* from meaning as *used*. It is only this latter that allows one to reason about synonymy and the inferential relations among words and sentences. Definition of terms, the strict meaning of logical connectives and the rules of inference are enabled by learning a metalanguage that makes the underlying unconscious structure of word and sentence meaning explicit. The implicit becomes the explicit through a metalanguage, and literacy is instrumental in creating and learning this metalanguage.

The distinction between the meaning in the language, that is, the "semantic meaning" or *sense*, and the intended meaning in the speaker's mind and communicated through language is not routinely made. Although Frege is usually credited with this distinction, Vygotsky, too, urged us in this direction. Katz and Fodor (1963), in their early theory of semantics, confined their account of meaning to definitional relations among terms such as "Bachelor is an unmarried male" as well as relations of synonymy and antonymy, that is, to properties of Fregean *sense*. But psychologists then and now remain unconvinced, insisting on a more inclusive concept of meaning that would include referential knowledge, knowledge about the world. For most ordinary discourse they are right to do so. But to fail to recognize the distinction bars one from an explanation of the implications of literacy. Thus, psychologists tended to insist that the meaning of "horse" must include something of what one knew about horses, the view I attributed to Dickens's Sissy Jupe. The metarepresentational view allows us to acknowledge that Sissy knows how to use words but not how to think about words. Although most of the time one thinks of typical horses, it is sometimes important to think of the meaning of the word "horse" and attempt to make a more formal definition such that necessary implications follow from it. Children are taught to do this in science class. Asked how many legs a bee has, schooled children may reply: "A bee is an insect. Insects have six legs, so a bee has six." Similarly, that is why "All elephants have trunks" is seen as a necessary truth, as part of the definition of the word "elephant," even if perhaps in nature there may be one that does not.

Attention to *sense* distinguishes ordinary language competence from literate language competence, namely, the ability to think about words and sentences apart from their normal contextual uses. All speakers of a language have acquired the ability to use the conventional, socially shared meanings of terms, but the linguistic knowledge remains implicit and unconscious, dominated by reference, what one is talking about. The *sense* of the expression, its semantic structure, contains no reference objects but only relations to other items in the linguistic code. This point is easy to grasp in regard to the underlying structure of phonological knowledge in that it consists of structured alternatives, unknown to the speaker, such as voiced–unvoiced and place of articulation. But the same is true of unconscious semantic knowledge in that it consists of structured alternatives in a semantic space. The concept of *wolf*, for example, is a location in a semantic space organized in terms of such dimensions as size, ferocity, friendliness, domesticated, carnivorous, as well as in terms of superordinate and subordinate relations (Abrahamsen, 1977). But all of this is implicit in the linguistic semantic system, while what one is conscious of is the animal referred to. What writing allows and invites is talk about these implicit properties, sorting them out and thus giving rise to definition and judgments of synonymy and of valid inference.[1]

It is, therefore, somewhat misleading to think of semantic knowledge in terms of a mental dictionary. A dictionary is an artifact that makes explicit what was implicit in semantic knowledge. Because semantic structure is implicit, when asked about the meaning of terms naive subjects talk about the object referred to, as Jung discovered to his disappointment with his word association test. When children offer a typical instance for the semantic meaning of a term, for example, that bird means robin, they are also providing a reference not a meaning. This is not surprising in that semantic

[1] Philosophical talk about "rigid designators" is a curious attempt to discover in the language the very features that literate thinkers have buried there through definition and then unearthed through reflection.

meaning is largely unconscious and brought into awareness through a literate metalanguage. Talking about words and their meanings is a practice monopolized by the school and by highly literate parents. On the other hand, it is the availability of implicit knowledge that makes the acquisition of explicit knowledge possible.

TRANSPARENCY: WHAT IS UNCONSCIOUS KNOWLEDGE OF LANGUAGE?

Although Saussure is credited with the claim that linguistic knowledge is unconscious, that claim was seconded by Vygotsky who added that writing turns language into an object of thought, with the implications I have pursued in this book. The claim that language is transparent to its users needs to be qualified in that pre-literate children and non-educated adults can and do comment on language, primarily but not exclusively on its reference, that is, what the discourse was about. But in addition they imitate speech, remember simple expressions, comment on anomalies such as mispronunciations, miswordings and the like, all of which indicate that language is not completely transparent, at least to some children. But which children? And in what context? S. B. Heath (1983) showed that language awareness was less a stage of development than an indication of the literacy practices of the families that the children grew up in. Hence, one can claim only that speech is normally used for social purposes and that ordinarily the properties and structures used in speaking are transparent to the messages conveyed. And further, that special means are required to divert attention from the message conveyed to the linguistic forms employed. The result is a pervasive shift as learners become readers and engage in the discourse about written language, a shift in consciousness from thinking about things in the world to thinking about the language used to describe the world. This double consciousness is a defining feature of literate consciousness.

So, what knowledge is unconscious? Unconscious cognitive processes are often described as instincts, behavioral habits, emotional states or brain processes. For language-based processes, on the other hand, the account is more specific in that the unconscious linguistic processes are described as structural, that is, underlying properties and rules that can be inferred from overt speech practices. Those features, including the semantic and grammatical features of the language, are what are described as unconscious. However, the only evidence for those underlying structures is the fact that explicit representations of them can be advanced and defended. To be specific, the primary evidence that a sentence is composed of *words*, or that the implicit meaning of a term is its *sense*, or that a paragraph has a *topic sentence* as part of its implicit or unconscious structure, is that the concepts of *word*, *sense* and *topic sentence* can be advanced, defined, taught and monitored as a normative standard by an expert community of readers and writers.

The availability of implicit or unconscious knowledge, what we may call intuition, namely the knowledge made explicit by concepts, also helps to explain how such concepts are ever learned. Here I departed somewhat from Vygotsky's concept of scientific concepts. Vygotsky seems to have thought that scientific concepts are simply taught and learned as a social practice and then work their way back into the consciousness of individual speakers. Social constructivists go further, suggesting that concepts are social inventions that become psychological only by internalization of the culture. The metarepresentational view, on the other hand, implies that any concept learned makes explicit some pattern or structure that was already in place in some form in the unconscious knowledge of the learner. Learning, on this view, is discovering something that was previously unacknowledged in practice and that the metarepresentational concept makes explicit. Thus in regard to the topic sentence, writers learn the concept only when they recognize in their speech practices something that has been organizing their discourse all along, namely, what they were talking about, even if they did not recognize it as a *topic*. The same is true for the concept of *word* and the *sense* of a word. The concept is not invented out of the blue; there is something in linguistic practice that the concept makes explicit.

Acknowledging the existence of implicit knowledge would go some distance to fill the gap in Vygotsky's account of how social practices become mental ones. Vygotsky had claimed that concepts appear on two planes, first in social interaction with others, later for use by a person him- or herself. The route from society to mind is sometimes described as internalization or "appropriation." Thus Wertsch (1991) suggests that language is a kind of mental meeting ground between novices and experts when he writes that any word in a language is "half someone else's" (p. 59). Admittedly, words exist only in a particular language, but the concepts they express only make explicit what was implicit in the learner's intuitions that have been shaped through participation in social practices. Concepts are socially validated as norms – it is other speakers who determine if a word is used correctly – but concepts are acquired only by individuals when they take up words and concepts to make explicit something they themselves already sensed or intuited implicitly as part of a social practice. Otherwise the concepts in question are merely verbal.

Vygotsky argued that the most important concept for talking about language was the concept of *word*. A word is one of the properties of speech that comes into awareness through writing a word-based script: "Writing brings awareness to speech," making words "abstract, voluntary and conscious" (1986, p. 183). This awareness does not develop all at once: "The word to the child is an integral part of the object it denotes," a view, he suggests, that is also found in "primitive linguistic consciousness" (p. 222). Children fail, he claimed, to distinguish meaning from reference. As we saw earlier, Fodor pointed out that if this were true they should not be able to understand a sentence such as "Daddy is a baker" because "daddy" and "the baker" have different meanings but the same reference. As I noted, if we restate the claim about transparency in terms of consciousness, Vygotsky's more general claim may be preserved. When agreeing that "Daddy is a baker," children's attention falls on the person designated while the means of designating that person, the *sense* of the expression, remains largely out of awareness. But not wholly. If asked "What did he say?" they may recall it, as Harris (2000) and Hedelin and Hjelmquist (1988) discovered, but after a delay, as with adults, the wording is soon forgotten while the reference or content of the expression remains. What remains out of awareness is not the wording but the *sense* of the word that would allow one to distinguish what was stated from what was merely implied. It is the semantic meaning of an expression that remains transparent, whereas the events referred to are conscious, something one can talk about. An important part of literacy development is to turn the *sense* of the expression into something to talk about. The *sense* of a term, recall, is what one attempts to capture in a definition.

If it can be granted that not only phonology but also syntax and semantic structures are largely unconscious or implicit knowledge embedded in the social practice of speaking, we can proceed to review how writing brings those implicit structures into consciousness. To bring something into consciousness is to be able to say something about it. So learning that the letter "t" says /t/ may be instrumental in bringing a phoneme into consciousness, as may the discovery that "cat" rhymes with "rat." The invention of visual/spatial features of the writing system, letters, word boundaries, punctuation and capitalization are devices useful for representing speech in such a way that a reader can recover what was said orally. Learning to recognize the visual signs as signs for aspects of speech brings those properties of speech into consciousness. Children actually learn to hear the distinctive phonemes in a word and thus pass tests of phonological awareness and to spell new words in the process of learning to read.

THE PSYCHOLOGY AND PEDAGOGY OF READING

In our earlier discussion of the so-called reading wars, a contrast was drawn between two perspectives, one that emphasized the implicit and automatic cognitive functions carried out unconsciously by the brain, and a second perspective that emphasized the conscious, deliberate actions and judgments of the learner. I advanced the notion of *metarepresentation* to explain how linguistic knowledge implicit in speech was made explicit in learning to read. For both listening and fluent reading the linguistic processes involved in assigning a meaning to an expression occur largely out of awareness; one is conscious of the story told. Metalinguistic concepts make some of those implicit processes explicit, something to think about and comment on. The concept *word* is one such concept; it picks out a piece of speech, turning it into an object of thought and discourse. But the same concept picks out a piece of print as a word. It is the metalinguistic concept that both discloses and unites the visual and the auditory as a comprehensible word. Grasping the relation expressed by the metalinguistic concept is essential to reading in that it defines the task. However, that metalinguistic understanding is *about* reading rather than an account of the processes of reading. Readers learn to integrate various sources of information to arrive at an understanding but those processes are largely implicit and unconscious in practice. Recall the analogy of learning to whistle; one recognizes the tune but has little awareness of how one achieved it. So too in fluent reading, attention falls on the story not on the means being employed in arriving at its meaning.

Recognizing the role of metarepresentation may help to resolve some of the traditional arguments about learning to read. Theories that emphasize Basic Skills treat reading as if reading were the application of explicit knowledge about language. Theories that emphasize meaning and understanding see reading as resting on implicit processes much like those involved in listening. What is missing from both is an account of the relation between the knowledge implicit in the social practices of talking and reading and the knowledge made explicit by metarepresentational concepts such as *letter* or *word*. These metarepresentations are essential for talking about reading, including explaining to learners what reading is and whether it is done correctly or incorrectly. It provides the conceptual base for reading. But reading and talking about reading are not the same thing. In actual fluent reading the metarepresentational slips to the background.

Thus, metarepresentational concepts including *letters* and *words* appear to function in two ways: first, to grasp what the reading task is, that is, to find a relation between oral speech and written signs, something that the learner must grasp; and second, to create a language about reading, shared by teacher and learner about what is being read and about how to do it correctly. I have argued that grasping the relation between visual sign and spoken word depends upon the invention of a concept. Nonetheless there are practices that make grasping the critical concepts more or less easy, among them, reading to children and playing with words. One appeals to the metarepresentational concepts themselves only when that the process is taken off-line for analysis and commentary: "What does that say?", "That says 'bed' not 'bad'" and so on. Indeed, much of this metalinguistic vocabulary is acquired by pre-reading children who live in a more literate environment. But it would be a mistake to assume that everyone knows such concepts.

The concept of metarepresentation was used both to explain what is critically involved in reading and to resolve one of the enduring perplexities of reading, namely, the role of linguistic awareness in learning to read. That such awareness is acquired in learning to read is well established and uncontroversial. Whereas in learning to speak underlying linguistic processes may remain implicit, in learning to read some of these underlying processes are brought into consciousness. Yet it is important to distinguish the practice of fluent reading from the metalinguistic discourse about reading. Advocates of Basic Skills regard knowledge of phonemes and words as a precondition for reading (Carroll, Snowling, Stevenson & Hulme, 2003), while others such as Valtin (2014) regard it as a consequence of reading. The argument advanced herein is that it is neither and both. Basic Skills, I have argued, are metalinguistic skills. They are means for talking about reading, not actual reading. Doing it and talking about it are two quite different things.

To learn to read is a skill or competence based on a conceptual understanding of the relation between visual signs and the structures of oral language. The concepts critical to learning to read allow learners to see, to become conscious of, what was already there (but implicit and previously unnoticed). This applies as well to the metalinguistic concept of *word* that creates a relation between a previously undistinguished visual sign and a previously undistinguished linguistic segment. It is the concept that allows the learner to see something and to hear something that was there all along. When they grasp this relation, they can understand what the reading task is. Non-readers literally cannot see or hear the structures that are there until they learn the concept that makes them explicit thereby bringing them into consciousness. Grasping this relation is the basis of learning to read.

On the other hand, metalinguistic concepts are *about* reading and bear only an indirect relation to the actual processes involved in reading, many of which remain out of awareness. Metalinguistic rules are rules for judgments of correctness and play a role in reading analogous to the role that logic plays in thinking. Metalinguistic concepts take something that is otherwise implicit in practice and make it subject to standards for judgments of correctness, of things one *ought* to do. This is what we are teaching children when we teach them to read.

Once metalinguistic concepts are recognized as being about reading rather than an account of the actual processes involved in reading comprehension, it becomes clear that the core competencies that make up Basic Skills are not those of the actual practice of reading but rather of those competencies taken off-line, what I earlier called "laboratory objects." Basic Skills are metarepresentational skills useful for examining underlying processes and for the diagnosis of difficulties, but function largely unconsciously and implicitly in the actual practice of fluent reading in which, for example, context and expectations become primary. The Basic Skills emphasis is misleading when those skills rather than the comprehension and production of written texts become the basis for judgments about reading competence.

The distinction between the language and metalanguage is overlooked by reading theorists, resulting in the misunderstandings at play in the reading "wars." Authors of the report of the National Reading Panel, like the inventors of the Common Core Curriculum, assume that reading competence is a matter of the metalinguistic knowledge taught and assessed as Basic Skills, ignoring the fact that Basic Skills are skills with language taken off-line. Their critics, such as Smith and Krashen, assume that reading competence, like speaking competence, is the ability to *use* language to arrive at a comprehensible meaning. Thus whereas the former treats language off-line, as *mentioned*, the latter treats language as *used* in context. The point, purpose, motivation and goal of reading is first and foremost to *use* language to construct a meaning. But the means involved in arriving at that meaning include just those explicated as Basic Skills and discovered by researchers in studying reading off-line. Thus both have a place once they are distinguished in terms of *use* and *mention*. Words *used* tend to be thought of in terms of their reference, words *mentioned* in terms of their semantic properties.

Theories of reading differ as well in their conception of the reader. Those who emphasize the unconscious implicit processes relegate agency not to the reader but to his or her brain. Educators, on the other hand, insist on the agency and autonomy of the learner and adjust their pedagogies accordingly. The goals and responsibilities of the learner play little role in the report of the National Reading Panel and the Common Core Curriculum based on that report. Agency and intentionality are presumed rather than addressed. Recognizing learners as agents who are responsible for not only their actions but also for their learning is important not only to learning to read but also to longer-term autonomy and self-control.

So there need be no great debate about reading and no balanced compromises. Rather there is a concept of a learner as an agent, a set of metalinguistic concepts shared by teacher and learner for talking about reading and misreading and that help to define what the reading task is, and there is a developing practical competence, features of which are discovered by reading researchers, that is acquired through teaching and through wide reading. The metalanguage shared by teacher and learner is critical for setting worthwhile goals, helping learners assemble the means for achieving them, detecting and eliminating confusions and providing assessments. All the while teachers must acknowledge that it is the learners who are learning and that their greatest satisfaction comes from achieving their goals.

THE LANGUAGES OF THINKING

A belief is just the "sincerity condition" for an assertion, the subjective side of an objective expression. The counterintuitive claim of the New Pragmatists is that the underlying thought, the sincerity condition, does not pre-exist the sentence; the sentence is not merely an expression of thought but the instrument of thought. Language competence is, as Chomsky insisted, generative. Furthermore, language allows predication (Bogdan, 2009), saying something about something. Anything that can be put into this linguistic frame is a thought. Consequently talking about beliefs and other mental states and activities is largely equivalent to talking about language. To talk about language requires a metalanguage; a language for talking about language is therefore a language for thinking about thinking. And an important part of that metalanguage derives from writing and the written tradition.

Concepts are expressible by words. But words only make conscious something already present implicitly as an intuition. This implicit knowledge serves as the meaning of a concept. But that implicit meaning may turn into a quasi-linguistic concept before one finds or learns the correct word for expressing it. Thus there is a fuzzy boundary between having a feeling of knowing, having a concept and knowing a word for expressing a concept. Peskin and Astington (2004) found that children on the margin of acquiring a theory of mind could attribute beliefs and intentions to actors in a story whether or not the explicit mental verb occurred in the story. Hence, in some cases, the concept appears to precede the word and may affect the learner's judgments. The metalinguistic term may be required to comment on the mental state, for example to judge it as true or false, but the understanding of those mental states seemed to precede the learning of a word. A similar reservation may be required to explain the role of the concept of *word* in learning to read. Some children may form an implicit understanding of the relation between visual signs and verbal forms even if they have not yet learned the metalinguistic concept for making that understanding explicit. The metalinguistic term is for talking about, making explicit, something implicit in practice.

Whereas learning a public language introduces one to what Sellars called "the space of reasons," learning a language about language introduces one to the language of literacy and of formal rationality. The study of thinking by psychological and educational theorists is conducted largely through the use of verbal tasks and verbal "test questions." Importantly, such tasks lift a piece of language from its ordinary embedded context to make it into an object of study in its own right. Words and sentences are taken "off-line," *mentioned* rather than *used*. On one hand, such test questions allow one to examine the underlying processes involved in making judgments, but at the same time their irreality raises questions as to the validity of such tasks and the generality of the findings. Why should it matter if Sissy Jupe cannot define the word "horse" so long as she uses the word correctly? Thus there are legitimate questions about the relevance of competence with such artifacts, such as definition of terms and correct responses to test questions, to judgment of the cognitive competencies of all speaking individuals. For one thing, it is primarily in literate cultures that persons engage in such analysis and it is in school contexts and in experimental tasks that one must rely on such analysis. To associate rationality with the ability to make such an analysis would seem to assign non-literate peoples to the class of the irrational. If, however, we assign competence with such analyses to a special style of using language in thinking "whose usefulness is manifest" (Turner & Thomas, 2011, p. 11), we can legitimately adopt such competence as important to cognitive development and a worthwhile goal of education.

I suggested that many cognitive tasks including test questions rely on knowledge of language taken off-line and thereby divorced from the ordinary context of use. Language out of context is more appropriately seen as a manufactured object, as an object created in the laboratory for research purposes rather than as a part of ordinary language competence. Although not occurring in nature, such objects may be created in the laboratory and their study may reveal underlying truths about nature. Words and sentences, along with prose and test questions, are laboratory objects that have revealed underlying properties of language important to our understanding of mind and rationality.

Yet, as I pointed out, there is a downside. Just as Galileo's laws of falling bodies hold only in a vacuum, so too the rules of inference that hold for abstracted words and statements may *not* hold in ordinary discourse because of altered contexts. Researchers have demonstrated that the rules of logic carefully worked out in the laboratory, whether Aristotle's *Modus ponens* or the logical meanings of "all" or "or" or "if," may fail to be observed in ordinary situations. These lapses are often seen as irrational, whereas in fact abstract rules and principles that apply to these decontextualized laboratory objects may not translate unequivocally back to real events. Ordinary language use is pragmatic, open to context and subject to a set of Cooperative Principles evolved to secure agreement between speaker and hearer. Rather than judging the failure to honor logical principles as failures of rationality, I followed Grice (1989) in distinguishing two logics, one formal, the other pragmatic. Conflict between the two occurs in tests of intelligence and in experimental reasoning tasks. Recall Sissy Jupe's inability to define "horse." And recall the test item: "Take two from three apples. How many do you have?" What looks like a subtraction problem actually depends on the logical implication of the imperative "take." If you took two, you have two. Similarly, the pragmatic principle expressed as Chekhov's gun insists that if some information is provided it must be essential and cannot be ignored, a rule violated in test questions as well as in Kahneman's famous "Linda" reasoning problem. Again this is not to deny that test questions provide important information; it is only to question the inferences drawn from such failures.

Failure to recognize the pragmatics of ordinary discourse may lead one to underestimate the rationality of children and the less educated, whose judgments tend to be more contextually sensitive and pragmatic. In order to answer correctly the laboratory-like test questions one must assume *ceteris paribus*, that of all things being equal. In ordinary discourse one cannot make such an assumption as any number of unmentioned considerations may turn out to be relevant. Language in practice, as we say, is embedded in a social context. It is primarily in special laboratory-like contexts that *probable* excludes *plausible*, that *some* dictates *not all*, that *all* excludes *most* and where the rules of logic apply strictly. This principle, it may be recalled, was critical to the pragmatists who saw thinking as problem solving rather than as the application of abstract rules. One member of the Metaphysical Club, jurist Oliver Wendell Holmes wrote: "All the pleasure of life is in general ideas but all the use of life is in specific solutions – which cannot be reached through generalities any more than a picture can be painted by knowing some rules of method. They are reached by insight, tact, and specific knowledge" (cited in Watson, 2014, p. 55). What has been gained by lifting words and sentences from their immediate context of use is the ability to say things about sameness of meanings and logical relations among terms and expressions. Such considerations provide new grounds for deciding on the interpretation of sentences that go beyond their ordinary pragmatic reference. With this new competence, the number of legs of a bee can be inferred from the fact that a bee is defined as an insect, and "Take one ..." can be seen as an imperative, and *some* implies *not all* and *all* now means *all*. These are some of the legacies of literacy.

Kahneman and Stanovich have drawn an important distinction between ordinary unreflective thought and action and its more deliberate, planfull and highly conscious cousin. I have drawn an equivalent distinction between the ordinary use of language and the metarepresentational use of language, the latter involving language about language and tied to literacy. To find a place for both language and literacy in a theory of thinking it was necessary to distinguish four types of cognition. First, there is that pre-verbal cognition we share with other animals that is tied to conditions and outcomes and driven directly by desires. Second, there is a special form of that pre-verbal cognition in human infants that is social and shared as ritual, imitation and play and that provides the basis for language learning. Third, there is the uniquely human, language-based cognition of everyday life in which many of our actions are represented as beliefs, goals and intentions that are knowingly acquired and to which one may appeal if asked or if problems arise. This is Sellars' "space of reasons." Even when acting fast, habitually and unconsciously those actions are supervised by more general goals and assumptions that are conscious. If asked, most persons in most contexts can provide a plausible explanation and in most cases a correct one. Yet reasons are not the direct causes of actions but rather their rational construal suited to the reason-giving practices of the society.

And fourth, my primary concern, there is that critical cognition, laboriously acquired by some, but familiar to those who grew up in a literate and language-rich environment, that is based on competence with a metalanguage suitable for reflecting on language, on the meaning of terms, the implications of words and sentences. This is the form of thinking that is useful for passing test questions, for reasoning about reasoning and for constructing Classical prose.

THINGS THAT THINK

Locke (1690) pointed out that:

> God has not been so sparing to men, to make them barely two-legged creatures, and left it to Aristotle to make them rational ... He has given them a mind that can reason without being instructed in the methods of syllogizing; the understanding is not taught to reason by these rules, it has a native faculty to perceive the coherence or incoherence of its ideas, and can range them right without any such perplexing repetitions. (pp. 264–265)

But even if persons are necessarily rational as Locke insisted, there is a kind of critical reasoning that is bound up with literacy. This reasoning depends upon the ability to think about, to metarepresent words, sentences and prose as objects divorced from their immediate use and then reapply the knowledge gained to the interpretation of expressions. One product is written prose, another is a correct response to a test question. Reasoning about such products is premised on exaggerated attention to linguistic form, primarily the precise meaning of words and the logical relations among sentences. And this reasoning is peculiarly literate both in invention and in acquisition. It is the form I have attempted to honor in writing this book.

The metalanguage for talking about words, sentences and prose discourse is vast. That for *word* ranges from *ambiguous* to *having the same meaning*; that for *sentence* ranges from *asserting* to *implying* and from *premise* to *conclusion*. Such concepts are instrumental not only to making ideas clear but also in providing a critical metalanguage for elaborating the norms and standards against which any inference or conclusion may be judged. To learn to manage this metalinguistic vocabulary is to learn to think about language, and consequently to think about thinking. I quoted Carruthers (2007, p. 206) as saying that most people "are bad at reasoning about reasoning." Good reasoning depends upon learning the linguistic distinctions based on the *sense* of terms including logical connectives and quantifiers. It includes those relevant to the scientific method such as what counts as a hypothesis and what counts as an observation, as well as the principles of validity as codified in systems of logic. All are metarepresentational, discourse about discourse.

The critical metalanguage taught through literacy has its roots in ordinary discourse. Although children may lack the concept of *inference* they express a complementary notion in the concept of *figuring it out.* Instead of saying *conclude* they may say *so*, instead of *imply* they may say *hint*, instead of *understand* they may say *get it*, instead of *hypothesis* they may say *guess* and instead of saying *evidence* they may say *another reason.* Yet using these devices is different from metarepresenting them. Young children claim to have known when what is actually a guess turns out to be correct. Only when metarepresented do such informal devices become objects that may be commented on and provide a basis for more formal distinctions. Once a guess is metarepresented as an *inference*, a *hypothesis* or an *assumption*, new norms and standards for judgment come into play that allow one to decide whether they are *informed*, *warranted*, *acknowledged* and so on. Consequently, when everyday concepts are treated metarepresentationally their meanings subtly change. Thus *probably* came to mean statistically *probable* rather than realistically *plausible. Foretell* became *predict* with its conspicuous non-mystical meaning.

The systematic reflection on words and sentence was sufficiently radical that the culture of Greece and Rome where it was invented is still taken as the dawn of modern consciousness. In the later Middle Ages, Abelard could expound on this knowledge to a large and newly developing intellectual and religious audience eager to learn about grammar and logic as a means of improving their thinking and reasoning. In the 17th century Francis Bacon and the Early Modern scientists created a new metalanguage for setting out in prose empirically valid knowledge organized by means of such concepts as *observation*, *assumption*, *hypothesis*, *inference*, *implication*, *premise* and *conclusion*, thereby altering the meaning and use of such traditional concepts as *truth* and *validity*.

New standards for the judgment of truth and the validity of judgments came, as we saw, with the establishment of a new standard for truth in the courts of law and in the scientific laboratory.

THE MIND ON PAPER

Although the importance of writing is widely acknowledged in society, and education remains at the top of the political agenda, writing has been slow to establish an appropriate place in the cognitive sciences, the sciences of the mind. Linguists since Saussure treat writing as simply a record of speech and of little conceptual importance. Cognitive scientists have shown how writing can serve as an add-on or extension to the mind, a cognitive tool for the economical storage and processing of information. These social uses of writing are extensive and important (Gee, 1990; Street, 1984). But to understand the cognitive implications of literacy it is also necessary, I have argued, to see writing not only as a tool for solving problems but rather as a generalized means or medium for representation and communication that give rise to those unique forms of human competence we in a modern society define as intelligence and rationality. Writing and reading creates a system of metarepresentational concepts linking visual signs to properties of speaking that were largely implicit, that is, transparent and unconscious, with the effect of bringing those features of language into consciousness as a subject of discourse. The real legacy of literacy is this new consciousness of language. The result is a doubling of consciousness, that of the world and that of how the world is represented in language. Thus is formed the mind on paper.

The historical and developmental evidence I reviewed shows that the processes of thinking and reasoning are products of the accumulation of cultural resources, primarily language but also language about language. These latter are not simply developmental, nor are they inevitable outcomes of ordinary discourse; they do not occur in the absence of teaching and learning, of demonstration and practice, and of careful monitoring by knowledgeable adults. The psychologist's habit of reporting cognitive changes in children and adolescents in terms of age hides the fact that age is often a proxy for years of schooling. Thus Leslie and Gelman's (2012, p. 211) interesting finding that statements containing the quantifier "all" are "cognitively more sophisticated" than general statements without the quantifier, is interpreted by them as indicating "a more general developmental trajectory." It is general trajectory only, I would add, in a particular culture of literacy with its fixed texts, its prolonged study, its habits of private silent reading and its accompanying critical commentary.

Cognitive theories of mind have yet to feel the effects of the "linguistic turn" that would turn the study of mental processes into the study of linguistic concepts. The linguistic turn is important to my account in that it allows the distinction between language and metalanguage. That distinction is essential to understanding the difference between contextually appropriate reasons that Kahneman has called "fast" and the explicitly logical reasons that he has called "slow." Subjects ordinarily reason pragmatically and contextually, but only when appropriately educated, tutored or warned do they reason formally and logically. If the former, subjects will treat the question as part of ordinary discourse; if the latter, they will examine the *sense* of the terms used in the question and derive an answer based on the strict implications of the terms employed. For it is only the *sense* of an expression that enters into the logical formulas developed by Aristotle. Both Luria's and Kahneman's questions require attention to the *sense* of the expression. Failure on such laboratory tasks should not be taken as evidence that one is outside the "space of reasons." It may, however, imply that one is outside the space of reasons about reasons. The linguistic turn would require that the psychological process be reconsidered in terms of the uses of language in both pragmatic contexts and in formal, metarepresentational ones.

The distinction between language and metalanguage is critical to an understanding of what in modern cultures is thought of as intelligence and rationality. It is only when words are lifted from their context that one can begin to think about words as objects and to define them so that the *sense* of the words becomes explicit. The metalanguage is also the language for criticism, for categorizing, formulating rules and principles and for making judgments about truth or falsity, validity or invalidity. It is less a matter of speaking or reading than of speaking *about* what is said or written. The metalanguage provides a guide and a standard for thinking about language and mind.

The linguistic turn would also go some distance to satisfy the concern of those who, like Vygotsky, insist that mind is a social and historical product and not only an individual and private function. Learning a language is a social practice in that the meanings of terms and expressions are social conventions monitored by adult speakers for their acceptability; there is no private language of thought. But language is generative, allowing the formation of an infinite set of sentences and, consequently, an infinite set of private thoughts. Thus, while we are constrained by the meaning of words we are not similarly constrained in what we believe. While language users share implicit knowledge of the sense of words and expressions allowing them to refer to things in the world, it is reading and literacy that makes some of that implicit knowledge explicit as an object of thought.

The error, if such it be, is to take the literate assumption that the verbal form of statements including that of test questions is a "given," a real event in nature, the kind of given both Sellars and Quine denied to nature and that psychologists mistakenly assign to written statements in the laboratory context of tests and textbooks as well as in models of text comprehension (van Dijk & Kintsch, 1983). Treating a test question as a "given" with a fixed interpretation and a correct answer violates the Gricean principle that the meaning depends upon the context and the interpretive assumptions of the reader. Yet such laboratory tasks and tests allow an analysis of the interpretive assumptions made by readers and listeners. The tests allow researchers to determine to what extent and in what contexts persons know and apply their metalinguistic knowledge to the task at hand. Acknowledging that reasoning processes are linguistic would invite the study of the metalinguistic concepts that turn aspects of language into objects of critical, reflective thinking.

I have attempted to set out some of the features of language brought into prominence by reading that are important to reflective thinking. Primary among them is the word with its Fregean *sense*, that aspect of meaning that is critical to defining a word in such a way that logical inferences may be derived from it. This is shift from thinking *with* language to thinking *about* language. This is the thinking sponsored by reading and elaborated by years of teaching and study.

What is true for words is also true for sentences, written prose, test questions and textbooks. Unlike living oral discourse, they are artifacts created for special purposes that require special metalinguistic knowledge if they are to be understood as intended by the writer. Understanding and appraising them appropriately is important not only for passing test questions but also for creating texts and for coping with the documentary practices of a modern bureaucratic literate culture.

The human mind is a linguistic mind that is tuned to the myriad influences inside and outside the person. The thinking of ordinary persons, as Locke noted, is not dependent on the single-mindedness dictated by the rules of logic. But that of educated adults is, or can be. Once brought to consciousness, words and expressions may be judged by the norms established by logic, science and statistics. Literate adults capable of thinking about language have learned a metalanguage that allows them to beware of unacknowledged assumptions, hidden premises and invalid inferences, especially when they occur in reading and writing texts.

Competence with ordinary language provides one with reasons, but specific metalinguistic distinctions are required to see reasons as reasons and to determine their status in a logical argument. Literacy education achieves its fuller significance when it accepts this larger mandate and the concept of mind will become more adequate when it acknowledges the role of literacy and education in its development.

The legacies of literacy are seen in the consciousness of language. It all begins with the metarepresentational concept of *word.* Indeed, Vygotsky concluded his magisterial *Thought and Language* with: "A word is a microcosm of human consciousness" (1986, p. 256). A suitable footnote would add that the metarepresentational concept of *word* is a microcosm of literate consciousness. Learning to read is an introduction to this new form of consciousness. But it is just the first step in the long road to the distinctive form of reasoning about reason, the rationality of the modern, literate mind.

References

Abrahamsen, A. A. (1977). *Child language: An interdisciplinary guide to theory and research*. Baltimore, MD: University Park Press.

Acocella, J. (November 11, 2013). Renaissance man: Boccaccio's Decameron. *The New Yorker*, 78–81.

Adams, M. J. (2011). Advancing our students' language and literacy: The challenge of complex texts. *American Educator, 34*(4), 3–11.

Adams, M. J., Treiman, R. & Pressley, M. (1998). Reading, writing, and literacy. In W. Damon (Ed.), *Handbook of child psychology* (Vol. 4, pp. 275–356). New York, NY: Wiley.

Adonis, A. (2012). *Education, education, education: Reforming England's schools*. London, UK: Biteback.

Allen, D. (2013). *Our declaration: A reading of the Declaration of Independence in defense of equality*. New York, NY: Liveright.

Apperly, I. (2011). *Mindreaders: The cognitive basis of "theory of mind."* New York, NY: Psychology Press.

Appleby, A. & Langer, J. (1987). *How writing shapes thinking*. Washington, DC: National Council for the Teaching of English.

Aram, D., Fine, Y. & Ziv, M. (2013). Enhancing parent–child shared book reading interaction. *Early Childhood Research Quarterly, 28*, 111–122.

Arendt, H. (1954). The crisis in education. *Between past and future*. New York, NY: Viking.

Assman, J. (2012). Cultural memory and the myth of the Axial Age. In R. N. Bellan & H. Joas (Eds.), *The Axial Age and its consequences* (pp. 366–407). Cambridge, MA: Belknap Press.

Astington, J. & Baird, J. (2005). *Why language matters for theory of mind*. Oxford, UK: Oxford University Press.

Astington, J., Harris, P. & Olson, D. R. (1988). *Developing theories of mind*. Cambridge, UK: Cambridge University Press.

Astington, J. W. & Hughes, C. (2013). Theory of mind: Self-reflection and social understanding. In P. D. Zelazo (Ed.), *The Oxford handbook of developmental psychology* (Vol. 2, pp. 398–424). New York, NY: Oxford University Press.

& Olson, D. R. (1990). Metacognitive and metalinguistic language: Learning to talk about thought. *Applied Psychology, 39*, 77–87.

Ayer, F. (1936). *Language, truth and logic*. London: Victor Gollancz.

Baines, J. (2008). The earliest Egyptian writing: development, context, purpose. In S. Houston (Ed.), *The first writing: Script invention as history and process* (pp. 150–189). Cambridge, UK: Cambridge University Press.

Bakhurst, D. (2011). *The formation of reason*. Malden, MA: Wiley-Blackwell.

Banfield, A. (1993). Where epistemology, style, and grammar meet literary history: The development of represented speech and thought. In J. Lucy (Ed.), *Reflexive language: Reported speech and metapragmatics* (pp. 339–364). Cambridge, UK: Cambridge University Press.

Bateson, G. (1972). *Steps to an ecology of mind*. New York, NY: Chandler Publishing.

Beal, C. (1990). Development of knowledge about the role of inference in text comprehension. *Child Development, 61*, 1011–1023.

Beal, C. R. & Flavell, J. H. (1984). Development of the ability to distinguish communicative intention and literal message meaning. *Child Development, 55*, 920–928.

Bereiter, C. & Scardamalia, M. (1987). *The psychology of written composition*. Mahwah, NJ: Lawrence Erlbaum.

Berman, R. & Ravid, D. (2009). Becoming a literate language user: Oral and written text construction across adolescence. In D. R. Olson & N. Torrance (Eds.), *The Cambridge handbook of literacy*. Cambridge, UK: Cambridge University Press.

Bernstein, R. (2010). *The pragmatic turn*. Cambridge, UK: Polity Press.

Bialystok, E. (2000). Symbolic representation across domains in preschool children. *Journal of Experimental Child Psychology, 76*, 173–189.

Biber, D. (1986). Spoken and written textual dimensions in English: Resolving the contradictory findings. *Language, 62*, 384–414.

(2009). Are there linguistic consequences of literacy? In D. R. Olson & N. Torrance (Eds.), *The Cambridge handbook of literacy*. Cambridge, UK: Cambridge University Press.

Bloom, A. (1968). *The Republic of Plato*. New York, NY: Basic Books.

Bogdan, R. (2009). *Predicative minds: The social ontogeny of propositional thinking*. Cambridge, MA: MIT Press.

Bradley, L. & Bryant, P. (1983). Categorizing sounds and learning to read: A causal connection. *Nature, 301*, 419–421.

Braine, M. & Rumain, B. (1981). Children's comprehension of "or": Evidence for a sequence of competencies. *Journal of Experimental Child Psychology, 31*, 46–70.

Brandom, R. (1994). *Making it explicit: Reasoning, representing and discursive commitment*. Cambridge, MA: Harvard University Press.

(2011). *Perspectives on Pragmatism: Classical, recent and contemporary*. Cambridge, MA: Harvard University Press.

Bredo, E. (1994). Reconstructing educational psychology: Situated cognition and Deweyan pragmatism. *Educational Psychologist, 29*, 23–35.

Brown, A. (1997). Transforming schools into communities of thinking and learning about serious matters. *American Psychologist, 52*, 399–413.

Bruner, J. S. (1960). *The process of education*. Cambridge, MA: Harvard University Press.

(1983). *Child's talk: Learning to use language*. New York, NY: Norton.

(2002). Narrative distancing: A foundation for literacy. In J. Brockmeier, M. Wang & D. R. Olson (Eds.), *Literacy, narrative and culture*. Richmond, UK: Curzon.

Bruner, J. S., Olver, R. & Greenfield, P. (Eds.). (1966). *Studies in cognitive growth*. New York, NY: Wiley.

Caines, M. (May 15, 2009). Arrange one's face: Review of H. Mantel's "Wolf Hall." *Times Literary Supplement*. Retrieved from www.the-tls.co.uk/tls/public/article758550.ece.

Calkins, L. (2006). *A guide to the writing workshop*. Portsmouth, NH: Heinemann.

Carlyle, E. I. (1947). *The life of William Cobbett*. London, UK: Home & Van Thal.

Carroll, J. M., Snowling, M. J., Stevenson, J. & Hulme, C. (2003). The development of phonological awareness in preschool children. *Developmental Psychology, 39*, 913–923.

Carruthers, M. (1990). *The book of memory: A study of memory in medieval culture*. Cambridge, UK: Cambridge University Press.

Carruthers, P. (2007). The illusion of conscious will. *Synthese, 159*, 197–213.

Chafe, W. (1985). Linguistic differences produced by differences between speaking and writing. In D. R. Olson, N. Torrance & A. Hildyard (Eds.), *Literacy, language and learning*. Cambridge, UK: Cambridge University Press.

Cheng, P. W. & Holyoak, K. J. (1985). Pragmatic reasoning schemas. *Cognitive Psychology, 17*, 391–416.

Chomsky, N. (1980). *Rules and representations*. New York, NY: Columbia University Press.

Clanchy, M. (1993). *From memory to written record: England 1066–1307* (2nd ed.). Oxford, UK: Oxford University Press.

(1997). *Abelard: A medieval life*. Oxford, UK: Blackwell.

Clark, A. (1988). Magic words: How language augments computation. In P. Carruthers & J. Boucher (Eds.), *Language and thought*. Cambridge, UK: Cambridge University Press.

(2008). *Supersizing the mind*. Oxford, UK: Oxford University Press.

& Chalmers, D. (1998). The extended mind. *Analysis, 58*, 7–19.

Cole, M. (1996). *Cultural psychology: A once and future discipline*. Cambridge, MA: Harvard University Press.

& Cole, J. (2006). Rethinking the Goody myth. In D. R. Olson & M. Cole (Eds.), *Technology, literacy, and the evolution of society*. Mahwah, NJ: Lawrence Erlbaum.

Cooper, J. S. (2008). Babylonian beginnings: The origin of the cuneiform writing system in comparative perspective. In S. Houston (Ed.), *The first writing: Script invention as history and process* (pp. 71–99). Cambridge, UK: Cambridge University Press.

Corson, D. (1985). *The lexical bar*. Oxford, UK: Pergamon.

Coulmas, F. (2013). *Writing and society*. Cambridge, UK: Cambridge University Press.

Council of Ministers of Education for Canada. (2013). *Measuring up: Canadian results of the OECD PISA study for 2012*. Toronto, ON: CMEC.

Cowen, J. (2003). *A balanced approach to beginning reading instruction*. Newark, DE: International Reading Association.

Crain, S. & Khlentzos, D. (2010). The logic instinct. *Mind and language, 25*, 30–65.

Cronin, V. S. (2002). The syntagmatic–paradigmatic shift and reading development. *Journal of Child Language, 29*(1), 189–204.

Crupi, V. & Tentori, K. (2016). Noisy probability judgment, the conjunction fallacy and rationality. *Psychological Review, 123*, 97–102.

Damasio, A. (2012). *Self comes to mind: Constructing the conscious brain*. New York, NY: Knopf Doubleday.

Daniels, P. (2009). Grammatology. In D. R. Olson & N. Torrance (Eds.), *The Cambridge handbook of literacy*. Cambridge, UK: Cambridge University Press.

Davidson, D. (2001). *Subjective, intersubjective, objective*. New York, NY: Oxford University Press.

Dehaene, S. (2009). *Reading in the brain*. New York, NY: Viking.

Dennett, D. (1991). *Consciousness explained*. Toronto, ON: Little, Brown and Company.

Derry, J. (2008). Abstract rationality in education: From Vygotsky to Brandom. *Studies in Philosophy and Education, 27*, 49–62.

(2013). *Vygotsky philosophy and education*. Oxford, UK: Wiley Blackwell.

de Villiers, J. (2005). Can language acquisition give children a point of view? In J. W. Astington & J. Baird (Eds.), *Why language matters for theory of mind*. Oxford, UK: Oxford University Press.

Dewey, J. (1986a). Experience and nature. In J. A. Boydston (Ed.), *John Dewey – The later works: Vol. 12. 1938*. Carbondale, IL: Southern Illinois University Press.

(1986b). Logic: The theory of inquiry. In J. A. Boydston (Ed.), *John Dewey – The later works: Vol. 12. 1938*. Carbondale, IL: Southern Illinois University Press.

(2003). Art as experience. In J. A. Boydston & L. Hickman (Eds.), *John Dewey – The later works: Vol. 30. 1934*. Carbondale, IL: Southern Illinois University Press.

Diringer, D. (1968). *The alphabet: A key to the history of mankind* (3rd ed.). New York, NY: Funk & Wagnalls.

Doherty, M. & Perner, J. (1998). Metalinguistic awareness and theory of mind. *Cognitive Development, 13*, 279–305.

Donald, M. (2012). An evolutionary approach to culture: Implications for the study of the Axial Age. In R. N. Bellah & H. Joas (Eds.), *The Axial Age and its consequences*. Cambridge, MA: Belknap Press.

Donaldson, M. (1978). *Children's minds*. Glasgow, UK: Fontana/Collins.

Downing, J. (1984). Task awareness in the development of reading skill. In J. Downing & R. Valtin (Eds.), *Language awareness and learning to read* (pp. 27–56). New York, NY: Springer.

& Valtin, R. (Eds.). (1984). *Language awareness and learning to read*. New York, NY: Springer.

Dummett, M. (1993). *Frege: Philosophy of language* (3rd ed.). Cambridge, MA: Harvard University Press.

Eagleman, D. (2011). *Incognito: The secret lives of the brain*. New York, NY: Vintage.

Edelman, G. (2004). *Wider than the sky: The phenomenological gift of consciousness*. New Haven, CT: Yale University Press.

Ehri, L. & Wilce, L. (1980). The influence of orthography on readers' conceptualization of the phonemic structure of words. *Applied Psycholinguistics, 1*, 371–385.

EQAO [Education Quality and Accountability Office]. (2014). (Source: EQAO: www.eqao.com/ProvincialReport/Files/14/PDF/provincial-report-elementary-findings-2014.pdf).

Erneling, C. (2010). *Towards discursive education*. Cambridge, UK: Cambridge University Press.

Eskritt, M. & Olson, D. R. (2012). From depiction to notation: How children use symbols to represent objects and events. *Journal of Cognition and Development, 13*, 189–207.

Feldman, C. (1991). Oral metalanguage. In D. R. Olson & N. Torrance (Eds.), *Literacy and orality*. Cambridge, UK: Cambridge University Press.

Ferreiro, E. (1985). Literacy development: A psychogenic perspective. In D. R. Olson, J. Torrance & A. Hildyard (Eds.), *Literacy, language and learning*. Cambridge, UK: Cambridge University Press.

& Teberosky, A. (1982). *Literacy before schooling*. Exeter, NY: Heinemann.

Flavell, J., Flavell, E. & Green, E. (1983). Development of the appearance–reality distinction. *Cognitive Psychology, 15*, 95–120.

Fodor, J. (1972). Some reflections on L. S. Vygotsky's Thought and Language. *Cognitive Psychology, 1*, 83–95.

Foucault, M. (1970). *The order of things: An archaeology of human sciences*. New York, NY: Pantheon Books.

Francis, H. (1973). Children's experience of reading and notions of units in language. *British Journal of Educational Psychology, 43*, 17–23.

Frank, T. (2015). Easy chair. *Harper's Magazine, 330*, p. 27.

Fromkin, V., Rodman, R. & Hymes, N. (2007). *An introduction to language*. Boston, MA: Thomson Publishing.

Frye, N. (1957). *Anatomy of criticism*. Princeton, NJ: Princeton University Press.

Gee, J. (1990). *Social linguistics and literacies: Ideology in discourses*. Brighton, UK: Falmer Press.

Gelb, I. J. (1963). *A study of writing* (2nd ed.). Chicago, IL: University of Chicago Press.

Giedion, S. (1948). *Mechanization takes command*. New York, NY: Norton.

Gigerenzer, G. (1991). How to make cognitive illusions disappear. *European Review of Social Psychology, 2*, 83–115.

Gigerenzer, G., Todd, P. & the ABC Research Group. (1999). *Simple heuristics that make us smart*. Oxford, UK: Oxford University Press.

Gillory, J. (2004). The memo and modernity. *Critical Inquiry, 31*, 108–132.

Ginzburg, C. (1980). *The cheese and the worms: The cosmos of a sixteenth-century miller*. Baltimore, MD: Johns Hopkins University Press.

Gleick, J. (1993). *Genius: The life and science of Richard Feynman*. New York, NY: Vintage.

Gleitman, L. R., Gleitman, H. & Shipley, E. F. (1972). The emergence of the child as grammarian. *Cognition, 1*, 137–164.

Goldhill, S. (2002). *The invention of prose*. Oxford, UK: Oxford University Press.

Goldstein, R. N. (October 8, 2015). What philosophers really know. *New York Review of Books, 62*, 48–50.

Goody, J. (1977). *The domestication of the savage mind*. Cambridge, UK: Cambridge University Press.

Gopnik, A. & Astington, J. (1988). Children's understanding of representational change and its relationship to the understanding of false belief and the appearance–reality distinction. *Child Development, 59*, 26–37.

Gopnik, A., Meltzoff, A. & Kuhl, P. (1999). *The scientist in the crib: Minds, brains, and how children learn.* New York, NY: William Morrow.

Greeno, J. G. (1997). On claims that answer the wrong questions. *Educational Researcher, 27*, 5–17.

Grendler, P. F. (1989). *Schooling in Renaissance Italy: Literacy and learning, 1300–1600.* Baltimore, MD: Johns Hopkins University Press.

Grice, H. P. (1989). *Studies in the ways with words.* Cambridge, MA: Harvard University Press.

Grieve, R. (1990). Children's awareness. In R. Grieve & M. Hughes (Eds.), *Understanding children: Essays in honour of Margaret Donaldson.* Oxford, UK: Blackwell.

Hass, C. & Flower, L. (1988). Rhetorical reading strategies and the recovery of meaning. *College Composition and Communication, 39*, 30–47.

Hacking, I. (1975). *Why does language matter to philosophy?* Cambridge, UK: Cambridge University Press.

(1983). *Representing and intervening.* Cambridge, UK: Cambridge University Press.

(1996). Normal people. In D. R. Olson & N. Torrance (Eds.), *Modes of thought.* Cambridge, UK: Cambridge University Press.

Halliday, M. A. K. (1985). *Spoken and written language.* Oxford, UK: Oxford University Press.

Halverson, J. (1991). Olson on literacy. *Language in Society, 20*, 619–640.

Hanson, N. R. (1958). *Patterns of discovery: An inquiry into the conceptual foundations of science.* New York, NY: Cambridge University Press.

Harris, P. (2000). *The work of the imagination.* Oxford, UK: Oxford University Press.

Harris, R. (2009). *Rationality and the literate mind.* London, UK: Routledge.

Havelock, E. A. (1982). *The literate revolution in Greece and its cultural consequences.* Princeton, NJ: Princeton University Press.

Hayes, J. R. & Flower, L. (1980). Identifying the organization of writing processes. In L. W. Gregg & E. R. Steinberg (Eds.), *Cognitive processes in writing.* Hillsdale, NJ: Erlbaum Associates.

Heath, J. (2011). *Enlightenment 2.0: Restoring sanity to our politics, our economy, and our lives.* Toronto, ON: HarperCollins.

Heath, S. (1983). *Ways with words: Language, life and work in communities and classrooms.* Cambridge, UK: Cambridge University Press.

Hedelin, E. & Hjelmquist, E. (1988). Preschool children's mastery of the form/content distinction in spoken language. In K. Ekberg & P. Mjaavatn (Eds.), *Growing into the modern world*. Trondheim: Norwegian Centre for Child Research.

Heeschen, V. (1978). The metalinguistic vocabulary of a speech community in the highlands of Irian Jaya (West New Guinea). In A. Sinclair, R. Jarvella & W. Levelt (Eds.), *The child's conception of language*. Berlin: Springer-Verlag.

Henle, M. (1962). On the relation between logic and thinking. *Psychological Review, 69*, 366–378.

Himmelmann, N. P. (2006). The challenges of segmenting spoken language. In N. P. Himmelmann & V. Mosel (Eds.), *Essentials of language documentation*. Berlin: Mouton de Gruyter.

Hirsch, E. D., Jr. (1987). *Cultural literacy: What every American needs to know*. Boston, MA: Houghton Mifflin.

Hoffman, M. & Murphy, P. (2005). Introduction. In M. Hoffman & P. Murphy (Eds.), *Essentials of the theory of fiction*. Durham, NC: Duke University Press.

Homer, B. (2009). Literacy and metalinguistic development. In D. R. Olson & N. Torrance (Eds.), *The Cambridge handbook of literacy*. Cambridge, UK: Cambridge University Press.

& Olson, D. R. (1999). Literacy and children's conception of words. *Written Language and Literacy, 2*, 113–140.

Householder, F. (1971). *Linguistic speculations*. Cambridge, UK: Cambridge University Press.

Huey, E. B. (1910). *The psychology and pedagogy of reading*. New York, NY: Appleton Century Croft.

Hume, D. (1978). *Treatise on human nature* (P. H. Nidditch, Ed.). Oxford, UK: Clarendon. (Original work published 1739.)

Huttenlocher, J. (1964). Children's language: Word–phrase relationship. *Science, 143*, 264–265.

Jackendoff, R. (2002). *Foundations of language*. Oxford, UK: Oxford University Press.

Janack, M. (2012). *What we mean by experience*. Stanford, CA: Stanford University Press.

Jaspers, K. (2011). *The origin and goal of history*. London, UK: Routledge Revivals. (Original work published 1949)

Jaynes, J. (1976). *The origin of consciousness in the breakdown of the bicameral mind*. New York, NY: Mifflin.

Johnson-Laird, P. N. (2006). *How we reason*. Oxford, UK: Oxford University Press.

Joos, M. (1967). *The five clocks: Five styles of English usage*. New York, NY: Harcourt, Brace and World.

Jung, C. G. (1969). *Studies in word association* (trans. M. D. Eder). London, UK: Routledge & Kegan Paul. (Original work published 1918)

Kafka, F. (1946). A little fable. In *The Great Wall of China: Stories and reflections*. Prague: Schocken Books.

Kahneman, D. (2011). *Thinking fast and slow*. Toronto, ON: Penguin.

Karanth, P. & Suchitra, M. (1993). Literacy acquisition and grammaticality judgments in children. In R. Scholes (Ed.), *Literacy and language analysis*. Hillsdale, NJ: Lawrence Erlbaum.

Karmiloff-Smith, A. (1992). *Beyond modularity: A developmental perspective on cognitive science*. Cambridge, MA: Bradford Books.

Katz, J. & Fodor, J. (1963). *The structure of a semantic theory*. Cambridge, MA: MIT Press.

Katz, S. (2001). *The knower and the known in folk pedagogies*. Unpublished doctoral dissertation, OISE/University of Toronto.

Kneale, W. & Kneale, M. (1984). *The development of logic* (Rev. ed.). Oxford, UK: Clarendon.

Koterski, A. (2015). The silhouette of ISOTYPE [Published in Polish as: Zarys ISOTYPE'u: Idea statystyki obrazkowej Metoda Wiedenska, *Przeglad Filozoficzny*, NS, nr 1 (2015), 227–250].

Kozulin, A. (1986). Introduction. In L. Vygotsky, *Thought and language*. Cambridge, MA: MIT Press.

Kramer, S. (2912). The "eye of the mind" and the eye of the body: Descartes and Leibniz on truth, mathematics, and visuality. In F. G. Barth, P. Giampieri Deutsch & H. D. Klein (Eds.), *Sensory perception: Mind and matter*. Vienna: Springer.

Krashen, S. D. (1989). We acquire vocabulary and spelling by reading: Additional evidence for the input hypothesis. *Modern Language Journal, 73*, 440–464.

Kuhn, D. (2005). *Education for thinking*. Cambridge, MA: Harvard University Press.
(2015). Thinking together and alone. *Educational Researcher, 44*, 46–53.

Lagemann, E. C. (2000). *The elusive science: The troubling history of educational research*. Chicago, IL: University of Chicago Press.

Lancashire, I. (2002). "Dumb significants" and Early Modern English definition. In J. Brockmeier, M. Wong & D. R. Olson (Eds.), *Literacy, narrative and culture*. Richmond, UK: Curzon.

Landgrafova, R. (2013). The classical art of memory as immaterial writing. *Pragmatics and Cognition, 21*, 505–520.

Lantolf, J. & Poehner, M. (1994). *Vygotskyan approaches to second language research*. Norwood, NJ: Ablex.

Lantolf, J. P. & Poehner, M. E. (2014). *Sociocultural theory and the pedagogical imperative in L2 education: Vygotskian praxis and the research/practice divide*. London, UK: Routledge.

Latour, B. & Woolgar, S. (1986). *Laboratory life: The construction of scientific facts*. Princeton, NJ: Princeton University Press.

Lee, E., Torrance, N. & Olson, D. R. (2001). Young children and the say/mean distinction: Verbatim and paraphrase recognition in narrative and nursery rhyme contexts. *Journal of Child Language, 28*, 531–543.

Leiper, K. (2013). *Education, literacy and its cognitive effects: Problem-solving and decision-making in Homer and archaic and fifth-century BC Athens*. Unpublished doctoral dissertation, Department of History, Macquarie University, Australia.

Leong, C. K. (1982). Reading in perspective. In J. Downing & C. K. Leong (Eds.), *Psychology of reading*. New York, NY: Macmillan.

Leslie, A. (1988). Some implications of pretense for mechanisms underlying the child's theory of mind. In J. W. Astington, P. Harris & D. R. Olson (Eds.), *Developing theories of mind*. Cambridge, UK: Cambridge University Press.

Leslie, S. J. & Gelman, S. A. (2012). Quantified statements are recalled as generics: Evidence from preschool children and adults. *Cognitive Psychology, 64*, 186–214.

Levinson, S. (1983). *Pragmatics*. Cambridge, UK: Cambridge University Press.

Levi-Strauss, C. (1961). *Tristes tropiques*. New York, NY: Atheneum.

(1963). *Structural anthropology*. New York, NY: Doubleday Anchor Books.

Liberman, I. Y. & Shankweiler, D. (1985). Phonology and the problems of learning to read and write. *Remedial and Special Education, 6*(6), 8–17.

Liberman, I. & Shankweiler, D. (1991). Phonology and beginning reading: A tutorial. In L. Rieben & C. Perfetti (Eds.), *Learning to read: Basic research and its implications*. Hillsdale, NJ: Erlbaum.

Linell, P. (2005). *The written language bias in linguistics: Its nature, origins and transformations*. London, UK: Routledge.

Locke, J. (1961). *An essay concerning human understanding*. London, UK: Dent. (Original work published 1690)

Logan, R. (2004). *The alphabet effect: A media ecology understanding of the making of Western civilization*. Cresskill, NJ: Hampton Press.

Lundberg, I., Olofsson, A. & Wall, S. (1980). Reading and spelling skills in the first years predicted from phonemic awareness skills in kindergarten. *Scandinavian Journal of Psychology, 21*, 159–173.

Luria, A. R. (1961). *The role of speech in the regulation of normal and abnormal behavior*. London, UK: Pergamon.

(1976). *Cognitive development: Its cultural and social foundations*. Cambridge, MA: Harvard University Press.

Lyotard, J.-F. (1984). *The postmodern condition*. Manchester, UK: Manchester University Press.

Macbeth, K. (2006). Diverse, unforeseen, and quaint difficulties: The sensible responses of novices learning to follow instructions in academic writing. *Research in the Teaching of English*, *41*, 180–207.

March, J. (1978). Bounded rationality, ambiguity, and the engineering of choice. *The Bell Journal of Economics*, *9*, 587–607.

McCallister, C. (2011). *Unison reading: Socially inclusive group instruction for equity and achievement*. Thousand Oaks, CA: Corwin Sage.

McCullers, C. (1953). *The heart is a lonely hunter*. New York, NY: Bantam Books.

McDowell, J. (1994). *Mind and world*. Cambridge, MA: Harvard University Press.

McLuhan, M. (1964). *Understanding media*. London, UK: Routledge.

Mead, G. H. (1934). *Mind, self and society*. Chicago, IL: University of Chicago Press.

Mehan, H. (1979). What time is it Denise? Some observations on the organization and consequences of asking known information questions in classroom discourse. *Theory into Practice*, *18*(4), 285–292.

Menand, L. (2001). *The Metaphysical Club: A story of ideas in America*. New York, NY: Farrer, Straus & Giroux.

Milligan, K., Astington, J. W. & Dack, L. A. (2007). Language and theory of mind: Meta-analysis of the relation between language ability and false-belief understanding. *Child Development*, *78*, 622–646.

Misak, S. (2013). *The American Pragmatists*. Oxford, UK: Oxford University Press.

Montaigne, M. de. (1993). *The complete essays*. London: Penguin. (Original work published 1580)

Moore, C. (2006). *The development of commonsense psychology*. Mahwah, NJ: LEA.

Moore, J. & Newell, A. (1973). How can MERLIN understand? In L. W. Gregg (Ed.), *Knowledge and cognition*. Baltimore, MD: Lawrence Erlbaum.

Morais, J., Alegria, J. & Content, A. (1987). The relationship between segmental analysis and alphabetic literacy: An interactive view. *Cahiers de Psychologie Cognitive*, *7*, 415–438.

Morison, E. (1966). *Men, machines, and modern times*. Cambridge, MA: MIT Press.

Murphy, J. P. (1990). *Pragmatism: From Peirce to Davidson*. San Francisco, CA: Westview Press.

Nagel, T. (1986). *The view from nowhere*. Oxford, UK: Oxford University Press.

Nagy, W. E. & Anderson, R. C. (1984). How many words are there in printed English? *Reading Research Quarterly, 19*, 304–330.

National Center for Educational Statistics. (2010). *The nation's report card: Grade 12 reading and mathematics 2009 national and pilot state results* (NCES 2011–455). Washington, DC: Institute of Education Sciences, U.S. Department of Education.

National Reading Panel and National Institute of Child Health and Human Development. (2000). *Report of the National Reading Panel: Teaching children to read*. Washington, DC: National Institute of Child Health and Human Development.

Nelson, K. (Ed.). (1989). *Narratives in the crib*. Cambridge, MA: Harvard University Press.

New York Times. (October 25, 2015). Obama administration, sharing blame, calls for limits on testing in schools (Kate Zernike, reporter).

Noveck, I. A. (2001). When children are more logical than adults: Experimental investigation of scalar implicatures. *Cognition, 78*, 165–188.

Nunez, T. & Bryant, P. (2009). *Children's reading and spelling: Beyond the first steps*. Malden, MA: Wiley-Blackwell.

Oatley, K. (1996). Inference in narrative and science. In D. R. Olson & N. Torrance (Eds.), *Modes of thought*. Cambridge, UK: Cambridge University Press.

(2013). Worlds of the possible: Abstraction, imagination, consciousness. *Pragmatics and Cognition, 21*, 448–468.

& Djikic, M. (2008). Writing as thinking. *Review of General Psychology, 12*, 9–27.

& Djikic, M. (in press). The creativity of literary writing. In J. Kaufman, J. Baer & V. Glaveanu (Eds.), *The Cambridge handbook of creativity across different domains*. Cambridge, UK: Cambridge University Press.

Olson, D. R. (1970). Language and thought: Aspects of a cognitive theory of semantics. *Psychological Review, 77*(4), 257–273.

(1975). The languages of experience: On natural language and formal education. *Bulletin of the British Psychological Society, 28*, 363–373.

(1977). From utterance to text: The bias of language in speech and writing. *Harvard Educational Review, 47*(3), 257–281.

(1994). *The world on paper: The conceptual and cognitive implications of writing and reading*. Cambridge, UK: Cambridge University Press.

Olson, D. R. (2003). *Psychological theory and educational reform: How schooling remakes mind and society*. Cambridge, UK: Cambridge University Press.

Olson, D. R. (2007). The self-ascription of intention: Responsibility, obligation and self-control. *Synthese, 159*, 297–314.

(2012). Narrative, cognition and rationality. In J. P. Gee & M. Handford (Eds.), *Routledge handbook of discourse analysis* (pp. 604–615). London, UK: Routledge.

& Astington, J. (1990). Talking about text: How literacy contributes to thought. *Journal of Pragmatics, 14*, 705–721.

Olson, D. R. & Astington, J. W. (2013). Preschool children conflate pragmatic agreement and semantic truth. *First Language, 33*, 617–627.

Olson, D. R. & Campbell, R. (1993). Constructing representations. In C. Pratt & A. F. Garton (Eds.), *Systems of representation in children: Development and use* (pp. 11–26). Chichester, UK: Wiley.

& Oatley, K. (2014). The quotation theory of writing. *Written Communication, 31*, 4–26.

Olver, R. & Hornsby, J. (1966). On equivalence. In J. S. Bruner, R. Olver & P. Greenfield (Eds.), *Studies in cognitive growth*. New York, NY: Wiley.

Ontario Teachers' Manuals: Primary Reading. (1920). Toronto: Copp Clark.

Osgood, C. E., Suci, G. & Tannenbaum, P. (1957). *The measurement of meaning*. Urbana, IL: University of Illinois Press.

Papafragou, A. & Musolino, J. (2003). Scalar implicatures: Experiments at the semantic–pragmatic interface. *Cognition, 86*, 253–282.

Papandropoulou, I. & Sinclair, H. (1974). What is a word? Experimental study of children's ideas on grammar. *Human Development, 17*, 241–258.

Pelletier, J. (2002). Young children's "clever misunderstandings" about print. In J. Brockmeier, M. Wong & D. R. Olson (Eds.), *Literacy, narrative and culture*. Richmond, UK: Curzon.

Perfetti, C. (1991). Representations and awareness in the acquisition of reading competence. In L. Riben & C. Perfetti (Eds.), *Learning to read: Basic research and its implications*. Hillsdale, NJ: Erlbaum.

Perner, J. (1991). *Understanding the representational mind*. Cambridge, MA: MIT Press.

& Roessler, J. (2012). From infants' to children's appreciation of belief. *Trends in Cognitive Sciences, 16*, 519–525.

Peskin, J. & Astington, J. W. (2004). The effects of adding metacognitive language to story texts. *Cognitive Development, 19*, 253–273.

Petsinis, T. (1997). *The French mathematician*. New York, NY: Walker and Company.

Piaget, J. (1962). *Play, dreams and imitation*. New York, NY: Norton.

Pinker, S. (1994). *The language instinct: How the mind creates language*. New York, NY: HarperCollins.

Popper, K. (1972). *Objective knowledge: An evolutionary approach.* Oxford, UK: Clarendon.

Powell, B. B. (1991). *Homer and the origin of the Greek alphabet.* Cambridge, UK: Cambridge University Press.

Premack, D. & Premack, A. (1996). Why animals lack pedagogy and why some cultures have more of it than others. In D. R. Olson & N. Torrance (Eds.), *The handbook of education and human development.* Oxford, UK: Blackwell.

Proctor, M. (2002). The essay as a literary and academic form: Closed gate or open door? In J. Brockmeier, M. Wang & D. R. Olson (Eds.), *Literacy, narrative and culture.* Richmond, UK: Curzon.

Proust, J. (2013). *The philosophy of metarepresentation: Mental agency and self-awareness.* Oxford, UK: Oxford University Press.

Proust, M. (1982). *Remembrance of things past: Vol. 1. Swann's Way.* New York, NY: Vintage.

Quine, W. (1960). *Word and object.* Cambridge, MA: MIT Press.

Ravitch, D. (2014, November 20). The myth of China's super schools. *New York Review of Books, 61,* 18.

Rayner, K., Foorman, B. R., Perfetti, C. A., Pesetsky, D. & Seidenberg, M. S. (2001). How psychological science informs the teacher of reading. *Psychological Science in the Public Interest, 2,* 31–74.

Read, C., Zhang, Y., Nie, H. & Ding, B. (1986). The ability to manipulate speech sounds depends on knowing alphabetic reading. *Cognition, 24,* 31–44.

Reid, J. (1960). Learning to think about reading. *Educational Research, 9,* 56–62.

Renfrew, C., Frith, C. & Malafouris, L. (2009). *The sapient mind: Archaeology meets neuroscience.* Oxford, UK: Oxford University Press.

Roberts, A. D. (2011). *The role of metalinguistic awareness in the effective teaching of foreign languages.* New York, NY: Peter Lang.

Robinson, E., Goelman, H. & Olson, D. R. (1983). Children's understanding of the relationship between expressions (what was said) and intentions (what was meant). *British Journal of Developmental Psychology, 1,* 75–86.

Rorty, R. (1981). Nineteenth-century idealism and twentieth-century textualism. *The Monist, 64,* 155–174.

Rose, S. (2011, February 12). Self comes to mind: Constructing the conscious brain by Antonio Damasio – Review. *Guardian.* Retrieved from www.theguardian.com/books/2011/feb/12/self-comes-mind-damasio-review.

Rosenthal, D. (1993). Thinking that one thinks. In M. Davis & G. Humphries (Eds.), *Consciousness.* Oxford, UK: Blackwell.

Rozeboom, W. (1972). Problems in the psycho-philosophy of knowledge. In J. Royce & W. Rozeboom (Eds.), *The psychology of knowing*. New York, NY: Gordon & Beach.

Sady, W. (2013). Quanta appeared not in Max Planck's mind, but on paper. *Pragmatics & Cognition, 21*(3), 521–529.

Saenger, P. (1982). Silent reading: Its impact on late medieval script and society. *Viator, 13*, 367–414.

Sahlberg, P. (2011). *Finnish lessons*. New York, NY: Teachers College, Columbia University.

Saussure, F. de. (1983). *Course in general linguistics*. London: Duckworth. (Original work published 1916)

Schmandt-Besserat, D. (1986). Tokens: Facts and interpretations. *Visible Language, 20*, 250–272.

(1992). *Before writing*. Austin, TX: University of Texas Press.

(2007). *When writing met art: From symbol to story*. Austin, TX: University of Texas Press.

Scribner, S. & Cole, M. (1981). *The psychology of literacy*. Cambridge, MA: Harvard University Press.

Searle, J. (1983). *Intentionality: An essay in the philosophy of mind*. Cambridge, UK: Cambridge University Press.

Sellars, W. (1997). *Empiricism and the philosophy of mind*. Introduction by R. Rorty and study guide by R. Brandom. Cambridge, MA: Harvard University Press. (Originally published in 1956)

Shallice, T. (1988). *From neuropsychology to mental structure*. Cambridge, UK: Cambridge University Press.

Shapin, S. (1985). Pump and circumstance: Robert Boyle's literary technology. *Social Studies of Science, 14*, 481–520.

Share, D. (2008). Orthographic learning, phonology, and the self-teaching hypothesis. *Advances in Child Development and Behavior, 36*, 31–82.

Simon, H. A. (1957). *Models of man*. New York, NY: Wiley.

(1996). *The sciences of the artificial* (3rd ed.). Cambridge, MA: MIT Press.

Small, J. P. (1997). *Wax tablets of the mind: Cognitive studies of memory and literacy in Classical Antiquity*. London, UK: Routledge.

Smith, D. (1990). *Texts, facts, and femininity: Exploring the relations of ruling*. London, UK: Routledge.

Smith, F. (1971). *Understanding reading*. Toronto, ON: Holt, Rinehart and Winston. (Sixth edition, Routledge Classics, 2014)

Snow, C. & Uccelli, P. (2009). The challenge of academic language. In D. R. Olson & N. Torrance (Eds.), *The Cambridge handbook of literacy*. Cambridge, UK: Cambridge University Press.

Snowling, M. & Hulme, C. (Eds.). (2005). *The science of reading: A handbook*. Malden, MA: Blackwell.

Sousa, R. de (2004). Rational animals. *Croatian Journal of Philosophy, 4*(3), 365–386.

Spelke, E. (1994). Initial knowledge: Six suggestions. *Cognition, 50*, 431–455.

(2003). What makes us smart? Core knowledge and natural language. In D. Gentner & S. Goldin-Meadow (Eds.), *Language in mind*. Cambridge, MA: MIT Press.

Spiro, R., DeSchryver, M., Hagerman, M., Morsink, M. & Thompson, P. (Eds.). (2015). *Reading at the crossroads?* New York, NY: Routledge/Taylor & Francis.

Spratt, T. (1966). *History of the Royal Society of London for the improving of natural knowledge* (J. Cope & H. Jones, Eds.). St. Louis, MO: Washington University Press. (Original work published 1667)

Standish, P. (2013). Series editor's preface. In J. Derry, *Vygotsky philosophy and education*. Oxford, UK: Wiley Blackwell.

Stanovich, K. (2009). *What intelligence tests miss: The psychology of rational thought*. New Haven, CT: Yale University Press.

& West, R. (2000). Individual differences in reasoning: Implications for the rationality debate. *Behavioral and Brain Sciences, 23*, 645–665.

Stewart, C. (1922). *Moonlight schools: For the emancipation of adult illiterates*. New York, NY: E. P. Dutton & Company.

Stock, B. (2015). Savoir lire et ecrire en perspective globale: Biologie, culture et societe. In M. Wieviorka, L. Levi-Strauss & G. Lieppe (Eds.), *Penser global: Internationalisation et globalization des sciences humaines et sociales*. Paris: Editions de la Maison des sciences de l'homme.

Street, B. (1984). *Literacy in theory and practice*. Cambridge, UK: Cambridge University Press.

Taylor, C. (2012). What was the Axial Revolution? In R. N. Bellah & H. Joas (Eds.), *The Axial Age and its consequences*. Cambridge, MA: Belknap Press.

Tetlock, P. E. & Gardner, D. (2014). *Superforecasting: The art and science of prediction*. New York, NY: Crown Publishers.

Theiner, G. (2011). *Res Cogitans Extensa*. Frankfurt: Peter Lang.

Tolchinsky, L. (2003). *The cradle of culture and what children know about writing and numbers before being taught*. Mahwah, NJ: Erlbaum.

Tolchinsky-Landsmann, L. & Levin, I. (1987). Writing in four- to six-year-olds: Representation of semantic and phonetic similarities and differences. *Journal of Child Language, 14*, 127–144.

Tomasello, M. (2014). *A natural history of human thinking*. Cambridge, MA: Harvard University Press.

Torrance, N. & Olson, D. R. (1985). Oral and literate competencies in the early school years. In D. R. Olson, N. Torrance & A. Hildyard (Eds.), *Literacy, language, and learning: The nature and consequences of reading and writing* (pp. 256–284). Cambridge, UK: Cambridge University Press.

Traugott, E. C. (1987). Literacy and language change. *Interchange: A Quarterly Review of Education, 18*, 32–47.

Treiman, R. & Zukowsky, A. (1991). Levels of phonological awareness. In S. A. Brady & D. P. Shankweiler (Eds.), *Phonological processes in literacy: A tribute to Isabelle Y. Liberman* (pp. 67–83). Hillsdale, NJ: Erlbaum.

Tunmer, W. & Bowey, J. (1984). Metalinguistic awareness and reading acquisition. In W. Tunmer, C. Pratt & M. Herriman (Eds.), *Metalinguistic awareness in children*. Berlin: Springer-Verlag.

Tunmer, W., Pratt, C. & Herriman, M. (1984). *Metalinguistic awareness in children: Theory, research, and implications*. Berlin: Springer-Verlag.

Turner, M. & Thomas, F.-N. (2011). *Clear and simple as the truth: Writing about prose*. Princeton, NJ: Princeton University Press.

Uccelli, P., Barr, C. D., Dodds, C. L., Phillips Galloway, E., Meneses, A. & Sanchez, E. (2014). Core academic language skills (CALS): An expanded operational construct and a novel instrument to chart school relevant language proficiency in pre-adolescent and adolescent learners. *Applied Psycholinguistics, 36*, 1077–1109.

Valtin, R. (2014). About the dubious role of phonological awareness in the discussion of literacy policies. Paper presented in the FELA endorsed symposium "Kindergarten literacy in Europe" at the 18th European Conference on Reading, Mons, Belgium, August 2011.

Van Dijk, T. & Kintsch, W. (1983). *Strategies of discourse comprehension*. New York, NY: Academic Press.

Vellutino, F. (1979). *Dyslexia: Theory and research*. Cambridge, MA: MIT Press.

Vendler, Z. (1970). Say what you think. In J. L. Cowan (Ed.), *Studies in thought and language*. Tucson: University of Arizona Press.

Vernon, S. (2002). Children's analysis of oral and written words. In J. Brockmeier, M. Wang & D. R. Olson (Eds.), *Literacy, narratives and culture*. London, UK: Curzon.

Vygotsky, L. S. (1962). *Thought and language*. Cambridge, MA: MIT Press.

(1978). *Mind in society: The development of higher psychological processes* (M. Cole et al., Eds.). Cambridge, MA: Harvard University Press.

(1986). *Thought and language* (A. Kozulin, Ed.). Cambridge, MA: MIT Press.

Watson, P. (2014). *The age of atheists: How we have sought to live since the death of God*. New York, NY: Simon & Schuster.

Watson, R. & Horowitz, W. (2011). *Writing science before the Greeks: A naturalistic analysis of the Babylonian astronomical treatise MUL. APIN*. Leiden: Brill.

Weir, R. (1962). *Language in the crib*. The Hague: Mouton.

Wells, G. (1999). *Dialogic inquiry: Towards a socio-cultural practice and theory of education*. Cambridge, UK: Cambridge University Press.

Wertsch, J. (1991). *Voices of the mind: A sociocultural approach to mediated action*. Cambridge, MA: Harvard University Press.

Wertsch, J., Tulviste, P. & Hagstrom, F. (1993). A sociocultural approach to agency. In E. Forman, N. Minick & C. Stone (Eds.),*Contexts for learning* (pp. 336–356). New York, NY: Oxford University Press.

Wiersbicka, A. (2010). *Experience, evidence, and sense: The hidden cultural legacy of English*. Oxford, UK: Oxford University Press.

Williams, J. (1965). *Stoner*. New York, NY: Viking.

Wilson, E. O. (2014). *The meaning of human existence*. New York, NY: Liveright/Norton.

Wilson, R. & Keil, F. (2000). The shadows and shallows of explanation. In F. Keil & R. Wilson (Eds.), *Explanation and cognition*. Cambridge, MA: MIT Press.

Wimmer, H. & Perner, J. (1983). Beliefs about beliefs: Representation and constraining function of wrong beliefs in young children's understanding of deception. *Cognition, 13*, 103–128.

Wiseberg, J. (2014). *Consciousness*. Cambridge, UK: Polity.

Wittgenstein, L. (1958). *Philosophical investigations*. Oxford, UK: Blackwell.

Wolf, M. (2008). *Proust and the squid: The story and science of the reading brain*. New York, NY: Harper Perennial.

Zelazo, P. D. & Jacques, S. (1996). Children's rule use: Representation, reflection, and cognitive control. *Annals of Child Development, 12*, 119–176.

Author Index

Subject Index

For EU product safety concerns, contact us at Calle de José Abascal, 56–1°, 28003 Madrid, Spain or eugpsr@cambridge.org.

www.ingramcontent.com/pod-product-compliance
Lightning Source LLC
LaVergne TN
LVHW011523200926
848484LV00001B/136

* 9 7 8 1 1 0 7 1 6 2 8 9 1 *